CONTENTS

INTRODUCTION

My entire life can be summed up in three words: Weight loss diets. I tried every diet known to men – from keto and paleo diet to the cabbage soup diet. Seriously, I did it all. But the results were, to put it mildly, devastating. I want to lose weight no matter what it took because I was desperate. Over the years, I have found a few strategies that seem to be effective. However, they were short-lived and I have experienced weight cycling, also known as "yo-yo dieting". However, I did not know anything about food and nutrition. I did not know anything about my body and weight loss process. I didn't know that restrictive diets lead to increased appetite as the body loses muscle mass, trying to resupply depleted fat stores. Moreover, yo-yo dieting has harmful effects on our health; it has been associated with increased risk of heart diseases, diabetes, and fatty liver; in fact, weight fluctuations may be worse than staying overweight.

With this in mind, I decided to break the cycle of weight fluctuations with temporary success, and start thinking in terms of long-term lifestyle changes. First things first, I decide to change the way I cook my favorite food. I like home-cooked meals but I don't want to be occupied in the kitchen for hours. On the other hand, I like popular fast-food items such as burgers, French fries, pizza, and donuts. I wanted to drop my pounds but not miss out on my guilty pleasure foods. Therefore, an Air Fryer seemed to be working. I must confess, I was skeptical at first, but this small countertop convection oven seemed like a perfect solution to my problems with obesity and a great way to avoid consuming excessive calories. Besides being economical and practical, I found an Air Fryer perfect tool for family gatherings and children's birthday parties. Today, I can't imagine healthy dieting without an Air Fryer. It delivers a crispy finished product and flavor-packed meals without all that unhealthy oil. Isn't it fantastic?

In this cookbook, I have a tendency to promote a healthy lifestyle and traditional values, without starving and nutrient depletion. Family dinners bring families together, contributing to our physical and mental health. Did you know that a child who is engaged in the cooking process with parents is more likely to grow to be an adult who has healthy eating habits? This is the recipe collection I wish I had when I started my weight loss journey. It is all about my favorite Air Fryer recipes, including my personal experience with this unique kitchen tool. I started by making fried vegetables and chicken wings in it. Then I ventured into more complicated meals such as casserole and pastry. For this recipe collection, I chose easy-to-follow recipes with fewer ingredients so a family dinner can be a reality any night of the week. Are you searching for a way to simplify your cooking routine? Do you want recipes for the best "make-it-again" fried food? Well, you are in the right place. The Air Fryer and this recipe collection are ready to be your reliable kitchen companions! The Air Fryer will spark your imagination and create heart-warming family kitchen memories! Enjoy!

Getting to Know Your Air Fryer and Must-Know Tips

I'm asked two questions time and time again, "Why use an Air Fryer? Is an Air Fryer worth buying?" Well, I have three words for you: Health, convenience, and versatility. Everyone likes the taste of fried foods. Nothing says Saturday movie night better than a big bowl of chips! An air fryer is a modern kitchen appliance, a type of a mini convection oven, used for making fried foods. It offers a flavorful, crispy finished product by circulating hot air in the cooking chamber. In other words, a super-heated air circulates around your food for faster and even cooking results. An Air Fryer promises to take a place of a convection oven, deep fryer, grill, and microwave; this magical appliance also lets you sauté and roast your foods. The best of all – your food does not taste like fat. The Air Fryer uses rapid air technology to cook foods to perfection (crispy exteriors and well-cooked, moist interiors) with a drizzle of healthy oil.

Here are a few tips and hacks you might benefit from:

➢Needless to say, read the user's manual to make the most of your Air Fryer, even if you are an experienced cook; moreover, it is recommended to consult the manual every now and then, since there are dozens of different models of Air Fryer on the market.

➢If you are not in a hurry, preheat your Air Fryer to ensure even cooking. Turn it to the desired temperature and allow it to run for around 3 minutes before adding ingredients to the cooking basket.

➢Do not forget to grease the cooking basket; just brush the cooking basket lightly with a healthy oil; most Air Fryer recipes call for 1/2 teaspoon or less per serving.

➢Don't overcrowd the basket to promote even cooking; simply cook in batches and shake the basket periodically; you can spritz your food with a nonstick spray halfway through cooking time. One more thing –

avoid cooking light items in the Air Fryer since it has a powerful fan on top of the unit, aggressively pushing hot air around your food, through the whole cooking basket. It includes leafy things like spinach and fresh herbs, seasonings, top slices of bread on sandwiches.

➢You can use your Air Fryer for healthy baked goods such as breakfast pastries and desserts. A 6-in round baking pan and bundt pan are worth investing in; bear in mind that baking pans should fit right inside the cooking basket.

Top Benefits of an Air Fryer You Need to Know

Fast and easy meals.

My Air Fryer helps me to avoid "there's-nothing-to-eat" situation on weeknights. Besides being a next-generation kitchen device, the Air Fryer frees up my time. It has automatic functions, so you don't need to stir food and watch the whole cooking process. Most of the recipes call for shaking the basket or flipping the ingredients halfway through the cooking time. That's it! When the cooking process ends, your Air Fryer will automatically turn off. The Air Fryer can deliver amazing results with minimal hands-on time.

Healthy fast food (improve your health and lose weight).

Really?! Is there such a thing as a healthy fast food? The truth is that it's practically impossible to follow a well-balanced diet when you're eating regularly junk food. On the other hand, cooking at home is associated with healthy eating habits. Your dietary patterns are extremely important on your weight loss journey. The good news is that you can cook French fries, donuts, fish, and burgers in your Air Fryer. This is only the beginning. Hearty casseroles, delicious appetizers, and delectable desserts will turn out great in your Air Fryer. When it comes to healthy weight loss that does not compromise flavor, this revolutionary kitchen gadget is a real winner!

A lower intake of unhealthy oil is one of the greatest benefits of the Air Fryer. Fried food tastes good, right?! But trans fats are harmful to our health. Fried foods such as chicken nuggets, refrigerated dough, and rolls are high in trans fats. There are numerous negative health effects of eating deep-fried foods such as cardiovascular and coronary diseases, diabetes, obesity, gut microbes, and so on. According to the leading experts, when it comes to healthy dieting, you should not be afraid of fats. You should avoid partially hydrogenated and genetically modified oils such as cottonseed oil, corn oil, and margarine. Good fats include olive oil, avocado oil, nuts and seeds.

There are numerous benefits of cooking at home. You can control your portion and count calories more precisely; you can cook with natural and local ingredients. As you probably already know, most pre-packaged foods are high in salt, sodium, sugar and artificial ingredients. Did you know that the spills of used oils injure wildlife, which has harmful effects on our environment? Therefore, our food choices have a direct impact on our health and well-being.

A practical solution to every cooking challenge.

One of the greatest things I love about my Air Fryer is the fact that it cooks food in the sealed environment; it means you can forget about unpleasant kitchen smells! The Air Fryer is good at performing multiple tasks in the kitchen - frying, roasting, grilling, and baking. Some extra-large models can be used for a rotisserie and dehydrating. Plus, unlike the heat in your oven, the heat in the Air Fryer cooking basket is constant; it promotes better and even cooking.

It saves you time and money.

In today's fast-paced world, it seems difficult to follow a healthy diet. I know it. The Air Fryer is a massive time saver. Its easy press-and-go functions save a lot of time in the kitchen. If you're a practical person who doesn't want to spend a fortune on takeaways, you should invest in an Air Fryer. There are many money-saving kitchen tips out there; opt for freezer-friendly recipes that call for local and seasonal ingredients. You can look for items on sale or buy them in bulk. If you have leftover grains or beans, you can make delicious vegan burgers and freeze them in storage containers. This is far less expensive than eating out. The Air Fryer is an energy-efficient kitchen appliance too. To sum up, this is a space, cost, and frustration-saving cooking solution!

Do not give up eating fried foods, your Air Fryer is the perfect alternative to your favorite take-outs and restaurant. If you are thinking of cutting down on fat consumption, the Air Fryer is your number one choice! This is arguably the best way to cook fast food at your own kitchen and eat healthier. I hope you won't run out of inspiration with these 600 recipes! Happy air frying!

VEGETABLES & SIDE DISHES

Simple Roasted Green Beans

(Ready in about 9 minutes | Servings 4)

Per serving: 45 Calories; 1.3g Fat; 7g Carbs; 2.1g Protein; 3.7g Sugars; 3.1g Fiber

Ingredients

1 pound fresh green beans, cleaned and trimmed
1/2 teaspoon garlic powder
1/2 teaspoon cumin powder
1/2 teaspoon onion powder
1/2 teaspoon dried dill weed
1 teaspoon olive oil
Sea salt and red pepper flakes, to taste

Directions

Toss the green beans with the remaining ingredients until they are well coated.
Arrange the green beans in the Air Fryer basket.
Cook the green beans at 375 degrees F for 7 minutes; make sure to check the green beans halfway through the cooking time.
Taste, adjust the seasonings, and serve warm. Bon appétit!

Garlicky and Lemony Mushrooms

(Ready in about 12 minutes | Servings 3)

Per serving: 114 Calories; 9.4g Fat; 5.8g Carbs; 3.8g Protein; 3.1g Sugars; 1.4g Fiber

Ingredients

3/4 pound button mushrooms, cleaned and cut into halves
2 tablespoons olive oil
1 garlic clove, pressed
Sea salt and ground black pepper, to taste
1 tablespoon fresh lemon juice
1 tablespoon fresh cilantro, chopped

Directions

Toss your mushrooms with the olive oil, garlic, salt, and black pepper.
Arrange them on a lightly oiled Air Fryer basket.
Air fry the mushrooms at 375 degrees F for about 11 minutes, shaking the basket halfway through the cooking time.
Drizzle fresh lemon juice over the mushroom and serve with the fresh cilantro. Enjoy!

Spicy Fingerling Potatoes

(Ready in about 22 minutes | Servings 3)

Per serving: 127 Calories; 4.6g Fat; 19.8g Carbs; 2.3g Protein; 1g Sugars; 2.4g Fiber

Ingredients

3/4 pound fingerling potatoes
1 tablespoon olive oil
1/2 teaspoon onion powder
1 teaspoon garlic powder
1 teaspoon chili pepper
Sea salt and ground black pepper, to taste

Directions

Toss the potatoes with the remaining ingredients until well coated on all sides.
Arrange the potatoes in the Air Fryer basket.
Cook the potatoes at 400 degrees F for about 20 minutes, shaking the basket halfway through the cooking time.
Garnish with fresh or dried herbs, if desired. Bon appétit!

Classic Broccoli Florets

(Ready in about 8 minutes | Servings 3)

Per serving: 79 Calories; 4.9g Fat; 7.5g Carbs; 3g Protein; 1.9g Sugars; 2.9g Fiber

Ingredients

3/4 pound broccoli florets
1 tablespoon olive oil
1 teaspoon garlic powder
Sea salt and ground black pepper, to taste

Directions

Toss the broccoli florets with the remaining ingredients until well coated.
Arrange the broccoli florets in the Air Fryer basket.
Cook the broccoli florets at 395 degrees F for 6 minutes, shaking the basket halfway through the cooking time.
Bon appétit!

Creamed Cauliflower Salad with Bacon

(Ready in about 15 minutes | Servings 3)

Per serving: 269 Calories; 23.3g Fat; 9.5g Carbs; 5.7g Protein; 3.5g Sugars; 2.8g Fiber

Ingredients

3/4 pound cauliflower florets
2 ounces bacon, diced
1/4 cup sour cream
1/4 cup mayonnaise
1 teaspoon Dijon mustard
1 tablespoon apple cider vinegar
1 garlic clove, minced
1 small red onion, thinly sliced
Kosher salt and freshly ground black pepper, to taste

Directions

Place the cauliflower florets in a lightly greased Air Fryer basket.
Cook the cauliflower florets at 400 degrees F for 12 minutes, shaking the basket halfway through the cooking time.
Thoroughly combine the cauliflower florets with the remaining ingredients. Serve well-chilled and enjoy!

Roasted Beet Salad

(Ready in about 45 minutes | Servings 4)

Per serving: 172 Calories; 13.3g Fat; 11.2g Carbs; 1.9g Protein; 3.2g Sugars; 7.7g Fiber

Ingredients

1 pound beets, whole
1/2 teaspoon cumin seeds
Sea salt and red pepper flakes, to taste
2 tablespoons apple cider vinegar
4 tablespoons olive oil
1 teaspoon garlic, pressed

Directions

Arrange your beats in the Air Fryer basket.
Cook the beats at 400 F for 40 minutes, shaking the basket halfway through the cooking time. Let them cool completely.
Peel the beets and cut them into thin slices; transfer to a salad bowl. Add in the remaining ingredients and stir to combine.
Bon appétit!

Butter Garlic Brussels Sprouts

(Ready in about 15 minutes | Servings 3)

Per serving: 121 Calories; 8g Fat; 10.2g Carbs; 4g Protein; 2.5g Sugars; 4.4g Fiber

Ingredients

3/4 pound Brussels sprouts
2 tablespoons butter, melted
2 garlic cloves, crushed
Kosher salt and ground black pepper, to taste

Directions

Toss the Brussels sprouts with the remaining ingredients until well coated.
Arrange the Brussels sprouts in the Air Fryer basket.
Cook the Brussels sprouts at 380 degrees F for 14 minutes, shaking the basket halfway through the cooking time.
Bon appétit!

Easy Roasted Eggplant

(Ready in about 18 minutes | Servings 3)

Per serving: 108 Calories; 9.2g Fat; 6.7g Carbs; 1.1g Protein; 4g Sugars; 3.4g Fiber

Ingredients

3/4 pound eggplant, peeled and diced
2 tablespoons sesame oil
1/2 teaspoon cumin powder
1/2 teaspoon onion powder
1 teaspoon granulated garlic

Directions

Toss the eggplant pieces with the remaining ingredients until they are well coated on all sides.
Arrange the eggplant in the Air Fryer basket.
Cook the potatoes at 400 degrees F for about 15 minutes, shaking the basket halfway through the cooking time.
Garnish with fresh herbs, if desired. Bon appétit!

Roasted Cauliflower with Onion

(Ready in about 15 minutes | Servings 3)

Per serving: 92 Calories; 4.8g Fat; 10.9g Carbs; 2.8g Protein; 4.3g Sugars; 3g Fiber

Ingredients

3/4 pound cauliflower florets
1 large onion, cut into wedges
2 cloves garlic, pressed
1 tablespoon olive oil
Sea salt and ground black pepper, to taste
1 teaspoon paprika

Directions

Toss the cauliflower florets and onion with the garlic, olive oil, and spices. Toss until they are well coated on all sides.
Arrange the vegetables in the Air Fryer basket.
Cook the vegetables at 400 degrees F for about 13 minutes, shaking the basket halfway through the cooking time.
Bon appétit!

Yellow Beans with Tomatoes

(Ready in about 9 minutes | Servings 3)

Per serving: 75 Calories; 4.8g Fat; 7.6g Carbs; 2g Protein; 4g Sugars; 2.8g Fiber

Ingredients

1/2 pound yellow beans, trimmed
2 small tomatoes, sliced
1 tablespoon sesame oil
Sea salt and ground black pepper, to taste

Directions

Toss the green beans and tomatoes with the olive oil, salt, and black pepper; toss until they are well coated.
Arrange the vegetables in the Air Fryer basket.
Cook the green beans at 390 degrees F for 8 minutes; make sure to stir your vegetables halfway through the cooking time.
Taste, adjust the seasonings, and serve immediately.
Bon appétit!

Roasted Cremini Mushrooms

(Ready in about 9 minutes | Servings 4)

Per serving: 95 Calories; 7g Fat; 6g Carbs; 2.7g Protein; 3.5g Sugars; 1.8g Fiber

Ingredients

1 pound cremini mushrooms, sliced
2 tablespoons olive oil
1/2 teaspoon shallot powder
1/2 teaspoon garlic powder
1 tablespoon coconut aminos
1 tablespoon white wine
Sea salt and ground black pepper, to taste
1 tablespoon fresh parsley, chopped

Directions

Toss the mushrooms with the remaining ingredients. Toss until they are well coated on all sides.
Arrange the mushrooms in the Air Fryer basket.
Cook your mushrooms at 400 degrees F for about 7 minutes, shaking the basket halfway through the cooking time.
Garnish with the fresh herbs, if desired. Bon appétit!

Roasted Gold Potatoes

(Ready in about 20 minutes | Servings 3)

Per serving: 127 Calories; 4.7g Fat; 19.6g Carbs; 2.5g Protein; 1g Sugars; 2.5g Fiber

Ingredients

3/4 pound Yukon Gold potatoes, peeled and cut into 1-inch chunks
1 tablespoon olive oil
Sea salt and ground black pepper, to taste
1/2 turmeric powder
1/2 teaspoon garlic powder
1/2 teaspoon paprika

Directions

Toss the potatoes with the remaining ingredients until well coated on all sides.
Arrange the potatoes in the Air Fryer basket.
Cook the potatoes at 400 degrees F for about 13 minutes, shaking the basket halfway through the cooking time.
Bon appétit!

Caponata with a Twist

(Ready in about 20 minutes | Servings 3)

Per serving: 153 Calories; 12.3g Fat; 9.9g Carbs; 1.8g Protein; 6.1g Sugars; 3.8g Fiber

Ingredients

3 bell peppers, sliced
1 medium-sized onion, sliced
2 tablespoons olive oil
2 ounces olives, pitted and sliced
1 large tomato, sliced
1 teaspoon capers, drained

Directions

Toss the peppers, onion, and olive oil in the Air Fryer cooking basket.
Cook the vegetables at 400 degrees F for about 10 minutes, shaking the basket halfway through the cooking time.
Add in the olives, tomato, and capers. Continue to cook an additional 5 minutes or until everything is cooked through.
Bon appétit!

Parmesan Broccoli Florets

(Ready in about 8 minutes | Servings 3)

Per serving: 158 Calories; 10.1g Fat; 10.2g Carbs; 8.3g Protein; 1.9g Sugars; 3g Fiber

Ingredients

3/4 pound broccoli florets
1 tablespoon olive oil
1/2 teaspoon dried dill weed
Coarse sea salt and freshly ground black pepper, to taste
2 ounces parmesan cheese, freshly grated

Directions

Toss the broccoli florets with the olive oil, dill, salt, and black pepper until well coated.
Arrange the broccoli florets in the Air Fryer basket.
Cook the broccoli florets at 395 degrees F for 6 minutes, shaking the basket halfway through the cooking time.
Top with the parmesan cheese and serve warm. Bon appétit!

Loaded Cauliflower Salad

(Ready in about 15 minutes | Servings 4)

Per serving: 192 Calories; 11.8g Fat; 17.2g Carbs; 6.1g Protein; 4.3g Sugars; 5.7g Fiber

Ingredients

1 pound cauliflower florets
1 cup chickpeas, canned or boiled
1/4 cup mayonnaise
1 teaspoon Dijon mustard
1 teaspoon ancho chili powder
Sea salt and ground black pepper, to taste
2 tablespoons fresh chives, chopped
2 tablespoons apple cider vinegar

Directions

Arrange the cauliflower florets in a lightly greased Air Fryer basket.
Cook the cauliflower florets at 400 degrees F for 12 minutes, shaking the basket halfway through the cooking time.
Thoroughly combine the cauliflower florets with the remaining ingredients. Serve well-chilled and enjoy!

Greek-Style Roasted Beets

(Ready in about 45 minutes | Servings 4)

Per serving: 252 Calories; 19.3g Fat; 13.2g Carbs; 6.1g Protein; 9.6g Sugars; 3.7g Fiber

Ingredients

1 pound beets, whole
Sea salt and red pepper flakes, to taste
2 tablespoons apple cider vinegar
4 tablespoons olive oil
1 teaspoon garlic powder
4 ounces feta cheese, crumbled

Directions

Arrange your beats in the Air Fryer basket.
Cook the beats at 400 F for 40 minutes, shaking the basket halfway through the cooking time. Let them cool completely.
Peel the beets and cut them into thin slices; transfer to a salad bowl. Add in the remaining ingredients and stir to combine.
Bon appétit!

Mediterranean-Style Green Beans

(Ready in about 10 minutes | Servings 3)

Per serving: 147 Calories; 9.3g Fat; 11.2g Carbs; 5.6g Protein; 5.5g Sugars; 3.6g Fiber

Ingredients

3/4 pound green beans, cleaned and trimmed
1 tablespoon olive oil
1 clove garlic, pressed
Sea salt and ground black pepper, to taste
2 ounces feta cheese, crumbled
1 tablespoon pistachio, chopped

Directions

Toss the green beans with the olive oil, garlic, salt, and black pepper until they are well coated.

Arrange the green beans in the Air Fryer basket.
Cook the green beans at 375 degrees F for 7 minutes; make sure to check the green beans halfway through the cooking time.
Taste, adjust the seasonings, and serve garnished with cheese and chopped pistachio. Enjoy!

Chinese-Style Brussels Sprouts

(Ready in about 15 minutes | Servings 2)
Per serving: 187 Calories; 14.3g Fat; 13.2g Carbs; 4.4g Protein; 3.8g Sugars; 4.9g Fiber
Ingredients
1/2 pound Brussels sprouts, trimmed
2 tablespoons sesame oil
Sea salt and ground black pepper, to taste
1 teaspoon Five-spice powder
1 teaspoon soy sauce
1 teaspoon rice vinegar
Directions
Toss the Brussels sprouts with the oil until well coated on all sides; then, arrange the Brussels sprouts in the Air Fryer basket.
Cook the Brussels sprouts at 380 degrees F for 10 minutes, shaking the basket halfway through the cooking time.
Toss them with the remaining ingredients and continue to cook for 3 to 4 minutes more. Serve warm and enjoy!

Italian-Style Eggplant Slices

(Ready in about 15 minutes | Servings 4)
Per serving: 210 Calories; 14.3g Fat; 10.2g Carbs; 11.4g Protein; 3.9g Sugars; 4.1g Fiber
Ingredients
2 eggs, whisked
1/2 cup almond flour
1/2 cup Parmesan cheese, grated
1 teaspoon Italian seasoning mix
3/4 pound eggplant, peeled and sliced
Directions
In a mixing bowl, thoroughly combine the eggs, almond flour, cheese, and Italian seasoning mix.
Dip the eggplant slices in the egg/flour mixture until they are well coated on all sides.
Arrange the eggplant in the Air Fryer basket.
Cook the eggplant at 400 degrees F for about 13 minutes, shaking the basket halfway through the cooking time.
Bon appétit!

Herbed Cauliflower Florets

(Ready in about 15 minutes | Servings 3)
Per serving: 70 Calories; 4.8g Fat; 5.6g Carbs; 2.4g Protein; 2.3g Sugars; 2.1g Fiber
Ingredients
3/4 pound cauliflower florets
1 tablespoon olive oil
1/2 teaspoon dried oregano
1 teaspoon dried basil
1 teaspoon dried rosemary
Sea salt and ground black pepper, to taste
Directions
Toss the cauliflower florets and onion with the olive oil and spices. Toss until they are well coated on all sides.
Arrange the cauliflower florets in the Air Fryer basket.
Cook the cauliflower florets at 400 degrees F for about 13 minutes, shaking the basket halfway through the cooking time.
Bon appétit!

Mom's Roasted Peppers

(Ready in about 15 minutes | Servings 3)
Per serving: 128 Calories; 9.3g Fat; 11.2g Carbs; 2g Protein; 0.7g Sugars; 1.6g Fiber
Ingredients
1 pound bell peppers, seeded and halved
1 chili pepper, seeded
2 tablespoons olive oil
Kosher salt and ground black pepper, to taste
1 teaspoon granulated garlic
Directions
Toss the peppers with the remaining ingredients; place them in the Air Fryer cooking basket.
Cook the peppers at 400 degrees F for about 15 minutes, shaking the basket halfway through the cooking time.
Taste, adjust the seasonings and serve at room temperature. Bon appétit!

Saucy Brown Mushrooms

(Ready in about 9 minutes | Servings 4)
Per serving: 88 Calories; 7g Fat; 5.5g Carbs; 2.9g Protein; 2.1g Sugars; 0.8g Fiber
Ingredients
1 pound brown mushrooms, quartered
2 tablespoons sesame oil
1 tablespoon tamari sauce
1 garlic clove, pressed
Sea salt and ground black pepper, to taste
Directions
Toss the mushrooms with the remaining ingredients. Toss until they are well coated on all sides.
Arrange the mushrooms in the Air Fryer basket.
Cook your mushrooms at 400 degrees F for about 7 minutes, shaking the basket halfway through the cooking time.
Bon appétit!

Country-Style Vegetables

(Ready in about 20 minutes | Servings 4)
Per serving: 119 Calories; 7g Fat; 15g Carbs; 1.2g Protein; 6.6g Sugars; 2.8g Fiber
Ingredients
1 carrot, trimmed and sliced
1 parsnip, trimmed and sliced
1 celery stalk, trimmed and sliced
1 onion, peeled and diced
2 tablespoons olive oil

Sea salt and ground black pepper, to taste
1 teaspoon red pepper flakes, crushed
Directions
Toss all ingredients in the Air Fryer basket.
Cook your mushrooms at 380 degrees F for about 15 minutes, shaking the basket halfway through the cooking time.
Bon appétit!

Classic Spicy Potatoes

(Ready in about 20 minutes | Servings 4)
Per serving: 117 Calories; 3.5g Fat; 19.5g Carbs; 2.3g Protein; 1g Sugars; 2.5g Fiber
Ingredients
1 pound potatoes, diced into bite-sized chunks
1 tablespoon olive oil
Sea salt and ground black pepper, to taste
1 teaspoon chili powder
Directions
Toss the potatoes with the remaining ingredients until well coated on all sides.
Arrange the potatoes in the Air Fryer basket.
Cook the potatoes at 400 degrees F for about 13 minutes, shaking the basket halfway through the cooking time.
Bon appétit!

Roasted Broccoli Florets with Pepitas

(Ready in about 8 minutes | Servings 3)
Per serving: 139 Calories; 10.3g Fat; 9.8g Carbs; 4.7g Protein; 2.1g Sugars; 3.6g Fiber
Ingredients
3/4 pound broccoli florets
1 ½ tablespoons olive oil
1 teaspoon garlic powder
1/2 teaspoon onion powder
1/2 teaspoon mustard seeds
Sea salt and freshly ground black pepper, to taste
2 tablespoons pepitas, lightly roasted
Directions
Toss the broccoli with the olive oil, garlic powder, onion powder, mustard seeds, salt, and black pepper.
Cook the broccoli florets at 395 degrees F for 6 minutes, shaking the basket halfway through the cooking time.
Top with roasted pepitas and serve warm. Bon appétit!

Paprika Sweet Potatoes

(Ready in about 40 minutes | Servings 4)
Per serving: 187 Calories; 10.1g Fat; 22.8g Carbs; 1.7g Protein; 4.7g Sugars; 3.6g Fiber
Ingredients
1 pound sweet potatoes, scrubbed and halved
3 tablespoons olive oil
1 teaspoon paprika
Sea salt and ground black pepper, to taste
Directions
Toss the sweet potatoes with the olive oil, paprika, salt, and black pepper.
Cook the sweet potatoes at 380 degrees F for 35 minutes, shaking the basket halfway through the cooking time.
Taste and adjust the seasonings. Bon appétit!

Refreshing Green Salad

(Ready in about 10 minutes | Servings 3)
Per serving: 132 Calories; 10g Fat; 11.4g Carbs; 3.7g Protein; 5.1g Sugars; 4g Fiber
Ingredients
3/4 pound fresh green beans, washed and trimmed
2 tablespoons olive oil
1/2 cup green onions, thinly sliced
2 cups baby spinach
1 tablespoon fresh basil, chopped
1 green pepper, sliced
2 tablespoons fresh lemon juice
Sea salt and ground black pepper, to taste
Directions
Toss the green beans with 1 tablespoon of the olive oil. Arrange the green beans in the Air Fryer basket.
Cook the green beans at 375 degrees F for 7 minutes; make sure to check the green beans halfway through the cooking time.
Add the green beans to a salad bowl; add in the remaining ingredients and stir to combine well.
Enjoy!

Chinese-Style Corn on the Cob

(Ready in about 10 minutes | Servings 2)
Per serving: 242 Calories; 15.2g Fat; 27.4g Carbs; 4.6g Protein; 4.6g Sugars; 4g Fiber
Ingredients
2 ears of corn, husked and halved
2 tablespoons Chinese chili oil
Sea salt and red pepper, to taste
2 tablespoons fresh cilantro, chopped
Directions
Toss the ears of corn with the oil, salt, and red pepper. Arrange the ears of corn in the Air Fryer cooking basket.
Cook the ears of corn at 390 degrees F for about 6 minutes, tossing them halfway through the cooking time.
Garnish the ears of corn with the fresh cilantro. Bon appétit!

Buttery Brussels Sprouts

(Ready in about 15 minutes | Servings 3)
Per serving: 85 Calories; 4.3g Fat; 10.2g Carbs; 4g Protein; 2.5g Sugars; 4.4g Fiber
Ingredients
3/4 pound Brussels sprouts, trimmed
1 tablespoon butter, melted
1 teaspoon red pepper flakes, crushed
Kosher salt and ground black pepper, to taste
Directions
Toss the Brussels sprouts with the butter and spices until they are well coated on all sides; then, arrange the Brussels sprouts in the Air Fryer basket.

Cook the Brussels sprouts at 380 degrees F for 10 minutes, shaking the basket halfway through the cooking time.
Serve warm and enjoy!

Easy Breaded Eggplant

(Ready in about 15 minutes | Servings 3)
Per serving: 187 Calories; 1.4g Fat; 36.5g Carbs; 8g Protein; 5.3g Sugars; 4.8g Fiber
Ingredients
Sea salt and freshly ground black pepper, to taste
1/2 cup all-purpose flour
2 eggs
3/4 pound eggplant, sliced
1/2 cup bread crumbs
Directions
In a shallow bowl, mix the salt, black pepper, and flour. Whisk the eggs in the second bowl, and place the breadcrumbs in the third bowl.
Dip the eggplant slices in the flour mixture, then in the whisked eggs; finally, roll the eggplant slices over the breadcrumbs until they are well coated on all sides.
Arrange the eggplant in the Air Fryer basket.
Cook the eggplant at 400 degrees F for about 13 minutes, shaking the basket halfway through the cooking time.
Bon appétit!

Easy Parsnips Provencal

(Ready in about 15 minutes | Servings 4)
Per serving: 117 Calories; 3.7g Fat; 20.5g Carbs; 1.3g Protein; 5.3g Sugars; 5.6g Fiber
Ingredients
1 pound parsnips, trimmed
1 tablespoon olive oil
1 teaspoon Herbs de province
1 teaspoon cayenne pepper
Sea salt and ground black pepper, to taste
Directions
Toss the parsnip with the olive oil and spices until they are well coated on all sides; then, arrange the parsnip in the Air Fryer basket.
Cook the parsnip at 380 degrees F for 10 minutes, shaking the basket halfway through the cooking time.
Bon appétit!

Crispy Portobello Mushrooms

(Ready in about 10 minutes | Servings 3)
Per serving: 297 Calories; 3.5g Fat; 48.5g Carbs; 10g Protein; 8.7g Sugars; 8.6g Fiber
Ingredients
1/2 cup flour
2 eggs
1 cup seasoned breadcrumbs
1 teaspoon smoked paprika
Sea salt and ground black pepper, to taste
3/4 pound Portobello mushrooms, sliced
Directions
Place the flour in a plate. Whisk the eggs in a shallow bowl. In a third bowl, mix the breadcrumbs, paprika, salt, and black pepper.
Dip your mushrooms in the flour, then dunk them in the whisked eggs, and finally toss them in the breadcrumb mixture. Toss until well coated on all sides.
Cook the mushrooms at 400 degrees F for about 7 minutes, turning them halfway through the cooking time.
Bon appétit!

Tomato and Cheese Stuffed Peppers

(Ready in about 13 minutes | Servings 3)
Per serving: 223 Calories; 6.5g Fat; 31.5g Carbs; 6.6g Protein; 17.7g Sugars; 8.5g Fiber
Ingredients
3 bell peppers, seeded and halved
1 tablespoon olive oil
1 small onion, chopped
2 garlic cloves, minced
Sea salt and ground black pepper, to taste
1 cup tomato sauce
2 ounces cheddar cheese, shredded
Directions
Toss the peppers with the oil; place them in the Air Fryer cooking basket.
Mix the onion, garlic, salt, black pepper, and tomato sauce. Spoon the sauce into the pepper halves.
Cook the peppers at 400 degrees F for about 10 minutes. Top the peppers with the cheese. Continue to cook for 5 minutes more.
Bon appétit!

Easy Parsnip Burgers

(Ready in about 20 minutes | Servings 3)
Per serving: 179 Calories; 2.2g Fat; 35.9g Carbs; 4.9g Protein; 5.6g Sugars; 6.5g Fiber
Ingredients
3/4 pound peeled parsnips, shredded
1/4 cup all-purpose flour
1/4 cup cornflour
1 egg, lightly beaten
1 teaspoon cayenne pepper
Sea salt and ground black pepper, to taste
Directions
Mix all ingredients until everything is well combined.
Form the mixture into three patties.
Cook the burgers at 380 degrees F for about 15 minutes or until cooked through.
Bon appétit!

Classic Broccoli Salad

(Ready in about 8 minutes | Servings 3)
Per serving: 293 Calories; 24.3g Fat; 16.2g Carbs; 6.2g Protein; 6g Sugars; 4.6g Fiber
Ingredients
3/4 pound broccoli florets
1/4 cup raw sunflower seeds
1 clove garlic, peeled and minced

1 small red onion, thinly sliced
1/4 cup dried cranberries
1/4 cup extra-virgin olive oil
2 tablespoons fresh lemon juice
1 tablespoon Dijon mustard
Sea salt and ground black pepper, to taste
Directions
Place the broccoli florets in a lightly greased Air Fryer basket.
Cook the broccoli florets at 395 degrees F for 6 minutes, shaking the basket halfway through the cooking time.
Toss the broccoli florets with the remaining ingredients. Serve at room temperature.
Bon appétit!

Parmesan Cauliflower Florets

(Ready in about 15 minutes | Servings 4)
Per serving: 213 Calories; 15.3g Fat; 10.9g Carbs; 10.5g Protein; 2.6g Sugars; 2.8g Fiber
Ingredients
1 pound cauliflower florets
2 tablespoons olive oil
1 teaspoon smoked paprika
Sea salt and ground black pepper, to taste
4 ounces parmesan cheese, grated
Directions
Toss the cauliflower florets with the olive oil and spices. Toss until they are well coated on all sides.
Arrange the cauliflower florets in the Air Fryer basket.
Cook the cauliflower florets at 400 degrees F for about 13 minutes, shaking the basket halfway through the cooking time.
Toss the warm cauliflower florets with cheese. Bon appétit!

Parmesan Paprika Potatoes

(Ready in about 20 minutes | Servings 3)
Per serving: 215 Calories; 10g Fat; 24.3g Carbs; 8g Protein; 1.8g Sugars; 3g Fiber
Ingredients
3/4 pound potatoes, diced
1 tablespoon olive oil
1 teaspoon smoked paprika
1 teaspoon red pepper flakes, crushed
Sea salt and ground black pepper, to taste
2 ounces parmesan cheese, grated
Directions
Toss the potatoes with the olive oil and spices until well coated on all sides.
Arrange the potatoes in the Air Fryer basket.
Cook the potatoes at 400 degrees F for about 15 minutes, shaking the basket halfway through the cooking time.
Top the warm potatoes with cheese and serve immediately. Enjoy!

Szechuan Green Beans

(Ready in about 9 minutes | Servings 4)
Per serving: 108 Calories; 6.8g Fat; 10.7g Carbs; 3.4g Protein; 5g Sugars; 3.8g Fiber
Ingredients
1 pound fresh green beans, trimmed
1 tablespoon sesame oil
1/2 teaspoon garlic powder
1 tablespoon soy sauce
Sea salt and Szechuan pepper, to taste
2 tablespoons sesame seeds, lightly toasted
Directions
Toss the green beans with the sesame oil and garlic powder; then, arrange them in the Air Fryer basket.
Cook the green beans at 380 degrees F for 7 minutes; make sure to check the green beans halfway through the cooking time.
Toss the green beans with the remaining ingredients and stir to combine well. Enjoy!

Carrots with Sesame Seeds

(Ready in about 20 minutes | Servings 3)
Per serving: 131 Calories; 9.5g Fat; 11.1g Carbs; 1.7g Protein; 5.3g Sugars; 3.5g Fiber
Ingredients
3/4 pound carrots, trimmed and cut into sticks
2 tablespoons butter, melted
Coarse sea salt and white pepper, to taste
1 tablespoon sesame seeds, lightly toasted
Directions
Toss the carrots with the butter, salt, and white pepper; then, arrange them in the Air Fryer basket.
Cook the carrots at 380 degrees F for 15 minutes; make sure to check the carrots halfway through the cooking time.
Top the carrots with the sesame seeds. Bon appétit!

Warm Brussels Sprout Salad

(Ready in about 12 minutes | Servings 3)
Per serving: 138 Calories; 9.3g Fat; 12g Carbs; 4g Protein; 3.4g Sugars; 4.6g Fiber
Ingredients
3/4 pound Brussels sprouts, trimmed
2 tablespoons olive oil
Sea salt and ground black pepper, to taste
1/2 teaspoon dried dill weed
1 tablespoon fresh lemon juice
1 tablespoon rice vinegar
Directions
Toss the Brussels sprouts with the olive oil and spices until they are well coated on all sides; then, arrange the Brussels sprouts in the Air Fryer basket.
Cook the Brussels sprouts at 380 degrees F for 10 minutes, shaking the basket halfway through the cooking time.
Toss the Brussels sprouts with lemon juice and vinegar. Enjoy!

Dilled Buttery Sweet Potatoes

(Ready in about 40 minutes | Servings 2)
Per serving: 163 Calories; 5.8g Fat; 26.2g Carbs; 2g Protein; 5.4g Sugars; 3.6g Fiber

Ingredients
2 sweet potatoes, peeled and halved
1 tablespoon butter, melted
1 teaspoon dried dill weed
Sea salt and red pepper flakes, crushed
Directions
Toss the sweet potatoes with the remaining ingredients.
Cook the sweet potatoes at 380 degrees F for 15 minutes, shaking the basket halfway through the cooking time.
Taste and adjust the seasonings. Bon appétit!

Easy Buttery Mushrooms with Tomatoes

(Ready in about 10 minutes | Servings 4)
Per serving: 84 Calories; 6.3g Fat; 6.1g Carbs; 2.8g Protein; 2g Sugars; 4.1g Fiber
Ingredients
1 pound cremini mushrooms, sliced
1 large tomato, sliced
2 tablespoons butter, melted
1 teaspoon rosemary, minced
1 teaspoon parsley, minced
1 teaspoon garlic, minced
Coarse sea salt and ground black pepper, to taste
Directions
Toss the mushrooms and tomatoes with the remaining ingredients. Toss until they are well coated on all sides.
Arrange the mushrooms in the Air Fryer basket.
Cook your mushrooms at 400 degrees F for about 7 minutes, shaking the basket halfway through the cooking time.
Bon appétit!

Winter Vegetable Patties

(Ready in about 20 minutes | Servings 3)
Per serving: 184 Calories; 3.3g Fat; 31.1g Carbs; 8g Protein; 5.6g Sugars; 4.3g Fiber
Ingredients
1 carrot, shredded
1 parsnip, shredded
1 onion, chopped
1 garlic clove, minced
1/2 cup all-purpose flour
1 teaspoon cayenne pepper
Sea salt and ground black pepper, to taste
2 eggs, whisked
Directions
Mix all ingredients until everything is well combined.
Form the mixture into three patties.
Cook the burgers at 380 degrees F for about 15 minutes or until cooked through.
Bon appétit!

Asian-Style Balsamic Fennel

(Ready in about 20 minutes | Servings 4)
Per serving: 114 Calories; 8.3g Fat; 9.1g Carbs; 2g Protein; 5.2g Sugars; 3.8g Fiber
Ingredients
1 pound fennel bulbs, trimmed and sliced
2 tablespoons sesame oil
Sea salt and ground black pepper, to taste
1 teaspoon red pepper flakes, crushed
1 tablespoon balsamic vinegar
1 tablespoon soy sauce
1 tablespoon sesame seeds, lightly toasted
Directions
Toss the fennel with the sesame oil, salt, black pepper, and red pepper flakes.
Cook the fennel at 370 degrees F for about 15 minutes or until cooked through; check your fennel halfway through the cooking time.
Toss the warm fennel with the vinegar, soy sauce, and sesame seeds.
Bon appétit!

Roasted Paprika Asparagus

(Ready in about 10 minutes | Servings 3)
Per serving: 110 Calories; 6.3g Fat; 9.2g Carbs; 2.9g Protein; 2.9g Sugars; 2.9g Fiber
Ingredients
3/4 pound fresh asparagus, trimmed
Coarse sea salt and ground black pepper, to taste
1 teaspoon paprika
2 tablespoons olive oil
Directions
Toss the asparagus with the salt, black pepper, paprika, and olive oil. Arrange the asparagus spears in the Air Fryer cooking basket.
Cook the asparagus at 400 degrees F for about 6 minutes, tossing them halfway through the cooking time.
Bon appétit!

Bean Buckwheat Burgers

(Ready in about 20 minutes | Servings 4)
Per serving: 198 Calories; 8.7g Fat; 24.2g Carbs; 8g Protein; 2.2g Sugars; 5.3g Fiber
Ingredients
1 cup buckwheat, soaked overnight and rinsed
1 cup canned kidney beans, drained and well rinsed
1/4 cup walnuts, chopped
1 tablespoon olive oil
1 small onion, chopped
1 teaspoon smoked paprika
Sea salt and ground black pepper, to taste
1/2 cup bread crumbs
Directions
Mix all ingredients until everything is well combined.
Form the mixture into four patties and arrange them in a lightly greased Air Fryer basket.
Cook the burgers at 380 degrees F for about 15 minutes or until cooked through. Tun them over halfway through the cooking time.
Bon appétit!

Asparagus with Pecorino Cheese

(Ready in about 10 minutes | Servings 4)

Per serving: 120 Calories; 8.5g Fat; 5.9g Carbs; 6.9g Protein; 2.6g Sugars; 2.8g Fiber

Ingredients

1 pound asparagus, trimmed
1 tablespoon sesame oil
1/2 teaspoon onion powder
1/2 teaspoon granulated garlic
Sea salt and cayenne pepper, to taste
1/2 cup Pecorino cheese, preferably freshly grated

Directions

Toss the asparagus with the sesame oil, onion powder, granulated garlic, salt, and cayenne pepper. Arrange the asparagus spears in the Air Fryer cooking basket.

Cook the asparagus at 400 degrees F for about 6 minutes, tossing them halfway through the cooking time.

Top the asparagus with the cheese. Bon appétit!

Cheesy Green Beans

(Ready in about 9 minutes | Servings 2)

Per serving: 154 Calories; 9.6g Fat; 13g Carbs; 6.4g Protein; 6.9g Sugars; 3.4g Fiber

Ingredients

1/2 pound green beans
1 tablespoon sesame oil
Sea salt and ground black pepper, to taste
2 ounces cheddar cheese, grated

Directions

Toss the green beans with the sesame oil; then, arrange them in the Air Fryer basket.

Cook the green beans at 380 degrees F for 7 minutes, tossing the basket halfway through the cooking time.

Toss the warm green beans with the salt, black pepper, and cheese; stir to combine well. Enjoy!

Italian Peppers with Herbs

(Ready in about 15 minutes | Servings 3)

Per serving: 77 Calories; 4.6g Fat; 7.2g Carbs; 1.4g Protein; 5g Sugars; 2.4g Fiber

Ingredients

3 Italian peppers, seeded and halved
1 tablespoon olive oil
Kosher salt and ground black pepper, to taste
1 teaspoon cayenne pepper
1 tablespoon fresh parsley, chopped
1 tablespoon fresh basil, chopped
1 tablespoon fresh chives, chopped

Directions

Toss the peppers with the olive oil, salt, black pepper, and cayenne pepper; place the peppers in the Air Fryer cooking basket.

Cook the peppers at 400 degrees F for about 13 minutes, shaking the basket halfway through the cooking time.

Taste, adjust the seasonings, and serve with the fresh herbs. Bon appétit!

Brussels Sprouts with Ham

(Ready in about 15 minutes | Servings 4)

Per serving: 93 Calories; 4.3g Fat; 10.2g Carbs; 6.2g Protein; 2.4g Sugars; 4.3g Fiber

Ingredients

1 pound Brussels sprouts, trimmed
1 tablespoon peanut oil
Sea salt and freshly ground black pepper, to season
2 ounces ham, diced

Directions

Toss the Brussels sprouts with the remaining ingredients; then, arrange the Brussels sprouts in the Air Fryer basket.

Cook the Brussels sprouts at 380 degrees F for 13 minutes, shaking the basket halfway through the cooking time.

Serve warm and enjoy!

Buttery Garlicky Potatoes

(Ready in about 20 minutes | Servings 3)

Per serving: 123 Calories; 4g Fat; 20.1g Carbs; 2.3g Protein; 0.9g Sugars; 2.5g Fiber

Ingredients

3/4 pound potatoes, quartered
1 tablespoon butter, melted
1 teaspoon garlic, pressed
1 teaspoon dried oregano
Sea salt and ground black pepper, to taste

Directions

Toss the potatoes with the remaining ingredients until well coated on all sides.

Arrange the potatoes in the Air Fryer basket.

Cook the potatoes at 400 degrees F for about 18 minutes, shaking the basket halfway through the cooking time.

Serve warm and enjoy!

Cheesy Chestnut Mushrooms

(Ready in about 10 minutes | Servings 4)

Per serving: 83 Calories; 5.1g Fat; 6.4g Carbs; 4g Protein; 3.4g Sugars; 1.7g Fiber

Ingredients

1 pound chestnut mushrooms, quartered
1 tablespoon olive oil
1 garlic clove, pressed
Sea salt and ground black pepper, to taste
4 tablespoons Pecorino Romano cheese, shredded

Directions

Toss the mushrooms with the oil, garlic, salt, and black pepper. Toss until they are well coated on all sides.

Arrange the mushrooms in the Air Fryer basket.

Cook your mushrooms at 400 degrees F for about 7 minutes, shaking the basket halfway through the cooking time.

Afterwards, toss the mushrooms with the cheese and serve immediately!

Mexican-Style Sweet Potatoes

(Ready in about 40 minutes | Servings 4)

Per serving: 128 Calories; 3.5g Fat; 22.1g Carbs; 3g Protein; 2.1g Sugars; 3g Fiber

Ingredients
1 pound sweet potatoes, scrubbed, prick with a fork
1 tablespoon olive oil
Coarse sea salt and ground black pepper, to taste
1/2 teaspoon cayenne pepper
4 tablespoons salsa
Directions
Sprinkle the sweet potatoes with olive oil, salt, black pepper, and cayenne pepper.
Cook the sweet potatoes at 380 degrees F for 35 minutes, checking them halfway through the cooking time.
Split the tops open with a knife. Top each potato with salsa and serve. Bon appétit!

Brown Mushroom Burgers

(Ready in about 15 minutes | Servings 3)
Per serving: 184 Calories; 11.1g Fat; 14g Carbs; 9.4g Protein; 4g Sugars; 1.5g Fiber
Ingredients
3/4 pound brown mushrooms, chopped
1 large eggs, whisked
1/2 cup breadcrumbs
1/2 cup parmesan cheese, grated
1 small onion, minced
1 garlic clove, minced
Sea salt and ground black pepper, to taste
1 tablespoon olive oil
Directions
Mix all ingredients until everything is well combined.
Form the mixture into three patties.
Cook the burgers at 380 degrees F for about 15 minutes or until cooked through.
Bon appétit!

Roasted Fennel Slices

(Ready in about 20 minutes | Servings 4)
Per serving: 97 Calories; 6.9g Fat; 8.4g Carbs; 1.4g Protein; 4.4g Sugars; 3.5g Fiber
Ingredients
1 pound fennel bulbs, trimmed and sliced
2 tablespoons olive oil
1 teaspoon fresh garlic, minced
1 teaspoon dried parsley flakes
Kosher salt and ground black pepper, to taste
Directions
Toss all ingredients in a mixing bowl.
Cook the fennel at 370 degrees F for about 15 minutes or until cooked through; check your fennel halfway through the cooking time.
Bon appétit!

Chinese Spicy Asparagus

(Ready in about 10 minutes | Servings 4)
Per serving: 75 Calories; 6g Fat; 5.6g Carbs; 2.8g Protein; 2.9g Sugars; 2.5g Fiber
Ingredients
1 pound asparagus
4 teaspoons Chinese chili oil
1/2 teaspoon garlic powder
1 tablespoon soy sauce
1/2 teaspoon red pepper flakes, crushed
Directions
Toss the asparagus with the remaining ingredients. Arrange the asparagus spears in the Air Fryer cooking basket.
Cook the asparagus at 400 degrees F for about 6 minutes, tossing them halfway through the cooking time.
Bon appétit!

Stuffed Breakfast Peppers

(Ready in about 15 minutes | Servings 3)
Per serving: 143 Calories; 9.1g Fat; 7.8g Carbs; 6.4g Protein; 5.4g Sugars; 2.6g Fiber
Ingredients
3 bell peppers, seeded and halved
1 tablespoon olive oil
3 eggs
3 tablespoons green onion, chopped
Sea salt and ground black pepper
Directions
Toss the peppers with the oil; place them in the Air Fryer cooking basket.
Crack an egg into each bell pepper half. Sprinkle your peppers with the salt and black pepper.
Cook the peppers at 400 degrees F for about 10 minutes. Top the peppers with green onions.
Continue to cook for 4 minutes more.
Bon appétit!

Indian Gujarati Green Beans

(Ready in about 10 minutes | Servings 3)
Per serving: 136 Calories; 10.4g Fat; 9.8g Carbs; 2.7g Protein; 4.9g Sugars; 3.3g Fiber
Ingredients
3/4 pound fresh green beans, trimmed
1 garlic clove, minced
2 tablespoons olive oil
1 tablespoon soy sauce
1 teaspoon black mustard seeds
1 dried red chile pepper, crushed
Sea salt and ground black pepper, to taste
Directions
Toss the green beans with the remaining ingredients; then, arrange them in the Air Fryer basket.
Cook the green beans at 380 degrees F for 8 minutes, tossing the basket halfway through the cooking time.
Enjoy!

Cheese Stuffed Mushrooms

(Ready in about 9 minutes | Servings 3)
Per serving: 124 Calories; 7.6g Fat; 8g Carbs; 7.7g Protein; 5g Sugars; 1.4g Fiber
Ingredients
3/4 pound button mushrooms, halved
1 tablespoon oil
Sea salt and ground black pepper, to taste
1/2 teaspoon garlic powder
3 ounces cheddar cheese, cubed

Directions

Toss the mushrooms with the olive oil, salt, black pepper, and garlic powder. Toss until they are well coated on all sides.

Arrange the mushrooms in the Air Fryer basket.

Cook your mushrooms at 400 degrees F for about 7 minutes, shaking the basket halfway through the cooking time.

Bon appétit!

Brussels Sprouts with Provolone Cheese

(Ready in about 13 minutes | Servings 4)

Per serving: 183 Calories; 11.3g Fat; 11.8g Carbs; 11.4g Protein; 3.2g Sugars; 4.5g Fiber

Ingredients

1 pound Brussels sprouts, trimmed
1 tablespoon olive oil
Sea salt and ground black pepper, to taste
4 ounces Provolone cheese, crumbled

Directions

Toss the Brussels sprouts with the olive oil and spices until they are well coated on all sides; then, arrange the Brussels sprouts in the Air Fryer basket.

Cook the Brussels sprouts at 380 degrees F for 10 minutes, shaking the basket halfway through the cooking time.

Toss the Brussels sprouts with the cheese and serve warm. Enjoy!

POULTRY

Easy Chicken Fingers

(Ready in about 13 minutes | Servings 4)

Per serving: 347 Calories; 10.4g Fat; 20.8g Carbs; 39.4g Protein; 2.2g Sugars; 1.4g Fiber

Ingredients

1 ½ pounds chicken tenders
1 tablespoon olive oil
1 egg, whisked
1 teaspoon fresh parsley, minced
1 teaspoon garlic, minced
Sea salt and black pepper, to taste
1 cup breadcrumbs

Directions

Pat the chicken dry with kitchen towels.
In a bowl, thoroughly combine the oil, egg, parsley, garlic, salt, and black pepper.
Dip the chicken tenders into the egg mixture. Then, roll the chicken over the breadcrumbs.
Cook the chicken tenders at 360 degrees F for 10 minutes, shaking the basket halfway through the cooking time.
Bon appétit!

Buttery Chicken Breasts

(Ready in about 15 minutes | Servings 4)

Per serving: 227 Calories; 13.4g Fat; 0.2g Carbs; 23.4g Protein; 0.2g Sugars; 1g Fiber

Ingredients

1 pound chicken breasts raw, boneless and skinless
1 tablespoon butter, room temperature
1 teaspoon garlic powder
Kosher salt and ground black pepper, to taste
1 teaspoon dried parsley flakes
1 teaspoon smoked paprika
1/2 teaspoon dried oregano

Directions

Pat the chicken dry with kitchen towels. Toss the chicken breasts with the remaining ingredients.
Cook the chicken at 380 degrees F for 12 minutes, turning them over halfway through the cooking time.
Bon appétit!

Hot Chicken Thighs

(Ready in about 25 minutes | Servings 4)

Per serving: 317 Calories; 25.4g Fat; 1.5g Carbs; 19.1g Protein; 0.6g Sugars; 1g Fiber

Ingredients

1 pound chicken thighs, bone-in
Sea salt and freshly ground black pepper, to taste
2 tablespoons olive oil
1 teaspoon stone-ground mustard
1/4 cup hot sauce

Directions

Pat the chicken dry with kitchen towels. Toss the chicken with the remaining ingredients.
Cook the chicken at 380 degrees F for 22 minutes, turning them over halfway through the cooking time.
Bon appétit!

Classic Chicken Legs

(Ready in about 35 minutes | Servings 4)

Per serving: 387 Calories; 18.1g Fat; 1.9g Carbs; 51.1g Protein; 0.6g Sugars; 0.4g Fiber

Ingredients

4 chicken legs, bone-in
2 tablespoons sesame oil
Coarse sea salt and ground black pepper, to taste
1/2 teaspoon mustard seeds
1 teaspoon cayenne pepper
1/2 teaspoon onion powder
1/2 teaspoon garlic powder

Directions

Pat the chicken dry with paper towels. Toss the chicken legs with the remaining ingredients.
Cook the chicken at 380 degrees F for 30 minutes, turning them over halfway through the cooking time.
Bon appétit!

Thanksgiving Turkey Breasts

(Ready in about 1 hour 5 minutes | Servings 4)

Per serving: 210 Calories; 10.1g Fat; 1.3g Carbs; 25.1g Protein; 0.6g Sugars; 0.4g Fiber

Ingredients

1 tablespoon butter, room temperature
Kosher salt and ground black pepper, to taste
1 teaspoon cayenne pepper
1 teaspoon Italian herb mix
1 pound turkey breast, bone-in

Directions

In a mixing bowl, thoroughly combine the butter, salt, black pepper, cayenne pepper, and herb mix.
Rub the mixture all over the turkey breast.
Cook the turkey breast at 350 degrees F for 1 hour, turning them over every 20 minutes.
Bon appétit!

Asian-Style Duck

(Ready in about 40 minutes | Servings 3)

Per serving: 345 Calories; 23.2g Fat; 5.7g Carbs; 27.1g Protein; 2.3g Sugars; 0.8g Fiber

Ingredients

1 pound duck breast
1 tablespoon Hoisin sauce
1 tablespoon Five-spice powder
Sea salt and black pepper, to taste
1/4 teaspoon ground cinnamon

Directions

Pat the duck breasts dry with paper towels. Toss the duck breast with the remaining ingredients.
Cook the duck breast at 330 degrees F for 15 minutes, turning them over halfway through the cooking time.

Turn the heat to 350 degrees F; continue to cook for about 15 minutes or until cooked through.
Let it rest for 10 minutes before carving and serving.
Bon appétit!

The Best Chicken Burgers Ever

(Ready in about 20 minutes | Servings 3)
Per serving: 373 Calories; 23.8g Fat; 11.7g Carbs; 27g Protein; 0.7g Sugars; 0.9g Fiber
Ingredients
3/4 pound chicken, ground
1/4 cup tortilla chips, crushed
1/4 cup Parmesan cheese, grated
1 egg, beaten
2 tablespoons onion, minced
2 garlic cloves, minced
1 tablespoon BBQ sauce
Directions
Mix all ingredients until everything is well combined. Form the mixture into three patties.
Cook the burgers at 380 degrees F for about 17 minutes or until cooked through; make sure to turn them over halfway through the cooking time.
Bon appétit!

Easy Chicken Salad

(Ready in about 20 minutes | Servings 3)
Per serving: 373 Calories; 23.8g Fat; 11.7g Carbs; 27g Protein; 0.7g Sugars; 0.9g Fiber
Ingredients
1 pound chicken breast
2 tablespoons scallions, chopped
1 carrot, shredded
1/2 cup mayonnaise
1 tablespoon mustard
Sea salt and ground black pepper, to taste
Directions
Pat the chicken dry with kitchen towels. Place the chicken in a lightly oiled cooking basket.
Cook the chicken at 380 degrees F for 12 minutes, turning them over halfway through the cooking time.
Chop the chicken breasts and transfer it to a salad bowl; add in the remaining ingredients and toss to combine well. Bon appétit!

Smoked Paprika Chicken Cutlets

(Ready in about 20 minutes | Servings 4)
Per serving: 229 Calories; 13.8g Fat; 1.9g Carbs; 24.1g Protein; 0.6g Sugars; 0.4g Fiber
Ingredients
1 pound chicken breasts, boneless, skinless, cut into 4 pieces
1 tablespoon butter, melted
1 teaspoon smoked paprika
Kosher salt and ground black pepper, to taste
1 teaspoon garlic powder
Directions
Flatten the chicken breasts to 1/4-inch thickness.
Toss the chicken breasts with the remaining ingredients.
Cook the chicken at 380 degrees F for 12 minutes, turning them over halfway through the cooking time.
Bon appétit!

Hawaiian Roll Chicken Sliders

(Ready in about 20 minutes | Servings 3)
Per serving: 490 Calories; 21.8g Fat; 46.7g Carbs; 28g Protein; 7g Sugars; 2.7g Fiber
Ingredients
3/4 pound chicken, ground
1 teaspoon garlic, minced
1 small onion, minced
2 tablespoons fresh parsley, minced
2 tablespoons fresh cilantro, minced
1/2 teaspoon mustard seeds
1/2 teaspoon ground cumin
1/2 teaspoon paprika
Sea salt and ground black pepper, to taste
2 tablespoons olive oil
6 Hawaiian rolls
Directions
Mix all ingredients , except for the burger buns, until everything is well combined. Shape the mixture into six patties.
Cook the burgers at 380 degrees F for about 17 minutes or until cooked through; make sure to turn them over halfway through the cooking time.
Serve your burgers over Hawaiian rolls and garnish with toppings of choice. Bon appétit!

Mediterranean-Style Chicken Fillets

(Ready in about 15 minutes | Servings 4)
Per serving: 227 Calories; 13.4g Fat; 0.2g Carbs; 23.4g Protein; 0.2g Sugars; 1g Fiber
Ingredients
1 ½ pounds chicken fillets
1 tablespoon olive oil
1 teaspoon garlic, minced
1 tablespoon Greek seasoning mix
1/2 teaspoon red pepper flakes, crushed
Sea salt and ground black pepper, to taste
Directions
Pat the chicken dry with paper towels. Toss the chicken with the remaining ingredients.
Cook the chicken fillets at 380 degrees F for 12 minutes, turning them over halfway through the cooking time.
Bon appétit!

Mexican Chicken Taquitos

(Ready in about 20 minutes | Servings 5)
Per serving: 256 Calories; 13g Fat; 14.2g Carbs; 20.4g Protein; 2.7g Sugars; 1.7g Fiber
Ingredients
3/4 pound chicken breasts, boneless and skinless
Kosher salt and ground black pepper, to taste
1/2 teaspoon red chili powder
5 small corn tortillas
5 ounces Cotija cheese, crumbled
Directions

Pat the chicken dry with kitchen towels. Toss the chicken breasts with the salt, pepper, and red chili powder.
Cook the chicken at 380 degrees F for 12 minutes, turning them over halfway through the cooking time.
Place the shredded chicken and cheese on one end of each tortilla. Roll them up tightly and transfer them to a lightly oiled Air Fryer basket.
Bake your taquitos at 360 degrees F for 6 minutes.
Bon appétit!

Hawaiian Chicken with Pineapple

(Ready in about 35 minutes | Servings 4)
Per serving: 267 Calories; 18.1g Fat; 6.5g Carbs; 19g Protein; 4.6g Sugars; 0.8g Fiber
Ingredients
1 pound chicken legs, boneless
Kosher salt and freshly ground black pepper, to taste
2 tablespoons tamari sauce
1 tablespoon hot sauce
1 cup pineapple, peeled and diced
1 tablespoon fresh cilantro, roughly chopped
Directions
Pat the chicken dry with paper towels. Toss the chicken legs with the salt, black pepper, tamari sauce, and hot sauce.
Cook the chicken at 380 degrees F for 30 minutes, turning them over halfway through the cooking time.
Top the chicken with the pineapple and continue to cook for 5 minutes more. Serve warm, garnished with the fresh cilantro.
Bon appétit!

Authentic Chicken Fajitas

(Ready in about 35 minutes | Servings 4)
Per serving: 330 Calories; 25.1g Fat; 6.1g Carbs; 19.6g Protein; 1.4g Sugars; 1g Fiber
Ingredients
1 pound chicken legs, boneless, skinless, cut into pieces
2 tablespoons canola oil
1 red bell pepper, sliced
1 yellow bell pepper, sliced
1 jalapeno pepper, sliced
1 onion, sliced
1/2 teaspoon onion powder
1/2 teaspoon garlic powder
Sea salt and ground black pepper, to taste
Directions
Pat the chicken dry with paper towels. Toss the chicken legs with 1 tablespoon of the canola oil.
Cook the chicken at 380 degrees F for 15 minutes, shaking the basket halfway through the cooking time.
Add the remaining ingredients to the Air Fryer basket and turn the heat to 400 degrees F. Let it cook for 15 minutes more or until cooked through.
Bon appétit!

Marinated Turkey Wings

(Ready in about 45 minutes + marinating time | Servings 5)
Per serving: 377 Calories; 22.5g Fat; 3.2g Carbs; 37.4g Protein; 1.3g Sugars; 0.6g Fiber
Ingredients
2 pounds turkey wings, bone-in
2 garlic cloves, minced
1 small onion, chopped
1 tablespoon Dijon mustard
1/2 cup red wine
Sea salt and ground black pepper, to taste
1 teaspoon poultry seasoning
Directions
Place the turkey wings, garlic, onion, mustard, and wine in a ceramic bowl. Cover the bowl and let the turkey marinate in your refrigerator overnight.
Discard the marinade and toss the turkey wings with the salt, black pepper, and poultry seasoning.
Cook the turkey wings at 400 degrees F for 40 minutes, turning them over halfway through the cooking time.
Bon appétit!

Zingy Duck Breast

(Ready in about 15 minutes | Servings 4)
Per serving: 295 Calories; 16.4g Fat; 2.2g Carbs; 31.4g Protein; 0.1g Sugars; 0.1g Fiber
Ingredients
2 tablespoons fresh lime juice
1 ½ pounds duck breast
2 tablespoons olive oil
1 teaspoon cayenne pepper
Kosher salt and freshly ground black pepper, to taste
Directions
Pat the duck breasts dry with paper towels. Toss the duck breast with the remaining ingredients.
Cook the duck breast at 330 degrees F for 15 minutes, turning them over halfway through the cooking time.
Turn the heat to 350 degrees F; continue to cook for about 15 minutes or until cooked through.
Let the duck breasts rest for 10 minutes before carving and serving. Bon appétit!

Restaurant-Style Fried Chicken

(Ready in about 15 minutes | Servings 4)
Per serving: 318 Calories; 23.3g Fat; 2.1g Carbs; 23.7g Protein; 0.8g Sugars; 0.3g Fiber
Ingredients
1 pound chicken fillets
1 egg
1 tablespoon olive oil
1 cup crackers, crushed
1 tablespoon fresh coriander, minced
1 tablespoon fresh parsley, minced
Sea salt and ground black pepper, to taste
1/4 teaspoon ground cumin
1/4 teaspoon mustard seeds
1 teaspoon celery seeds
Directions

Pat the chicken fillets dry with paper towels. Whisk the egg in a shallow bowl.
Mix the remaining ingredients in a separate shallow bowl.
Dip the chicken breasts into the egg mixture. Then, roll the chicken breasts over the breadcrumb mixture.
Cook the chicken at 380 degrees F for 12 minutes, turning them over halfway through the cooking time.
Bon appétit!

Old-Fashioned Chicken Schnitzel

(Ready in about 25 minutes | Servings 3)

Per serving: 477 Calories; 21.2g Fat; 14.8g Carbs; 53.3g Protein; 1.9g Sugars; 1.4g Fiber

Ingredients

3 chicken legs, boneless and skinless
2 tablespoons olive oil
1 teaspoon dried basil
1 teaspoon dried oregano
1 teaspoon dried sage
Sea salt and freshly cracked black pepper
1/2 cup breadcrumbs

Directions

Pat the chicken dry with paper towels. Toss the chicken legs with the remaining ingredients.
Cook the chicken at 370 degrees F for 20 minutes, turning them over halfway through the cooking time.
Bon appétit!

Mozzarella Stuffed Chicken

(Ready in about 25 minutes | Servings 4)

Per serving: 257 Calories; 13.9g Fat; 2.7g Carbs; 28.3g Protein; 1.4g Sugars; 0.6g Fiber

Ingredients

1 pound chicken breasts, boneless, skinless, cut into four pieces
2 tablespoons sundried tomatoes, chopped
1 garlic clove, minced
2 ounces mozzarella cheese, crumbled
Sea salt and ground black pepper, to taste
1 tablespoon olive oil

Directions

Flatten the chicken breasts with a mallet.
Stuff each piece of chicken with the sundried tomatoes, garlic, and cheese. Roll them up and secure with toothpicks.
Season the chicken with the salt and pepper and drizzle the olive oil over them.
Place the stuffed chicken in the Air Fryer cooking basket. Cook the chicken at 400 degrees F for about 20 minutes, turning them over halfway through the cooking time.
Bon appétit!

Balsamic Chicken Drumettes

(Ready in about 25 minutes | Servings 4)

Per serving: 265 Calories; 11.4g Fat; 2.4g Carbs; 34.4g Protein; 1.7g Sugars; 0.2g Fiber

Ingredients

1 ½ pounds chicken drumettes
2 tablespoons olive oil
2 tablespoons balsamic vinegar
Kosher salt and ground black pepper, to taste

Directions

Toss the chicken drumettes with the remaining ingredients.
Cook the chicken drumettes at 380 degrees F for 22 minutes, turning them over halfway through the cooking time.
Bon appétit!

Kid-Friendly Chicken Fingers

(Ready in about 20 minutes | Servings 4)

Per serving: 475 Calories; 28.6g Fat; 14.4g Carbs; 36.4g Protein; 0.7g Sugars; 0.8g Fiber

Ingredients

1 egg, whisked
1/2 cup all-purpose flour
1 teaspoon garlic powder
1 teaspoon cayenne pepper
Sea salt and ground black pepper, to taste
1/4 cup breadcrumbs
1/4 cup parmesan cheese, grated
1 ½ pounds chicken breast boneless, skinless and cut into strips

Directions

Mix the egg and flour in a shallow bowl. In a separate bowl, whisk the garlic powder, cayenne pepper, salt, black pepper, breadcrumbs, and parmesan cheese.
Dip the chicken breasts into the egg mixture. Then, roll the chicken breasts over the breadcrumb mixture.
Cook the chicken at 380 degrees F for 12 minutes, turning them over halfway through the cooking time.
Bon appétit!

Classic Breaded Chicken

(Ready in about 15 minutes | Servings 4)

Per serving: 316 Calories; 16.4g Fat; 11.8g Carbs; 28.1g Protein; 1.6g Sugars; 1g Fiber

Ingredients

1 pound chicken breasts, boneless and skinless
1 tablespoon butter, room temperature
1 egg, whisked
1 teaspoon cayenne pepper
1 teaspoon garlic powder
Kosher salt and ground black pepper, to taste
1/2 cup breadcrumbs

Directions

Pat the chicken dry with paper towels.
In a bowl, thoroughly combine the butter, egg, cayenne pepper, garlic powder, kosher salt, black pepper.
Dip the chicken breasts into the egg mixture. Then, roll the chicken breasts over the breadcrumbs.
Cook the chicken at 380 degrees F for 12 minutes, turning them over halfway through the cooking time.
Bon appétit!

Parmesan Chicken Wings

(Ready in about 25 minutes | Servings 3)

Per serving: 349 Calories; 19.1g Fat; 4.4g Carbs; 38.3g Protein; 1.1g Sugars; 0.3g Fiber

Ingredients

1 pound chicken wings, bone-in
Sea salt and red pepper flakes, to taste
2 tablespoons olive oil
1/2 cup parmesan cheese, grated
2 cloves garlic, pressed

Directions

Pat the chicken dry with kitchen towels. Toss the chicken breasts with the remaining ingredients.
Cook the chicken at 380 degrees F for 22 minutes, turning them over halfway through the cooking time.
Bon appétit!

Crispy Chicken Drumsticks

(Ready in about 25 minutes | Servings 3)

Per serving: 324 Calories; 22.8g Fat; 3.5g Carbs; 24.3g Protein; 2g Sugars; 0.3g Fiber

Ingredients

3 chicken drumsticks, bone-in
Kosher salt and ground black pepper, to taste
2 tablespoons olive oil
2 tablespoons soy sauce
1 tablespoon rice vinegar
1 teaspoon garlic powder

Directions

Pat the chicken drumsticks dry with paper towels. Toss the chicken drumsticks with the remaining ingredients.
Cook the chicken at 370 degrees F for 20 minutes, turning them over halfway through the cooking time.
Bon appétit!

BBQ Turkey Breasts

(Ready in about 1 hour 5 minutes | Servings 5)

Per serving: 342 Calories; 18g Fat; 1.6g Carbs; 40.3g Protein; 0.6g Sugars; 0.6g Fiber

Ingredients

2 tablespoons olive oil
Sea salt and freshly cracked black pepper, to taste
1 tablespoon Dijon mustard
1 tablespoon hot sauce
1 teaspoon smoked paprika
1 teaspoon dried basil
1 teaspoon dried thyme
2 pounds turkey breast, bone-in

Directions

In a mixing bowl, thoroughly combine the olive oil, salt, black pepper, mustard, hot sauce, paprika, basil, and thyme.
Rub the mixture all over the turkey breast.
Cook the turkey breast at 350 degrees F for 1 hour, turning them over every 20 minutes.
Bon appétit!

Classic Turkey Drumettes

(Ready in about 50 minutes | Servings 4)

Per serving: 247 Calories; 12g Fat; 1.4g Carbs; 31.2g Protein; 0.5g Sugars; 0.2g Fiber

Ingredients

1 ½ pounds turkey drumettes
1 tablespoon sesame oil
1 teaspoon poultry seasoning mix
Sea salt and ground black pepper, to taste

Directions

Toss the turkey drumettes with the remaining ingredients.
Cook the turkey drumettes at 400 degrees F for 40 minutes, turning them over halfway through the cooking time.
Let the turkey rest for 10 minutes before carving and serving. Bon appétit!

Rustic Duck Fillet

(Ready in about 40 minutes | Servings 4)

Per serving: 383 Calories; 26.2g Fat; 4.7g Carbs; 30.1g Protein; 4g Sugars; 0.2g Fiber

Ingredients

1 ½ pounds duck fillet
1 tablespoon honey
2 tablespoons dark soy sauce
1 tablespoon soybean paste

Directions

Toss the duck fillets with the remaining ingredients.
Cook the duck fillets at 330 degrees F for 15 minutes, turning them over halfway through the cooking time.
Turn the heat to 350 degrees F; continue to cook for about 15 minutes or until cooked through.
Let it rest for 10 minutes before carving and serving.
Bon appétit!

Chinese Chicken Patties

(Ready in about 20 minutes | Servings 4)

Per serving: 224 Calories; 12.5g Fat; 2.7g Carbs; 20.1g Protein; 14g Sugars; 0.6g Fiber

Ingredients

1 pound chicken, ground
1 tablespoon olive oil
1 small onion, chopped
1 teaspoon garlic, minced
1 tablespoon chili sauce
Kosher salt and ground black pepper, to taste

Directions

Mix all ingredients until everything is well combined.
Form the mixture into four patties.
Cook the patties at 380 degrees F for about 17 minutes or until cooked through; make sure to turn them over halfway through the cooking time.
Bon appétit!

Greek Chicken Salad

(Ready in about 20 minutes | Servings 4)

Per serving: 314 Calories; 21g Fat; 3.2g Carbs; 24.8g Protein; 2.1g Sugars; 0.6g Fiber

Ingredients

1 pound chicken breasts, boneless, skinless
1 red onion, thinly sliced
1 bell pepper, sliced
4 Kalamata olives, pitted and minced

1 small Greek cucumber, grated and squeezed
4 tablespoons Greek yogurt
4 tablespoons mayonnaise
1 tablespoon fresh lemon juice
Coarse sea salt and red pepper flakes, to taste

Directions

Pat the chicken dry with paper towels. Place the chicken breasts in a lightly oiled Air Fryer basket.
Cook the chicken at 380 degrees F for 12 minutes, turning them over halfway through the cooking time.
Chop the chicken breasts and transfer it to a salad bowl; add in the remaining ingredients and toss to combine well.
Serve well-chilled and enjoy!

Chicken English Muffin Sandwiches

(Ready in about 20 minutes | Servings 4)

Per serving: 439 Calories; 21g Fat; 26.2g Carbs; 35.3g Protein; 1g Sugars; 2.8g Fiber

Ingredients

1 pound chicken breasts
1 tablespoon olive oil
Sea salt and black pepper, to taste
4 slices cheddar cheese
4 teaspoons yellow mustard
4 English muffins, lightly toasted

Directions

Pat the chicken dry with kitchen towels. Toss the chicken breasts with the olive oil, salt, and pepper.
Cook the chicken at 380 degrees F for 12 minutes, turning them over halfway through the cooking time.
Shred the chicken using two forks and serve with cheese, mustard, and English muffins. Bon appétit!

Bacon Stuffed Chicken

(Ready in about 25 minutes | Servings 4)

Per serving: 361 Calories; 27.6g Fat; 2g Carbs; 24.9g Protein; 1.2g Sugars; 0.2g Fiber

Ingredients

1 pound chicken breasts
4 tablespoons goat cheese
4 tablespoons bacon
1 tablespoon olive oil
1/2 teaspoon garlic powder
1 teaspoon dried basil
1 teaspoon dried oregano
1 teaspoon dried parsley flakes

Directions

Flatten the chicken breasts with a mallet.
Stuff each piece of chicken with cheese and bacon. Roll them up and secure with toothpicks.
Then, sprinkle the chicken with olive oil, garlic powder, basil, oregano, and parsley.
Place the stuffed chicken breasts in the Air Fryer cooking basket. Cook the chicken at 400 degrees F for about 20 minutes, turning them over halfway through the cooking time.
Bon appétit!

Greek-Style Chicken Fillets

(Ready in about 15 minutes | Servings 4)

Per serving: 380 Calories; 24g Fat; 11.2g Carbs; 26.5g Protein; 2.2g Sugars; 2.9g Fiber

Ingredients

1 pound chicken fillets, boneless, skinless
2 eggs, whisked
1 teaspoon dried basil
1/2 teaspoon dried rosemary
1/2 teaspoon dried oregano
1/2 teaspoon red pepper flakes, crushed
1/2 cup seasoned breadcrumbs
2 ounces Kalamata olives, pitted and sliced

Directions

Pat the chicken dry with paper towels.
In a shallow bowl, thoroughly combine the eggs and spices. Place the breadcrumbs in a separate shallow bowl.
Dip the chicken fillets into the egg mixture. Then, roll the chicken fillets over the breadcrumbs.
Cook the chicken fillets at 380 degrees F for 12 minutes, turning them over halfway through the cooking time.
Serve with Kalamata olives and enjoy!

Spinach and Feta Stuffed Chicken

(Ready in about 25 minutes | Servings 4)

Per serving: 355 Calories; 27g Fat; 2.7g Carbs; 23.5g Protein; 1.2g Sugars; 0.9g Fiber

Ingredients

1 pound chicken breasts, skinless, boneless and cut into pieces
2 tablespoons olives, chopped
1 garlic clove, minced
2 cups spinach, torn into pieces
2 ounces feta cheese
Sea salt and ground black pepper, to taste
2 tablespoons olive oil

Directions

Flatten the chicken breasts with a mallet.
Stuff each piece of chicken with olives, garlic, spinach, and cheese. Roll them up and secure with toothpicks.
Sprinkle the chicken with the salt, black pepper, and olive oil.
Place the stuffed chicken breasts in the Air Fryer cooking basket. Cook the chicken at 400 degrees F for about 20 minutes, turning them over halfway through the cooking time.
Bon appétit!

Chinese-Style Chicken Drumsticks

(Ready in about 25 minutes | Servings 3)

Per serving: 314 Calories; 22g Fat; 3.5g Carbs; 24.2g Protein; 1.8g Sugars; 0.5g Fiber

Ingredients

3 chicken drumsticks
2 tablespoons sesame oil
Kosher salt and ground black pepper, to taste
1 tablespoon soy sauce
1 teaspoon Five-spice powder

Directions

Pat the chicken drumsticks dry with paper towels. Toss the chicken drumsticks with the remaining ingredients.
Cook the chicken drumsticks at 370 degrees F for 22 minutes, turning them over halfway through the cooking time.
Bon appétit!

Sriracha Herb Turkey

(Ready in about 1 hour 5 minutes | Servings 5)
Per serving: 367 Calories; 21.9g Fat; 0.1g Carbs; 40g Protein; 0.2g Sugars; 0.2g Fiber
Ingredients
2 pounds turkey breasts, rib bones trimmed
4 tablespoons butter, melted
1 teaspoon Sriracha sauce
1 tablespoon fresh cilantro, chopped
1 tablespoon fresh parsley, chopped
1 tablespoon fresh thyme, chopped
Kosher salt and freshly ground black pepper, to taste
Directions
Pat the turkey breasts dry with paper towels. Toss the turkey breasts with the remaining ingredients.
Cook the turkey breasts at 350 degrees F for 1 hour, turning them over every 20 minutes.
Bon appétit!

Ranch Chicken Drumsticks

(Ready in about 25 minutes | Servings 4)
Per serving: 309 Calories; 17.2g Fat; 13.4g Carbs; 22.8g Protein; 0.4g Sugars; 0.8g Fiber
Ingredients
1/2 cup all-purpose flour
1 tablespoon Ranch seasoning mix
1 pound chicken drumsticks
1 tablespoon hot sauce
Sea salt and ground black pepper, to taste
Directions
Pat the chicken drumsticks dry with paper towels. Toss the chicken drumsticks with the remaining ingredients.
Cook the chicken drumsticks at 370 degrees F for 20 minutes, turning them over halfway through the cooking time.
Bon appétit!

Holiday Duck Roast

(Ready in about 45 minutes | Servings 5)
Per serving: 356 Calories; 11.7g Fat; 23.5g Carbs; 38.8g Protein; 15g Sugars; 5.1g Fiber
Ingredients
2 pounds duck breasts
1 tablespoon butter, melted
2 tablespoons pomegranate molasses
2 tablespoons miso paste
1 teaspoon garlic, minced
1 teaspoon ginger, peeled and minced
1 teaspoon Five-spice powder
Directions
Pat the duck breasts dry with paper towels. Toss the duck breast with the remaining ingredients.
Cook the duck breasts at 330 degrees F for 15 minutes, turning them over halfway through the cooking time.
Turn the heat to 350 degrees F; continue to cook for about 15 minutes or until cooked through.
Let it rest for 10 minutes before carving and serving.
Bon appétit!

Sicilian Chicken Fillets

(Ready in about 20 minutes | Servings 4)
Per serving: 434 Calories; 32.4g Fat; 1.8g Carbs; 31.8g Protein; 0.7g Sugars; 0.5g Fiber
Ingredients
1 ½ pounds chicken fillets
2 tablespoons olive oil
1 teaspoon smoked paprika
1 teaspoon Italian seasoning mix
Sea salt and ground black pepper, to taste
1/2 cup Pecorino Romano cheese, grated
Directions
Pat the chicken fillets dry with paper towels. Toss the chicken fillets with the olive oil and spices.
Cook the chicken fillets at 380 degrees F for 12 minutes, turning them over halfway through the cooking time.
Top the chicken fillets with grated cheese and serve warm. Bon appétit!

Restaurant-Style Chicken Nuggets

(Ready in about 15 minutes | Servings 4)
Per serving: 467 Calories; 19.4g Fat; 26.8g Carbs; 38.8g Protein; 4.3g Sugars; 4.9g Fiber
Ingredients
1 egg, whisked
1/4 cup all-purpose flour
1 cup seasoned breadcrumbs
1 tablespoon olive oil
Sea salt and ground black pepper, to taste
1 ½ pounds chicken breasts, cut into small pieces
Directions
Mix the egg and flour in a shallow bowl. In a separate bowl, whisk the breadcrumbs, olive oil, salt, and black pepper.
Dip the chicken breasts into the egg mixture. Then, roll the chicken breasts over the breadcrumb mixture.
Cook the chicken at 380 degrees F for 12 minutes, turning them over halfway through the cooking time.
Bon appétit!

The Best Turkey Taquitos Ever

(Ready in about 30 minutes | Servings 6)
Per serving: 249 Calories; 11.4g Fat; 13.3g Carbs; 22.8g Protein; 1.6g Sugars; 2g Fiber
Ingredients
1 pound turkey breasts, boneless and skinless
Kosher salt and freshly ground black pepper, to taste
1 clove garlic, minced
1 habanero pepper, minced

4 ounces Mexican cheese blend, shredded
6 small corn tortillas
1/2 cup salsa

Directions

Pat the turkey breasts dry with kitchen towels. Toss the turkey breasts with the salt and black pepper.
Cook the turkey breasts at 380 degrees F for 18 minutes, turning them over halfway through the cooking time.
Place the shredded chicken, garlic, habanero pepper, and cheese on one end of each tortilla. Roll them up tightly and transfer them to a lightly oiled Air Fryer basket.
Bake your taquitos at 360 degrees F for 6 minutes.
Serve your taquitos with salsa and enjoy!

Mexican Taco Chicken Fingers

(Ready in about 20 minutes | Servings 4)

Per serving: 427 Calories; 23.1g Fat; 11.1g Carbs; 41.4g Protein; 0.6g Sugars; 0.9g Fiber

Ingredients

1 egg, whisked
1/2 cup parmesan cheese, preferably freshly grated
1/2 cup tortilla chips, crushed
1/2 teaspoon onion powder
1/2 teaspoon garlic powder
1 teaspoon red chili powder
1 ½ pounds chicken breasts, boneless skinless cut into strips

Directions

Whisk the egg in a shallow bowl. In a separate bowl, whisk the parmesan cheese, tortilla chips, onion powder, garlic powder, and red chili powder.
Dip the chicken pieces into the egg mixture. Then, roll the chicken pieces over the breadcrumb mixture.
Cook the chicken at 380 degrees F for 12 minutes, turning them over halfway through the cooking time.
Bon appétit!

Classic Turkey Schnitzel

(Ready in about 25 minutes | Servings 3)

Per serving: 579 Calories; 27.4g Fat; 30.3g Carbs; 51g Protein; 2g Sugars; 1.6g Fiber

Ingredients

1 ½ pounds turkey thighs, skinless, boneless
1 egg, beaten
1/2 cup all-purpose flour
1/2 cup seasoned breadcrumbs
1/2 teaspoon red pepper flakes, crushed
Sea salt and ground black pepper, to taste
1 tablespoon olive oil

Directions

Flatten the turkey thighs with a mallet.
Whisk the egg in a shallow bowl. Place the flour in a second bowl.
Then, in a third shallow bowl, place the breadcrumbs, red pepper, salt, and black pepper. Dip the turkey first in the flour, then, in the beaten egg, and roll them in the breadcrumb mixture.
Place the breaded turkey thighs in the Air Fryer basket. Mist your schnitzel with the olive oil and transfer them to the cooking basket.
Cook the schnitzel at 380 degrees F for 22 minutes, turning them over halfway through the cooking time.
Bon appétit!

The Best Marinated Chicken Ever

(Ready in about 15 minutes + marinating time | Servings 2)

Per serving: 313 Calories; 16g Fat; 3.7g Carbs; 36.5g Protein; 2g Sugars; 0.9g Fiber

Ingredients

3/4 pound chicken breasts, boneless, skinless
1 teaspoon garlic, minced
1/2 cup red wine
1/4 cup hot sauce
1 tablespoon Dijon mustard
Sea salt and cayenne pepper, to taste

Directions

Place the chicken, garlic, red wine, hot sauce, and mustard in a ceramic bowl. Cover the bowl and let the chicken marinate for about 3 hours in your refrigerator.
Discard the marinade and place the chicken breasts in the Air Fryer cooking basket.
Cook the chicken breasts at 380 degrees F for 12 minutes, turning them over halfway through the cooking time.
Season the chicken with the salt and cayenne pepper to taste. Bon appétit!

Crispy Chicken Wings

(Ready in about 15 minutes | Servings 2)

Per serving: 265 Calories; 11.7g Fat; 0.5g Carbs; 37.5g Protein; 0.5g Sugars; 0.9g Fiber

Ingredients

3/4 pound chicken wings, boneless
1 tablespoon butter, room temperature
1/2 teaspoon garlic powder
1/2 teaspoon shallot powder
1/2 teaspoon mustard powder

Directions

Toss the chicken wings with the remaining ingredients.
Cook the chicken wings at 380 degrees F for 18 minutes, turning them over halfway through the cooking time.
Bon appétit!

Country-Style Turkey Drumsticks

(Ready in about 45 minutes | Servings 5)

Per serving: 341 Calories; 21.7g Fat; 0.5g Carbs; 35.5g Protein; 0.1g Sugars; 0.1g Fiber

Ingredients

2 pounds turkey drumsticks, bone-in
2 tablespoons olive oil
Kosher salt and freshly ground black pepper, to taste
1 teaspoon dried thyme
1 teaspoon dried rosemary

1 teaspoon garlic, minced
Directions
Toss the turkey drumsticks with the remaining ingredients.
Cook the turkey drumsticks at 400 degrees F for 40 minutes, turning them over halfway through the cooking time.
Bon appétit!

Peppery Chicken Fillets

(Ready in about 20 minutes | Servings 4)
Per serving: 305 Calories; 22.8g Fat; 2.3g Carbs; 21.6g Protein; 1.1g Sugars; 0.4g Fiber
Ingredients
1 pound chicken fillets
2 tablespoons butter
2 bell peppers, seeded and sliced
1 teaspoon garlic, minced
Sea salt and ground black pepper, to taste
1 teaspoon red pepper flakes
Directions
Toss the chicken fillets with the butter and place them in the Air Fryer basket. Top the chicken with bell peppers, garlic, salt, black pepper, and red pepper flakes.
Cook the chicken and peppers at 380 degrees F for 15 minutes, tossing the basket halfway through the cooking time.
Serve warm and enjoy!

Traditional Orange Duck

(Ready in about 45 minutes | Servings 4)
Per serving: 471 Calories; 44.1g Fat; 2.9g Carbs; 13.3g Protein; 2.1g Sugars; 0.3g Fiber
Ingredients
1 pound duck legs
1/4 cup orange sauce
Sea salt and red pepper flakes, crushed
Directions
Toss the duck legs with the remaining ingredients.
Cook the duck legs at 400 degrees F for 40 minutes, turning them over halfway through the cooking time.
Bon appétit!

Chicken Dinner Rolls

(Ready in about 20 minutes | Servings 4)
Per serving: 575 Calories; 25.3g Fat; 37g Carbs; 49.7g Protein; 4.6g Sugars; 3.2g Fiber
Ingredients
1 pound chicken, ground
1/2 cup tortilla chips, crushed
2 ounces cheddar cheese, grated
1 teaspoon dried parsley flakes
1 teaspoon cayenne pepper
1/2 teaspoon paprika
Kosher salt and ground black pepper, to taste
4 dinner rolls
Directions
Mix the chicken, tortilla chips, cheese, and spices until everything is well combined. Now, roll the mixture into four patties.
Cook the burgers at 380 degrees F for about 17 minutes or until cooked through; make sure to turn them over halfway through the cooking time.
Serve your burgers in dinner rolls. Bon appétit!

Ham and Cheese Stuffed Chicken

(Ready in about 25 minutes | Servings 4)
Per serving: 486 Calories; 32.3g Fat; 7.9g Carbs; 39.3g Protein; 0.8g Sugars; 0.2g Fiber
Ingredients
1 pound chicken breasts, skinless, boneless and cut into 4 slices
4 ounces goat cheese, crumbled
4 ounces ham, chopped
1 egg
1/4 cup all-purpose flour
1/4 cup parmesan cheese, grated
1/2 teaspoon onion powder
1/2 teaspoon garlic powder
Directions
Flatten the chicken breasts with a mallet.
Stuff each piece of chicken with cheese and ham. Roll them up and secure with toothpicks.
In a shallow bowl, mix the remaining ingredients until well combined. Dip the chicken rolls into the egg/flour mixture.
Place the stuffed chicken in the Air Fryer cooking basket. Cook the stuffed chicken breasts at 400 degrees F for about 22 minutes, turning them over halfway through the cooking time.
Bon appétit!

Parsley Lemon Turkey

(Ready in about 45 minutes | Servings 5)
Per serving: 411 Calories; 27.8g Fat; 1.3g Carbs; 36.5g Protein; 0.3g Sugars; 0.2g Fiber
Ingredients
2 pounds turkey wings
2 tablespoons olive oil
1/2 teaspoon garlic powder
1/2 teaspoon onion powder
1 teaspoon poultry seasoning mix
2 tablespoons fresh parsley, roughly chopped
1 lemon, cut into slices
Directions
Toss the turkey wings with the olive oil, garlic powder, onion powder, and poultry seasoning mix.
Cook the turkey wings at 400 degrees F for 40 minutes, turning them over halfway through the cooking time.
Let the turkey rest for 10 minutes before carving and serving. Garnish the turkey wings with the parsley and lemon slices.
Bon appétit!

Chicken Cutlets with Broccoli

(Ready in about 15 minutes | Servings 4)

Per serving: 313 Calories; 20.8g Fat; 7.5g Carbs; 24.5g Protein; 1.9g Sugars; 2g Fiber

Ingredients

1 pound chicken cutlets
1 pound broccoli florets
1 tablespoon olive oil
Sea salt and ground black pepper, to taste

Directions

Pat the chicken dry with kitchen towels. Place the chicken cutlets in a lightly greased Air Fryer basket.
Cook the chicken cutlets at 380 degrees F for 6 minutes, turning them over halfway through the cooking time.
Turn the heat to 400 degrees F and add in the remaining ingredients. Continue to cook for 6 minutes more.
Bon appétit!

Creamed Chicken Salad

(Ready in about 20 minutes | Servings 4)

Per serving: 315 Calories; 23g Fat; 2.8g Carbs; 24.5g Protein; 0.9g Sugars; 0.4g Fiber

Ingredients

1 pound chicken breasts, skinless and boneless
1/4 cup mayonnaise
1/4 cup sour cream
1 tablespoon lemon juice
Sea salt and ground black pepper
1/2 cup celery, chopped

Directions

Pat the chicken dry with paper towels. Place the chicken in a lightly oiled cooking basket.
Cook the chicken breasts at 380 degrees F for 12 minutes, turning them over halfway through the cooking time.
Shred the chicken breasts using two forks; transfer it to a salad bowl and add in the remaining ingredients. Toss to combine and serve well chilled. Bon appétit!

Tender Spicy Chicken

(Ready in about 15 minutes + marinating time | Servings 4)

Per serving: 206 Calories; 11g Fat; 1g Carbs; 24.2g Protein; 0.4g Sugars; 0.2g Fiber

Ingredients

1 pound chicken breasts, boneless, skinless
1/2 cup rice wine
1 tablespoon stone-ground mustard
1 teaspoon garlic, minced
1 teaspoon black peppercorns, whole
1 teaspoon chili powder
1/4 teaspoon sea salt, or more to taste

Directions

Place the chicken, wine, mustard, garlic, and whole peppercorns in a ceramic bowl. Cover the bowl and let the chicken marinate for about 3 hours in your refrigerator.
Discard the marinade and place the chicken breasts in the Air Fryer cooking basket.
Cook the chicken breasts at 380 degrees F for 12 minutes, turning them over halfway through the cooking time.
Season the chicken with the chili powder and salt. Serve immediately and enjoy!

Ranch Chicken Wings

(Ready in about 25 minutes | Servings 3)

Per serving: 273 Calories; 14.3g Fat; 0.5g Carbs; 33.2g Protein; 0.4g Sugars; 0.5g Fiber

Ingredients

1 pound chicken wings, boneless
2 tablespoons olive oil
1 teaspoon Ranch seasoning mix
Kosher salt and ground black pepper, to taste

Directions

Pat the chicken dry with kitchen towels. Toss the chicken with the remaining ingredients.
Cook the chicken wings at 380 degrees F for 22 minutes, turning them over halfway through the cooking time.
Bon appétit!

Roasted Turkey Legs with Scallions

(Ready in about 45 minutes | Servings 4)

Per serving: 279 Calories; 14.4g Fat; 1.8g Carbs; 33.6g Protein; 0.7g Sugars; 0.5g Fiber

Ingredients

1 ½ pounds turkey legs
1 tablespoon butter, melted
1 teaspoon hot paprika
1 teaspoon garlic, pressed
Sea salt and ground black pepper, to taste
2 tablespoons scallions, chopped

Directions

Toss the turkey legs with the remaining ingredients, except for the scallions.
Cook the turkey legs at 400 degrees F for 40 minutes, turning them over halfway through the cooking time.
Garnish the roasted turkey legs with the fresh scallions and enjoy!

Turkey and Avocado Sliders

(Ready in about 25 minutes | Servings 4)

Per serving: 519 Calories; 22.4g Fat; 48g Carbs; 31.6g Protein; 6.7g Sugars; 5g Fiber

Ingredients

1 pound turkey, ground
1 tablespoon olive oil
1 avocado, peeled, pitted and chopped
2 garlic cloves, minced
1/2 cup breadcrumbs
Kosher salt and ground black pepper, to taste
8 small rolls

Directions

Mix the turkey, olive oil, avocado, garlic, breadcrumbs, salt, and black pepper until everything is well combined. Form the mixture into eight small patties.

Cook the patties at 380 degrees F for about 20 minutes or until cooked through; make sure to turn them over halfway through the cooking time.
Serve your patties in the prepared rolls and enjoy!

Chicken Salad Sandwich

(Ready in about 20 minutes | Servings 4)
Per serving: 522 Calories; 31.4g Fat; 27.1g Carbs; 31.6g Protein; 5.2g Sugars; 2.5g Fiber
Ingredients
1 pound chicken breasts, boneless and skinless
1 stalks celery, chopped
1 carrot, chopped
1 small onion, chopped
1 cup mayonnaise
Sea salt and ground black pepper, to taste
4 sandwich buns
Directions
Pat the chicken dry with paper towels. Place the chicken in a lightly oiled cooking basket.
Cook the chicken breasts at 380 degrees F for 12 minutes, turning them over halfway through the cooking time.
Shred the chicken breasts using two forks; transfer it to a salad bowl and add in the celery, carrot, onion, mayo, salt, and pepper.
Toss to combine and serve in sandwich buns. Enjoy!

Italian-Style Chicken Drumsticks

(Ready in about 25 minutes | Servings 4)
Per serving: 235 Calories; 14.8g Fat; 0.3g Carbs; 23.2g Protein; 0.1g Sugars; 0.3g Fiber
Ingredients
4 chicken drumsticks, bone-in
1 tablespoon butter
1/2 teaspoon cayenne pepper
1 teaspoon Italian herb mix
Sea salt and ground black pepper, to taste
Directions
Pat the chicken drumsticks dry with paper towels.
Toss the chicken drumsticks with the remaining ingredients.
Cook the chicken drumsticks at 370 degrees F for 20 minutes, turning them over halfway through the cooking time.
Bon appétit!

Thai Hot Chicken Drumettes

(Ready in about 25 minutes | Servings 3)
Per serving: 260 Calories; 13.3g Fat; 0.5g Carbs; 31.2g Protein; 0.4g Sugars; 0.5g Fiber
Ingredients
1 pound chicken drumettes, bone-in
Sea salt and freshly ground black pepper, to taste
1/4 cup Thai hot sauces
2 tablespoons sesame oil
1 teaspoon tamari sauce
Directions
Toss the chicken drumettes with the remaining ingredients.
Cook the chicken drumettes at 380 degrees F for 22 minutes, turning them over halfway through the cooking time.
Bon appétit!

Buttermilk Fried Chicken

(Ready in about 15 minutes + marinating time | Servings 4)
Per serving: 266 Calories; 3.9g Fat; 26.7g Carbs; 28.2g Protein; 3g Sugars; 0.8g Fiber
Ingredients
1 pound chicken breast halves
Sea salt and ground black pepper, to taste
1 cup buttermilk
1 cup all-purpose flour
1/2 teaspoon onion powder
1 teaspoon garlic powder
1 teaspoon smoked paprika
Directions
Toss together the chicken pieces, salt, and black pepper in a large bowl to coat. Stir in the buttermilk until the chicken is coated on all sides. Place the chicken in your refrigerator for about 6 hours.
In a shallow bowl, thoroughly combine the flour, onion powder, garlic powder, and smoked paprika. Then, dredge the chicken in the seasoned flour; shake off any excess and transfer them to a lightly oiled Air Fryer basket.
Cook the chicken breasts at 380 degrees F for 12 minutes, turning them over halfway through the cooking time.
Enjoy!

BEEF

Herb and Onion Beef Roast

(Ready in about 55 minutes | Servings 4)
Per serving: 268 Calories; 13.6g Fat; 1.2g Carbs; 35.2g Protein; 0.6g Sugars; 0.2g Fiber
Ingredients
1 ½ pounds beef eye round roast
1 tablespoon olive oil
Sea salt and ground black pepper, to taste
1 onion, sliced
1 rosemary sprig
1 thyme sprig
Directions
Toss the beef with the olive oil, salt, and black pepper; place the beef in the Air Fryer cooking basket.
Cook the beef eye round roast at 390 degrees F for 45 minutes, turning it over halfway through the cooking time.
Top the beef with the onion, rosemary, and thyme. Continue to cook an additional 10 minutes.
Enjoy!

Easy Fried Porterhouse

(Ready in about 15 minutes | Servings 4)
Per serving: 326 Calories; 19.6g Fat; 1.9g Carbs; 35.6g Protein; 0.6g Sugars; 0.4g Fiber
Ingredients
1 ½ pounds Porterhouse steak
1 tablespoon olive oil
Kosher salt and ground black pepper, to taste
1/2 teaspoon cayenne pepper
1 teaspoon dried parsley
1 teaspoon dried oregano
1/2 teaspoon dried basil
2 tablespoons butter
2 garlic cloves, minced
Directions
Toss the steak with the remaining ingredients; place the steak in the Air Fryer cooking basket.
Cook the steak at 400 degrees F for 12 minutes, turning it over halfway through the cooking time.
Bon appétit!

Restaurant-Style Beef Burgers

(Ready in about 20 minutes | Servings 3)
Per serving: 392 Calories; 16.6g Fat; 32.3g Carbs; 28.2g Protein; 5.3g Sugars; 1.8g Fiber
Ingredients
3/4 pound ground beef
2 cloves garlic, minced
1 small onion, chopped
Kosher salt and ground black pepper, to taste
3 hamburger buns
Directions
Mix the beef, garlic, onion, salt, and black pepper until everything is well combined. Form the mixture into three patties.
Cook the burgers at 380 degrees F for about 15 minutes or until cooked through; make sure to turn them over halfway through the cooking time.
Serve your burgers on the prepared buns and enjoy!

The Best London Broil Ever

(Ready in about 30 minutes + marinating time| Servings 3)
Per serving: 220 Calories; 9.6g Fat; 6.3g Carbs; 24.9g Protein; 3.6g Sugars; 1g Fiber
Ingredients
1 pound London broil
1/4 cup soy sauce
1/4 cup fresh lemon juice
2 garlic cloves, minced
1 tablespoon paprika
Sea salt and ground black pepper, to taste
Directions
Toss the beef with the remaining ingredients and let it marinate for an hour.
Place the beef in a lightly oiled Air Fryer cooking basket and discard the marinade.
Cook the beef at 400 degrees F for 28 minutes, turning it over halfway through the cooking time.
Bon appétit!

New York Strip Steak

(Ready in about 20 minutes | Servings 4)
Per serving: 218 Calories; 12.6g Fat; 1.4g Carbs; 23.6g Protein; 0.6g Sugars; 0.4g Fiber
Ingredients
1 ½ pounds New York strip steak
2 tablespoons butter, melted
Sea salt and ground black pepper, to taste
1 teaspoon paprika
1 teaspoon dried thyme
1 teaspoon dried rosemary
Directions
Toss the beef with the remaining ingredients; place the beef in the Air Fryer cooking basket.
Cook the beef at 400 degrees F for 15 minutes, turning it over halfway through the cooking time.
Enjoy!

Italian Herb Filet Mignon

(Ready in about 20 minutes | Servings 4)
Per serving: 300 Calories; 17.4g Fat; 0.7g Carbs; 35.3g Protein; 0.1g Sugars; 0.2g Fiber
Ingredients
1 ½ pounds filet mignon
2 tablespoons olive oil
2 cloves garlic, pressed
1 tablespoon Italian herb mix
1 teaspoon cayenne pepper
Kosher salt and freshly ground black pepper, to taste
Directions

Toss the beef with the remaining ingredients; place the beef in the Air Fryer cooking basket.
Cook the beef at 400 degrees F for 14 minutes, turning it over halfway through the cooking time. Enjoy!

Rosemary Ribeye Steak

(Ready in about 20 minutes | Servings 4)

Per serving: 263 Calories; 17.8g Fat; 3.7g Carbs; 22.7g Protein; 0.5g Sugars; 0.2g Fiber

Ingredients

1 pound ribeye steak, bone-in
2 tablespoons butter, room temperature
2 garlic cloves, minced
Sea salt and ground black pepper, to taste
2 rosemary sprigs, leaves picked, chopped

Directions

Toss the ribeye steak with the butter, garlic, salt, black pepper, and rosemary; place the steak in the Air Fryer cooking basket.
Cook the ribeye steak at 400 degrees F for 15 minutes, turning it over halfway through the cooking time.
Bon appétit!

Mustard Steak Sliders

(Ready in about 20 minutes | Servings 4)

Per serving: 541 Calories; 20.7g Fat; 44g Carbs; 44g Protein; 6.1g Sugars; 2.3g Fiber

Ingredients

1 ½ pounds skirt steak
1 teaspoon steak dry rub
1/2 teaspoon cayenne pepper
Sea salt and ground black pepper, to taste
2 tablespoons olive oil
2 tablespoons Dijon mustard
8 Hawaiian buns

Directions

Toss the beef with the spices and olive oil; place the beef in the Air Fryer cooking basket.
Cook the beef at 400 degrees F for 15 minutes, turning it over halfway through the cooking time.
Cut the beef into slices and serve them with mustard and Hawaiian buns. Bon appétit!

Herb Roast Beef

(Ready in about 55 minutes | Servings 4)

Per serving: 301 Calories; 16.7g Fat; 0.4g Carbs; 35.4g Protein; 0.1g Sugars; 0.1g Fiber

Ingredients

1 ½ pounds bottom round roast
2 tablespoons olive oil
2 garlic cloves, minced
1 teaspoon rosemary
1 teaspoon parsley
1 teaspoon oregano
Sea salt and freshly ground black pepper

Directions

Toss the beef with the spices, garlic, and olive oil; place the beef in the Air Fryer cooking basket.
Cook the roast beef at 390 degrees F for 50 minutes, turning it over halfway through the cooking time.
Cut the beef into slices and serve them with dinner rolls. Bon appétit!

Classic Beef Brisket

(Ready in about 1 hour 10 minutes | Servings 4)

Per serving: 401 Calories; 32.1g Fat; 2.4g Carbs; 25.4g Protein; 0.6g Sugars; 0.4g Fiber

Ingredients

1 ½ pounds beef brisket
2 tablespoons olive oil
1 teaspoon onion powder
1 teaspoon garlic powder
Sea salt and ground black pepper, to taste
1 teaspoon dried parsley flakes
1 teaspoon dried thyme

Directions

Toss the beef with the remaining ingredients; place the beef in the Air Fryer cooking basket.
Cook the beef at 390 degrees F for 15 minutes, turn the beef over and turn the temperature to 360 degrees F.
Continue to cook the beef for 55 minutes more. Bon appétit!

Classic Pulled Beef

(Ready in about 1 hour 10 minutes | Servings 4)

Per serving: 414 Calories; 32.4g Fat; 25g Carbs; 3.4g Protein; 1.6g Sugars; 0.8g Fiber

Ingredients

1 ½ pounds beef brisket
2 tablespoons olive oil
3 garlic cloves, pressed
Sea salt and ground black pepper, to taste
1 teaspoon red pepper flakes, crushed
2 tablespoons tomato ketchup
2 tablespoons Dijon mustard

Directions

Toss the beef brisket with the olive oil, garlic, salt, black pepper, and red pepper; now, place the beef brisket in the Air Fryer cooking basket.
Cook the beef brisket at 390 degrees F for 15 minutes, turn the beef over and reduce the temperature to 360 degrees F.
Continue to cook the beef brisket for approximately 55 minutes or until cooked through.
Shred the beef with two forks; add in the ketchup and mustard and stir to combine well. Bon appétit!

Spicy Top Round Roast

(Ready in about 55 minutes | Servings 5)

Per serving: 270 Calories; 10.9g Fat; 0.5g Carbs; 42.2g Protein; 0.1g Sugars; 0.2g Fiber

Ingredients

2 pounds top round roast
2 tablespoons extra-virgin olive oil
2 cloves garlic, pressed
1 tablespoon fresh rosemary, chopped
1 tablespoon fresh parsley, chopped

1 teaspoon red chili powder
Kosher salt and freshly ground black pepper, to taste
Directions
Toss the beef with the remaining ingredients; place the beef in the Air Fryer cooking basket.
Cook the beef at 390 degrees F for 55 minutes, turning it over halfway through the cooking time.
Enjoy!

Dad's Spicy Burgers

(Ready in about 20 minutes | Servings 3)
Per serving: 270 Calories; 10.9g Fat; 0.5g Carbs; 42.2g Protein; 0.1g Sugars; 0.2g Fiber
Ingredients
3/4 pound ground beef
2 tablespoons onion, minced
1 teaspoon garlic, minced
1 teaspoon cayenne pepper
Sea salt and ground black pepper, to taste
1 teaspoon red chili powder
3 hamburger buns
Directions
Mix the beef, onion, garlic, cayenne pepper, salt, black pepper, and red chili powder until everything is well combined. Form the mixture into three patties.
Cook the burgers at 380 degrees F for about 15 minutes or until cooked through; make sure to turn them over halfway through the cooking time.
Serve your burgers on the prepared buns and enjoy!

Marinated London Broil

(Ready in about 30 minutes | Servings 4)
Per serving: 227 Calories; 13.6g Fat; 2.7g Carbs; 23.8g Protein; 0.9g Sugars; 0.3g Fiber
Ingredients
1 pound London broil
Kosher salt and ground black pepper, to taste
2 tablespoons olive oil
1 small lemon, freshly squeezed
3 cloves garlic, minced
1 tablespoon fresh parsley, chopped
1 tablespoon fresh coriander, chopped
Directions
Toss the beef with the remaining ingredients and let it marinate for an hour.
Place the beef in a lightly oiled Air Fryer cooking basket and discard the marinade.
Cook the beef at 400 degrees F for 28 minutes, turning it over halfway through the cooking time.
Bon appétit!

Old-Fashioned Meatloaf

(Ready in about 30 minutes | Servings 4)
Per serving: 373 Calories; 23.1g Fat; 5g Carbs; 36.8g Protein; 1.4g Sugars; 0.6g Fiber
Ingredients
1 ½ pounds ground chuck
1 egg, beaten
2 tablespoons olive oil
4 tablespoons crackers, crushed
1/2 cup shallots, minced
2 garlic cloves, minced
1 tablespoon fresh rosemary, chopped
1 tablespoon fresh thyme, chopped
Sea salt and ground black pepper, to taste
Directions
Thoroughly combine all ingredients until everything is well combined.
Scrape the beef mixture into a lightly oiled baking pan and transfer it to the Air Fryer cooking basket.
Cook your meatloaf at 390 degrees F for 25 minutes.
Bon appétit!

Mom's Skirt Steak

(Ready in about 15 minutes | Servings 4)
Per serving: 305 Calories; 17.5g Fat; 1.8g Carbs; 35.2g Protein; 0.6g Sugars; 0.3g Fiber
Ingredients
1 ½ pounds skirt steak
Kosher salt and freshly cracked black pepper, to taste
1 teaspoon cayenne pepper
1/4 teaspoon cumin powder
2 tablespoons olive oil
2 garlic cloves, minced
Directions
Toss the steak with the other ingredients; place the steak in the Air Fryer cooking basket.
Cook the steak at 400 degrees F for 12 minutes, turning it over halfway through the cooking time.
Bon appétit!

Traditional French Chateaubriand

(Ready in about 15 minutes | Servings 4)
Per serving: 249 Calories; 15.5g Fat; 1.8g Carbs; 26.2g Protein; 0.8g Sugars; 0.4g Fiber
Ingredients
1 pound beef filet mignon
Sea salt and ground black pepper, to taste
1 teaspoon cayenne pepper
3 tablespoons olive oil
1 tablespoon Dijon mustard
4 tablespoons dry French wine
Directions
Toss the filet mignon with the rest of the ingredients; place the filet mignon in the Air Fryer cooking basket.
Cook the filet mignon at 400 degrees F for 14 minutes, turning it over halfway through the cooking time.
Enjoy!

Montreal Ribeye Steak

(Ready in about 20 minutes | Servings 4)
Per serving: 357 Calories; 23.5g Fat; 2.7g Carbs; 33.5g Protein; 0.2g Sugars; 0.4g Fiber
Ingredients
1 ½ pounds ribeye steak, bone-in
2 tablespoons butter
1 Montreal seasoning mix
Sea salt and ground black pepper, to taste
Directions

Toss the ribeye steak with the remaining ingredients; place the ribeye steak in a lightly oiled Air Fryer cooking basket.
Cook the ribeye steak at 400 degrees F for 15 minutes, turning it over halfway through the cooking time.
Bon appétit!

Italian Rump Roast

(Ready in about 55 minutes | Servings 4)
Per serving: 297 Calories; 16.9g Fat; 0.7g Carbs; 35.2g Protein; 0.2g Sugars; 0.1g Fiber
Ingredients
1 ½ pounds rump roast
2 tablespoons olive oil
Sea salt and ground black pepper, to taste
1 teaspoon Italian seasoning mix
1 onion, sliced
2 cloves garlic, peeled
1/4 cup red wine
Directions
Toss the rump roast with the rest of the ingredients; place the rump roast in a lightly oiled Air Fryer cooking basket.
Cook the rump roast at 390 degrees F for 55 minutes, turning it over halfway through the cooking time.
Bon appétit!

Tenderloin Steaks with Mushrooms

(Ready in about 20 minutes | Servings 4)
Per serving: 310 Calories; 17g Fat; 3.7g Carbs; 41.2g Protein; 1.6g Sugars; 1.7g Fiber
Ingredients
1 ½ pounds tenderloin steaks
2 tablespoons butter, melted
1 teaspoon garlic powder
1/2 teaspoon mustard powder
1 teaspoon cayenne pepper
Sea salt and ground black pepper, to taste
1/2 pound cremini mushrooms, sliced
Directions
Toss the beef with 1 tablespoon of the butter and spices; place the beef in the Air Fryer cooking basket.
Cook the beef at 400 degrees F for 10 minutes, turning it over halfway through the cooking time.
Add in the mushrooms along with the remaining 1 tablespoon of the butter. Continue to cook an additional 5 minutes. Serve warm.
Bon appétit!

BBQ Beef Brisket

(Ready in about 1 hour 10 minutes | Servings 4)
Per serving: 391 Calories; 26.7g Fat; 9.5g Carbs; 25.2g Protein; 7g Sugars; 0.3g Fiber
Ingredients
1 ½ pounds beef brisket
1/4 cup barbecue sauce
2 tablespoons soy sauce
Directions
Toss the beef with the remaining ingredients; place the beef in the Air Fryer cooking basket.
Cook the beef at 390 degrees F for 15 minutes, turn the beef over and turn the temperature to 360 degrees F.
Continue to cook the beef for 55 minutes more. Bon appétit!

Roast Beef with Carrots and Herbs

(Ready in about 55 minutes | Servings 5)
Per serving: 293 Calories; 15.7g Fat; 0.9g Carbs; 37.2g Protein; 0.5g Sugars; 0.2g Fiber
Ingredients
2 pounds top sirloin roast
2 tablespoons olive oil
Sea salt and ground black pepper, to taste
2 carrots, sliced
1 tablespoon fresh coriander
1 tablespoon fresh thyme
1 tablespoon fresh rosemary
Directions
Toss the beef with the olive oil, salt, and black pepper; place the beef in the Air Fryer cooking basket.
Cook the beef eye round roast at 390 degrees F for 45 minutes, turning it over halfway through the cooking time.
Top the beef with the carrots and herbs. Continue to cook an additional 10 minutes.
Enjoy!

Classic BBQ Cheeseburgers

(Ready in about 20 minutes | Servings 3)
Per serving: 394 Calories; 17.5g Fat; 26.5g Carbs; 32.5g Protein; 6.4g Sugars; 1.3g Fiber
Ingredients
3/4 pound ground chuck
1 teaspoon garlic, minced
2 tablespoons BBQ sauce
Sea salt and ground black pepper, to taste
3 slices cheese
3 hamburger buns
Directions
Mix the ground chuck, garlic, BBQ sauce, salt, and black pepper until everything is well combined. Form the mixture into four patties.
Cook the burgers at 380 degrees F for about 15 minutes or until cooked through; make sure to turn them over halfway through the cooking time.
Top each burger with cheese. Serve your burgers on the prepared buns and enjoy!

Garlic Butter London Broil

(Ready in about 30 minutes | Servings 4)
Per serving: 432 Calories; 24.2g Fat; 1.6g Carbs; 52g Protein; 0.6g Sugars; 0.4g Fiber
Ingredients
1 ½ pounds London broil
Kosher salt and ground black pepper, to taste
1/4 teaspoon ground bay leaf
3 tablespoons butter, cold

1 tablespoon Dijon mustard
1 teaspoon garlic, pressed
1 tablespoon fresh parsley, chopped
Directions
Toss the beef with the salt and black pepper; place the beef in a lightly oiled Air Fryer cooking basket.
Cook the beef at 400 degrees F for 28 minutes, turning over halfway through the cooking time.
In the meantime, mix the butter with the remaining ingredients and place it in the refrigerator until well-chilled.
Serve warm beef with the chilled garlic butter on the side. Bon appétit!

Classic Mexican Carnitas

(Ready in about 1 hour 10 minutes | Servings 4)
Per serving: 542 Calories; 34.2g Fat; 25.6g Carbs; 29.1g Protein; 2.1g Sugars; 1.6g Fiber
Ingredients
1 ½ pounds beef brisket
2 tablespoons olive oil
Sea salt and ground black pepper, to taste
1 teaspoon chili powder
4 medium-sized flour tortillas
Directions
Toss the beef brisket with the olive oil, salt, black pepper, and chili powder; now, place the beef brisket in the Air Fryer cooking basket.
Cook the beef brisket at 390 degrees F for 15 minutes, turn the beef over and reduce the temperature to 360 degrees F.
Continue to cook the beef brisket for approximately 55 minutes or until cooked through.
Shred the beef with two forks and serve with tortillas and toppings of choice. Bon appétit!

Paprika Flank Steak

(Ready in about 15 minutes | Servings 5)
Per serving: 299 Calories; 14.5g Fat; 0.3g Carbs; 38.5g Protein; 0g Sugars; 0.2g Fiber
Ingredients
2 pounds flank steak
2 tablespoons olive oil
1 teaspoon paprika
Sea salt and ground black pepper, to taste
Directions
Toss the steak with the remaining ingredients; place the steak in the Air Fryer cooking basket.
Cook the steak at 400 degrees F for 12 minutes, turning over halfway through the cooking time.
Bon appétit!

Mexican-Style Meatloaf

(Ready in about 30 minutes | Servings 4)
Per serving: 368 Calories; 22.4g Fat; 5.4g Carbs; 36.5g Protein; 2g Sugars; 0.7g Fiber
Ingredients
1 ½ pounds ground chuck
1/2 onion, chopped
1 teaspoon habanero pepper, minced
1/4 cup tortilla chips, crushed
1 teaspoon garlic, minced
Sea salt and ground black pepper, to taste
2 tablespoons olive oil
1 egg, whisked
Directions
Thoroughly combine all ingredients until everything is well combined.
Scrape the beef mixture into a lightly oiled baking pan and transfer it to the Air Fryer cooking basket.
Cook your meatloaf at 390 degrees F for 25 minutes.
Bon appétit!

Mediterranean Filet Mignon

(Ready in about 15 minutes | Servings 4)
Per serving: 385 Calories; 26g Fat; 2.2g Carbs; 36.2g Protein; 0.5g Sugars; 0.3g Fiber
Ingredients
1 ½ pounds filet mignon
Sea salt and ground black pepper, to taste
2 tablespoons olive oil
1 teaspoon dried rosemary
1 teaspoon dried thyme
1 teaspoon dried basil
2 cloves garlic, minced
Directions
Toss the beef with the remaining ingredients; place the beef in the Air Fryer cooking basket.
Cook the beef at 400 degrees F for 14 minutes, turning it over halfway through the cooking time.
Enjoy!

Beef Breakfast Cups

(Ready in about 30 minutes | Servings 4)
Per serving: 355 Calories; 18.6g Fat; 14.2g Carbs; 27.5g Protein; 6.2g Sugars; 2.3g Fiber
Ingredients
Meatloaves:
1 pound ground beef
1/4 cup seasoned breadcrumbs
1/4 cup parmesan cheese, grated
1 small onion, minced
2 garlic cloves, pressed
1 egg, beaten
Sea salt and ground black pepper, to taste
Glaze:
4 tablespoons tomato sauce
1 tablespoon brown sugar
1 tablespoon Dijon mustard
Directions
Thoroughly combine all ingredients for the meatloaves until everything is well combined.
Scrape the beef mixture into lightly oiled silicone cups and transfer them to the Air Fryer cooking basket.
Cook the beef cups at 380 degrees F for 20 minutes.
In the meantime, mix the remaining ingredients for the glaze. Then, spread the glaze on top of each muffin; continue to cook for another 5 minutes.
Bon appétit!

Blue Cheese Ribeye Steak

(Ready in about 15 minutes | Servings 4)

Per serving: 399 Calories; 29.4g Fat; 4.6g Carbs; 29.2g Protein; 0.7g Sugars; 0.3g Fiber

Ingredients

1 pound ribeye steak, bone-in
Sea salt and ground black pepper, to taste
2 tablespoons olive oil
1/2 teaspoon onion powder
1 teaspoon garlic powder
1 cup blue cheese, crumbled

Directions

Toss the ribeye steak with the salt, black pepper, olive oil, onion powder, and garlic powder; place the ribeye steak in the Air Fryer cooking basket.
Cook the ribeye steak at 400 degrees F for 15 minutes, turning it over halfway through the cooking time.
Top the ribeye steak with the cheese and serve warm.
Bon appétit!

Dad's Rump Roast

(Ready in about 55 minutes | Servings 4)

Per serving: 390 Calories; 22.4g Fat; 1.4g Carbs; 35.2g Protein; 0.6g Sugars; 0.4g Fiber

Ingredients

1 ½ pounds rump roast
Ground black pepper and kosher salt, to taste
1 teaspoon paprika
2 tablespoons olive oil
1/4 cup brandy
2 tablespoons cold butter

Directions

Toss the rump roast with the black pepper, salt, paprika, olive oil, and brandy; place the rump roast in a lightly oiled Air Fryer cooking basket.
Cook the rump roast at 390 degrees F for 50 minutes, turning it over halfway through the cooking time.
Serve with the cold butter and enjoy!

Classic Coulotte Roast

(Ready in about 55 minutes | Servings 5)

Per serving: 306 Calories; 16.7g Fat; 1.3g Carbs; 37.7g Protein; 0.4g Sugars; 0.2g Fiber

Ingredients

2 pounds Coulotte roast
2 tablespoons olive oil
1 tablespoon fresh parsley, finely chopped
1 tablespoon fresh cilantro, finely chopped
2 garlic cloves, minced
Kosher salt and ground black pepper, to taste

Directions

Toss the roast beef with the remaining ingredients; place the roast beef in the Air Fryer cooking basket.
Cook the roast beef at 390 degrees F for 55 minutes, turning over halfway through the cooking time.
Enjoy!

Chinese Beef Tenderloin

(Ready in about 55 minutes | Servings 4)

Per serving: 326 Calories; 18.7g Fat; 3g Carbs; 35.7g Protein; 1.6g Sugars; 0.3g Fiber

Ingredients

1 ½ pounds beef tenderloin, sliced
2 tablespoons sesame oil
1 teaspoon Five-spice powder
2 garlic cloves, minced
1 teaspoon fresh ginger, peeled and grated
2 tablespoons soy sauce

Directions

Toss the beef tenderloin with the remaining ingredients; place the beef tenderloin in the Air Fryer cooking basket.
Cook the beef tenderloin at 400 degrees F for 20 minutes, turning it over halfway through the cooking time.
Enjoy!

Juicy Peppery Beef

(Ready in about 15 minutes | Servings 4)

Per serving: 299 Calories; 15.6g Fat; 4.3g Carbs; 33.1g Protein; 2.2g Sugars; 0.7g Fiber

Ingredients

1 ½ pounds Tomahawk steaks
2 bell peppers, sliced
2 tablespoons butter, melted
2 teaspoons Montreal steak seasoning
2 tablespoons fish sauce
Sea salt and ground black pepper, to taste

Directions

Toss all ingredients in the Air Fryer cooking basket.
Cook the steak and peppers at 400 degrees F for about 14 minutes, turning it over halfway through the cooking time.
Bon appétit!

Mushroom and Beef Patties

(Ready in about 15 minutes | Servings 4)

Per serving: 305 Calories; 10.4g Fat; 25.3g Carbs; 27.7g Protein; 4.5g Sugars; 1.7g Fiber

Ingredients

1 pound ground chuck
2 garlic cloves, minced
1 small onion, chopped
1 cup mushrooms, chopped
1 teaspoon cayenne pepper
Sea salt and ground black pepper, to taste
4 brioche rolls

Directions

Mix the ground chuck, garlic, onion, mushrooms, cayenne pepper, salt, and black pepper until everything is well combined. Form the mixture into four patties.
Cook the patties at 380 degrees F for about 15 minutes or until cooked through; make sure to turn them over halfway through the cooking time.
Serve your patties on the prepared brioche rolls and enjoy!

Classis Steak Salad

(Ready in about 15 minutes | Servings 5)

Per serving: 316 Calories; 16g Fat; 3.7g Carbs; 38.2g Protein; 1.7g Sugars; 0.7g Fiber

Ingredients

2 pounds T-bone steak
1 teaspoon garlic powder
Sea salt and ground black pepper, to taste
2 tablespoons lime juice
1/4 cup extra-virgin olive oil
1 bell pepper, seeded and sliced
1 red onion, sliced
1 tomato, diced

Directions

Toss the steak with the garlic powder, salt, and black pepper; place the steak in the Air Fryer cooking basket.
Cook the steak at 400 degrees F for 12 minutes, turning it over halfway through the cooking time.
Cut the steak into slices and add in the remaining ingredients. Serve at room temperature or well-chilled.
Bon appétit!

Easy Beef Sliders

(Ready in about 20 minutes | Servings 4)

Per serving: 406 Calories; 16.2g Fat; 27g Carbs; 35.2g Protein; 1.5g Sugars; 2.6g Fiber

Ingredients

1 pound ground beef
1/2 teaspoon garlic powder
1/2 teaspoon onion powder
1 teaspoon paprika
Sea salt and ground black pepper, to taste
8 dinner rolls

Directions

Mix all ingredients , except for the dinner rolls. Shape the mixture into four patties.
Cook the burgers at 380 degrees F for about 15 minutes or until cooked through; make sure to turn them over halfway through the cooking time.
Serve your burgers on the prepared dinner rolls and enjoy!

Tender Buttery Filet Mignon

(Ready in about 20 minutes | Servings 4)

Per serving: 393 Calories; 26.2g Fat; 2.7g Carbs; 36.2g Protein; 1.5g Sugars; 0.2g Fiber

Ingredients

1 ½ pounds filet mignon
2 tablespoons soy sauce
2 tablespoons butter, melted
1 teaspoon mustard powder
1 teaspoon garlic powder
Sea salt and ground black pepper, to taste

Directions

Toss the filet mignon with the remaining ingredients; place the filet mignon in the Air Fryer cooking basket.
Cook the filet mignon at 400 degrees F for 14 minutes, turning it over halfway through the cooking time.
Enjoy!

Christmas Corned Beef

(Ready in about 1 hour 10 minutes | Servings 4)

Per serving: 410 Calories; 32.4g Fat; 2.9g Carbs; 25.6g Protein; 0.8g Sugars; 0.9g Fiber

Ingredients

1 ½ pounds beef brisket
2 tablespoons olive oil
1 tablespoon smoked paprika
1 tablespoon English mustard powder
1 teaspoon ground
1 teaspoon chili pepper flakes
2 garlic cloves, pressed

Directions

Toss the beef with the remaining ingredients; place the beef in the Air Fryer cooking basket.
Cook the beef at 390 degrees F for 15 minutes, turn the beef over and reduce the temperature to 360 degrees F.
Continue to cook the beef for 55 minutes more. Bon appétit!

Beef Shoulder with Onion

(Ready in about 55 minutes | Servings 4)

Per serving: 309 Calories; 16.2g Fat; 2.2g Carbs; 36.2g Protein; 0.7g Sugars; 0.4g Fiber

Ingredients

1 ½ pounds beef shoulder
Sea salt and ground black pepper, to taste
1 teaspoon cayenne pepper
1/2 teaspoon ground cumin
2 tablespoons olive oil
2 cloves garlic, minced
1 teaspoon Dijon mustard
1 onion, cut into slices

Directions

Toss the beef with the spices, garlic, mustard, and olive oil; place the beef in a lightly oiled Air Fryer cooking basket.
Cook the beef at 390 degrees F for 45 minutes, turning it over halfway through the cooking time.
Add in the onion and continue to cook an additional 10 minutes.
Bon appétit!

Greek Pulled Beef (Gyros)

(Ready in about 1 hour 10 minutes | Servings 4)

Per serving: 402 Calories; 32.2g Fat; 1.2g Carbs; 25.2g Protein; 0.1g Sugars; 0.3g Fiber

Ingredients

1 ½ pounds beef brisket
2 tablespoons olive oil
Sea salt and freshly ground black pepper, to season
1 teaspoon dried oregano
1 teaspoon mustard powder
1/2 teaspoon ground cumin
2 cloves garlic, minced
2 tablespoons chives, chopped
2 tablespoons cilantro, chopped

Directions
Toss the beef brisket with the rest of the ingredients; now, place the beef brisket in the Air Fryer cooking basket.
Cook the beef brisket at 390 degrees F for 15 minutes, turn the beef over and reduce the temperature to 360 degrees F.
Continue to cook the beef brisket for approximately 55 minutes or until cooked through.
Shred the beef with two forks and serve with toppings of choice. Bon appétit!

Holiday Chuck Roast

(Ready in about 4 hours | Servings 5)
Per serving: 267 Calories; 11.5g Fat; 3g Carbs; 38.1g Protein; 0.8g Sugars; 0.4g Fiber
Ingredients
1/2 cup red wine
1 tablespoon Dijon mustard
1 tablespoon fresh garlic, minced
1 teaspoon red pepper flakes, crushed
Sea salt and ground black pepper, to taste
2 pounds chuck roast
1 tablespoon corn flour
Directions
Place the wine, mustard, garlic, red pepper, salt, black pepper, and chuck roast in a ceramic bowl.
Cover the bowl and let the meat marinate for 3 hours in your refrigerator.
Toss the roast beef with the corn flour; place the roast beef in the Air Fryer cooking basket.
Cook the roast beef at 390 degrees F for 55 minutes, turning them over halfway through the cooking time.
Enjoy!

Chuck Eye Roast with Tomatoes

(Ready in about 55 minutes | Servings 4)
Per serving: 299 Calories; 17g Fat; 1.4g Carbs; 36.1g Protein; 0.8g Sugars; 0.4g Fiber
Ingredients
1 ½ pounds chuck eye roast
Sea salt and ground black pepper, to taste
1 teaspoon red pepper flakes, crushed
2 tablespoons olive oil, melted
1 jalapeno pepper, chopped
1 large-sized tomato, sliced
Directions
Toss the roast beef with the salt, black pepper, salt, red pepper flakes, and olive oil; place the roast beef in a lightly oiled Air Fryer cooking basket.
Cook the roast beef at 390 degrees F for 45 minutes, turning it over halfway through the cooking time.
Top the roast beef with the tomato and jalapeno pepper. Continue to cook for 10 minutes more. Enjoy!

Smoked Beef Sausage with Peppers

(Ready in about 20 minutes | Servings 4)
Per serving: 464 Calories; 42g Fat; 3.5g Carbs; 16.1g Protein; 1g Sugars; 0.5g Fiber
Ingredients
1 pound smoked beef sausage
2 bell peppers, sliced
2 garlic cloves, pressed
2 tablespoons olive oil
1 teaspoon sage
1 teaspoon thyme
Sea salt and red pepper, to season
Directions
Toss all ingredients in a lightly oiled Air Fryer cooking basket.
Cook the sausage and peppers at 380 degrees F for 15 minutes, tossing the basket halfway through the cooking time.
Serve warm and enjoy!

Home-Style Mini Meatloaves

(Ready in about 25 minutes | Servings 4)
Per serving: 279 Calories; 14.5g Fat; 11.4g Carbs; 25.3g Protein; 0.8g Sugars; 0.6g Fiber
Ingredients
1 pound ground chuck
1 tablespoon olive oil
1 small-sized onion, chopped
2 garlic cloves, minced
1/4 cup breadcrumbs
1 egg, beaten
Sea salt and ground black pepper, to taste
1/2 cup ketchup
Directions
Thoroughly combine all ingredients , except for the ketchup; mix until everything is well combined.
Scrape the beef mixture into a lightly oiled muffin tin and transfer it to the Air Fryer cooking basket.
Cook your meatloaves at 380 degrees F for 20 minutes. Then, spread the ketchup over the top of the meatloaves. Continue cooking for another 5 minutes.
Bon appétit!

Herb Butter Steak

(Ready in about 15 minutes | Servings 5)
Per serving: 316 Calories; 18.1g Fat; 0.7g Carbs; 37.2g Protein; 0.1g Sugars; 0.1g Fiber
Ingredients
2 pounds ribeye steaks, bone-in
Kosher salt and freshly ground black pepper, to taste
3 tablespoons butter
1 tablespoon fresh basil, minced
1 tablespoon fresh parsley, minced
2 tablespoons fresh scallions, minced
2 cloves garlic, minced
Kosher salt and freshly ground black pepper, to taste
Directions
Toss the steak with the salt and black pepper; place the steak in a lightly oiled Air Fryer cooking basket.
Cook the steak at 400 degrees F for 12 minutes, turning it over halfway through the cooking time.
In the meantime, mix the butter with the remaining ingredients and place it in the refrigerator until well-chilled.

Serve the warm steak with the chilled herb butter and enjoy!

Restaurant-Style Ribeye Steak

(Ready in about 20 minutes | Servings 4)

Per serving: 451 Calories; 34.1g Fat; 3.4g Carbs; 33.2g Protein; 0.1g Sugars; 0.1g Fiber

Ingredients

1 ½ pounds ribeye steak
Sea salt and freshly ground black pepper, to taste
1 tablespoon olive oil
2 garlic cloves, minced
1/2 stick butter, cold and cut into cubes

Directions

Toss the ribeye steak with the salt, black pepper, olive oil, and garlic; place the ribeye steak in the Air Fryer cooking basket.
Cook the ribeye steak at 400 degrees F for 15 minutes, turning it over halfway through the cooking time.
Top the ribeye steak with the butter and serve warm. Bon appétit!

Beef and Broccoli Patties

(Ready in about 20 minutes | Servings 4)

Per serving: 252 Calories; 14.7g Fat; 7g Carbs; 24.2g Protein; 2.4g Sugars; 2.1g Fiber

Ingredients

1 pound beef
1/2 pound broccoli, minced
1 small onion, chopped
2 garlic cloves, minced
Sea salt and ground black pepper, to taste
1 tablespoon tamari sauce

Directions

In a mixing bowl, thoroughly combine all ingredients . Shape the mixture into four patties.
Cook the burgers at 380 degrees F for about 15 minutes or until cooked through; make sure to turn them over halfway through the cooking time.
Serve the warm patties with the topping of choice. Bon appétit!

Glazed Corned Beef

(Ready in about 1 hour 10 minutes | Servings 4)

Per serving: 362 Calories; 25.6g Fat; 5.9g Carbs; 25.8g Protein; 2.7g Sugars; 1.2g Fiber

Ingredients

1 ½ pounds beef brisket
2 tablespoons tomato ketchup
1 tablespoon brown mustard
1 teaspoon chili powder
2 tablespoons salt
1 teaspoon garlic powder
1 teaspoon onion powder
1 tablespoon ground black pepper
1 tablespoon brown sugar

Directions

Toss the beef with the remaining ingredients; place the beef in the Air Fryer cooking basket.
Cook the beef at 390 degrees F for 15 minutes, turn the beef over and reduce the temperature to 360 degrees F.
Continue to cook the beef for 55 minutes more or until cooked through Bon appétit!

Garlicky Roast Beef

(Ready in about 4 hours | Servings 4)

Per serving: 301 Calories; 11.5g Fat; 3g Carbs; 38.1g Protein; 0.8g Sugars; 0.4g Fiber

Ingredients

1 ½ pounds eye round roast
4 cloves garlic, peeled and thinly sliced
2 tablespoons olive oil
Kosher salt and ground black pepper, to taste

Directions

Pierce the beef with a sharp knife and insert the garlic slices into the holes.
Toss the meat with the oil, salt, and black pepper and transfer it to the Air Fryer cooking basket.
Cook the roast beef at 390 degrees F for 55 minutes, turning it over halfway through the cooking time.
Enjoy!

Butter and Allspice Coulotte Roast

(Ready in about 55 minutes | Servings 5)

Per serving: 300 Calories; 15.5g Fat; 1.3g Carbs; 37.1g Protein; 0.4g Sugars; 0.2g Fiber

Ingredients

2 pounds Coulotte roast
2 tablespoons butter
Kosher salt and ground black pepper, to taste
1 teaspoon ground allspice
1 teaspoon garlic, minced

Directions

Toss the beef with the remaining ingredients; place the beef in the Air Fryer cooking basket.
Cook the beef at 390 degrees F for 55 minutes, turning it over halfway through the cooking time.
Enjoy!

Parmesan Filet Mignon

(Ready in about 15 minutes | Servings 4)

Per serving: 382 Calories; 26.5g Fat; 4.9g Carbs; 31.1g Protein; 0.6g Sugars; 0.2g Fiber

Ingredients

1 pound filet mignon
Sea salt and ground black pepper, to season
1 teaspoon red pepper flakes
1 teaspoon rosemary, finely chopped
2 tablespoons olive oil
1 cup parmesan cheese, preferably freshly grated

Directions

Toss the filet mignon with the salt, black pepper, red pepper, rosemary, and olive oil; place the filet mignon in the Air Fryer cooking basket.
Cook the filet mignon at 400 degrees F for 14 minutes, turning it over halfway through the cooking time.
Enjoy!

Italian Pulled Pork Ragu

(Ready in about 1 hour 10 minutes | Servings 5)

Per serving: 259 Calories; 10.9g Fat; 2.5g Carbs; 37g Protein; 0.6g Sugars; 0.4g Fiber

Ingredients

2 pounds beef shoulder
Kosher salt and ground black pepper, to taste
2 garlic cloves, minced
1 tablespoon Italian seasoning mix

Directions

Toss the beef shoulder with the remaining ingredients; now, place the beef shoulder in the Air Fryer cooking basket.
Cook the beef shoulder at 390 degrees F for 15 minutes, turn the beef shoulder over and reduce the temperature to 360 degrees F.
Continue to cook the beef shoulder for approximately 55 minutes or until cooked through.
Shred the beef shoulder with two forks and serve with toppings of choice. Bon appétit!

Beef Sausage with Baby Potatoes

(Ready in about 20 minutes | Servings 4)

Per serving: 625 Calories; 33g Fat; 62.1g Carbs; 20.7g Protein; 2.6g Sugars; 7.4g Fiber

Ingredients

8 baby potatoes, scrubbed and halved
4 smoked beef sausages
1 teaspoon Italian seasoning mix

Directions

Toss all ingredients in a lightly oiled Air Fryer cooking basket.
Cook the sausage and potatoes at 400 degrees F for 15 minutes, tossing the basket halfway through the cooking time.
Serve warm and enjoy!

Beef Mushroom Breakfast Muffins

(Ready in about 30 minutes | Servings 4)

Per serving: 305 Calories; 17.1g Fat; 12.5g Carbs; 25.6g Protein; 8.1g Sugars; 0.8g Fiber

Ingredients

1 pound ground beef
1 egg, beaten
1 teaspoon Dijon mustard
Sea salt and ground black pepper, to taste
1/2 onion, minced
1/2 cup mushrooms
1/4 cup seasoned bread crumbs
1 teaspoon Italian seasoning mix
1/2 cup ketchup

Directions

Thoroughly combine all ingredients , except for the ketchup; mix until everything is well combined.
Scrape the beef mixture into lightly oiled silicone cups and transfer them to the Air Fryer cooking basket.
Cook your muffins at 380 degrees F for 20 minutes. Then, spread the ketchup on the top of each muffin and continue cooking for another 5 minutes.
Bon appétit!

Dijon Chuck Eye Steak

(Ready in about 15 minutes | Servings 4)

Per serving: 300 Calories; 17.5g Fat; 0.5g Carbs; 35.1g Protein; 0.1g Sugars; 0.4g Fiber

Ingredients

1 ½ pounds chuck eye steak
2 tablespoons olive oil
1 teaspoon paprika
1 tablespoon Dijon mustard
Kosher salt and ground black pepper, to taste

Directions

Toss the steak with the remaining ingredients; place the steak in the Air Fryer cooking basket.
Cook the steak at 400 degrees F for 12 minutes, turning it over halfway through the cooking time.
Bon appétit!

Roasted Short Loin

(Ready in about 15 minutes | Servings 5)

Per serving: 315 Calories; 14g Fat; 6.5g Carbs; 41.1g Protein; 5.1g Sugars; 0.2g Fiber

Ingredients

2 pounds short loin, sliced
2 tablespoons butter, room temperature
1 tablespoon dark brown sugar
1 teaspoon coarse sea salt
1 teaspoon ground black pepper
1 teaspoon cayenne pepper
1 teaspoon ground coriander

Directions

Toss the short loin with the remaining ingredients; place the short loin in the Air Fryer cooking basket.
Cook the short loin at 400 degrees F for 14 minutes, turning it over halfway through the cooking time.
Bon appétit!

Herb Butter London Broil

(Ready in about 30 minutes | Servings 4)

Per serving: 368 Calories; 29.5g Fat; 2.8g Carbs; 24.1g Protein; 0.9g Sugars; 0.5g Fiber

Ingredients

1 pound London broil
1/4 cup freshly squeezed lemon juice
1/4 cup olive oil
2 tablespoons tamari sauce
1 tablespoon stone-ground mustard
1 teaspoon mixed peppercorns, whole
3 tablespoons butter, cold
2 tablespoons fresh Italian herbs
1 teaspoon garlic powder
1/2 teaspoon kosher salt

Directions

Toss the beef with the lemon juice, olive oil, tamari sauce, mustard, and peppercorns; let it marinate for an hour.
Place the beef in a lightly oiled Air Fryer cooking basket and discard the marinade.

Cook the beef at 400 degrees F for 28 minutes, turning it over halfway through the cooking time.
Meanwhile, mix the butter, herbs, garlic powder, and salt. Serve warm beef with the chilled herb butter on the side.
Bon appétit!

Old-Fashioned Scotch Tender

(Ready in about 55 minutes | Servings 4)

Per serving: 339 Calories; 19.3g Fat; 4.8g Carbs; 36.4g Protein; 2.8g Sugars; 0.5g Fiber

Ingredients

1 ½ pounds Scotch tender
2 garlic cloves, pressed
1 tablespoon stone-ground mustard
2 tablespoons balsamic vinegar
2 tablespoons soy sauce
2 tablespoons olive oil
1 teaspoon garlic powder
Kosher salt and ground black pepper, to taste

Directions

Toss the Scotch tender with the remaining ingredients; place the Scotch tender in the Air Fryer cooking basket.
Cook the Scotch tender at 390 degrees F for 55 minutes, turning it over halfway through the cooking time.
Enjoy!

Hawaiian Roll Sliders

(Ready in about 20 minutes | Servings 4)

Per serving: 490 Calories; 17.3g Fat; 45g Carbs; 28.4g Protein; 4.6g Sugars; 6.5g Fiber

Ingredients

1 pound beef, ground
1 cup seasoned breadcrumbs
1 tablespoon fresh cilantro, finely chopped
1 tablespoon fresh parsley, finely chopped
8 Hawaiian butter dinner rolls

Directions

Mix all ingredients , except for the rolls. Shape the mixture into four patties.
Cook the burgers at 380 degrees F for about 15 minutes or until cooked through; make sure to turn them over halfway through the cooking time.
Serve your burgers on the prepared rolls and enjoy!

PORK

Smoked Paprika Pork Loin Chops

(Ready in about 20 minutes | Servings 4)

Per serving: 332 Calories; 13.3g Fat; 1.9g Carbs; 23.4g Protein; 0.7g Sugars; 0.8g Fiber

Ingredients

1 pound pork loin chops
1 tablespoon olive oil
Sea salt and ground black pepper, to taste
1 tablespoon smoked paprika

Directions

Place all ingredients in a lightly greased Air Fryer cooking basket.
Cook the pork loin chops at 400 degrees F for 15 minutes, turning them over halfway through the cooking time.
Bon appétit!

Classic Center Cut Pork Roast

(Ready in about 55 minutes | Servings 4)

Per serving: 330 Calories; 14.3g Fat; 1g Carbs; 37.4g Protein; 0g Sugars; 0.3g Fiber

Ingredients

1 ½ pounds center-cut pork roast
1 tablespoon olive oil
Sea salt and freshly ground black pepper, to taste
1 teaspoon garlic powder
1 teaspoon hot paprika
1/2 teaspoon dried parsley flakes
1/2 teaspoon dried rosemary

Directions

Toss all ingredients in a lightly greased Air Fryer cooking basket.
Cook the pork at 360 degrees F for 55 minutes, turning it over halfway through the cooking time.
Serve warm and enjoy!

Classic Pork Spareribs

(Ready in about 40 minutes | Servings 4)

Per serving: 301 Calories; 8.5g Fat; 2.8g Carbs; 50.1g Protein; 2g Sugars; 0.2g Fiber

Ingredients

2 pounds pork spareribs
1 teaspoon coarse sea salt
1/3 teaspoon freshly ground black pepper
1 tablespoon brown sugar
1 teaspoon cayenne pepper
1 teaspoon garlic powder
1 teaspoon mustard powder

Directions

Toss all ingredients in a lightly greased Air Fryer cooking basket.
Cook the pork ribs at 350 degrees F for 35 minutes, turning them over halfway through the cooking time.
Bon appétit!

Country-Style Pork Belly

(Ready in about 20 minutes | Servings 6)

Per serving: 603 Calories; 60.1g Fat; 3.3g Carbs; 11.1g Protein; 1.7g Sugars; 0.8g Fiber

Ingredients

1 ½ pounds pork belly, cut into pieces
1/4 cup tomato sauce
1 tablespoon tamari sauce
2 tablespoons dark brown sugar
1 teaspoon garlic, minced
Sea salt and ground black pepper, to season

Directions

Toss all ingredients in your Air Fryer cooking basket.
Cook the pork belly at 400 degrees F for about 17 minutes, shaking the basket halfway through the cooking time.
Bon appétit!

Italian-Style Burgers

(Ready in about 20 minutes | Servings 4)

Per serving: 593 Calories; 38.9g Fat; 30.2g Carbs; 27.6g Protein; 5g Sugars; 2.7g Fiber

Ingredients

1 pound ground pork
Sea salt and ground black pepper, to taste
1 tablespoon Italian herb mix
1 small onion, chopped
1 teaspoon garlic, minced
1/4 cup parmesan cheese, grated
1/4 cup seasoned breadcrumbs
1 egg
4 hamburger buns
4 teaspoons Dijon mustard
4 tablespoons mayonnaise

Directions

In a mixing bowl, thoroughly combine the pork, spices, onion, garlic, parmesan, breadcrumbs, and egg. Form the mixture into four patties.
Cook the burgers at 380 degrees F for about 15 minutes or until cooked through; make sure to turn them over halfway through the cooking time.
Serve your burgers with hamburger buns, mustard, and mayonnaise. Enjoy!

Blue Cheese Pork Loin Filets

(Ready in about 20 minutes | Servings 4)

Per serving: 408 Calories; 18.3g Fat; 5g Carbs; 53.4g Protein; 2.8g Sugars; 1.3g Fiber

Ingredients

1 ½ pounds pork loin filets
Sea salt and ground black pepper, to taste
2 tablespoons olive oil
1 pound mushrooms, sliced
2 ounces blue cheese

Directions

Place the pork, salt, black pepper, and olive oil in a lightly greased Air Fryer cooking basket.

Cook the pork loin filets at 400 degrees F for 10 minutes, turning them over halfway through the cooking time.
Top the pork loin filets with the mushrooms. Continue to cook for about 5 minutes longer. Top the warm pork with blue cheese.
Bon appétit!

Bacon Salad with Croutons

(Ready in about 20 minutes | Servings 5)
Per serving: 419 Calories; 36.3g Fat; 10.3g Carbs; 13.4g Protein; 2.5g Sugars; 1g Fiber
Ingredients
1 pound bacon, cut into thick slices
1 head lettuce, torn into leaves
1 tablespoon fresh chive, chopped
1 tablespoon fresh tarragon, chopped
1 tablespoon fresh parsley, chopped
2 tablespoons freshly squeezed lemon juice
2 garlic cloves, minced
Coarse sea salt and ground black pepper, to taste
1 teaspoon red pepper flakes, crushed
2 cups bread cubes
Directions
Place the bacon in the Air Fryer cooking basket. Then, cook the bacon at 400 degrees F for approximately 10 minutes, tossing the basket halfway through the cooking time; reserve.
Air fry the bread cubes at 390 degrees F for approximately 6 minutes or until the bread is toasted.
Toss the remaining ingredients in a salad bowl; top your salad with the bacon and croutons. Bon appétit!

Pork Sausage with Brussels Sprouts

(Ready in about 20 minutes | Servings 4)
Per serving: 444 Calories; 35.8g Fat; 11.5g Carbs; 20.1g Protein; 2.5g Sugars; 4.4g Fiber
Ingredients
1 pound sausage links, uncooked
1 pound Brussels sprouts, halved
1 teaspoon dried thyme
1 teaspoon dried rosemary
1 teaspoon dried parsley flakes
1 teaspoon garlic powder
Directions
Place the sausage and Brussels sprouts in a lightly greased Air Fryer cooking basket.
Air fry the sausage and Brussels sprouts at 380 degrees F for approximately 15 minutes tossing the basket halfway through the cooking time.
Bon appétit!

Holiday Picnic Ham

(Ready in about 1 hour | Servings 4)
Per serving: 344 Calories; 21.8g Fat; 7.5g Carbs; 28.4g Protein; 0.5g Sugars; 2.4g Fiber
Ingredients
1 ½ pounds picnic ham
2 tablespoons olive oil
2 garlic cloves, minced
2 tablespoons rice vinegar
1 tablespoon tamari sauce
Directions
Start by preheating your Air Fryer to 400 degrees F for about 13 minutes.
Toss the ham with the remaining ingredients; wrap the ham in a piece of aluminum foil and lower it into the Air Fryer cooking basket.
Reduce the temperature to 375 degrees F and cook the ham for about 30 minutes.
Remove the foil, turn the temperature to 400 degrees F, and continue to cook an additional 15 minutes or until cooked through.
Bon appétit!

Rosemary and Garlic Pork Butt

(Ready in about 1 hour | Servings 4)
Per serving: 338 Calories; 22g Fat; 0.7g Carbs; 29.7g Protein; 0.2g Sugars; 0.2g Fiber
Ingredients
1 ½ pounds pork butt
1 teaspoon butter, melted
2 garlic cloves, pressed
2 tablespoons fresh rosemary, chopped
Coarse sea salt and freshly ground black pepper, to taste
Directions
Toss all ingredients in a lightly greased Air Fryer cooking basket.
Cook the pork at 360 degrees F for 55 minutes, turning it over halfway through the cooking time.
Serve warm and enjoy!

Fall-Off-The-Bone Ribs with Zucchini

(Ready in about 40 minutes | Servings 4)
Per serving: 303 Calories; 13.5g Fat; 7.2g Carbs; 37.1g Protein; 4.1g Sugars; 0.9g Fiber
Ingredients
1 ½ pounds pork loin ribs
2 cloves garlic, minced
1 tablespoon olive oil
4 tablespoons whiskey
1 teaspoon onion powder
Sea salt and ground black pepper, to taste
1/2 pound zucchini, sliced
Directions
Toss the pork ribs with the garlic, olive oil, whiskey and spices; place the ingredients in a lightly greased Air Fryer cooking basket.
Cook the pork ribs at 350 degrees F for 25 minutes, turning them over halfway through the cooking time.
Top the pork ribs with the sliced zucchini and continue cooking an additional 12 minutes. Serve immediately.
Bon appétit!

Dijon Pork Loin Roast

(Ready in about 20 minutes | Servings 4)
Per serving: 352 Calories; 21.2g Fat; 1.9g Carbs; 36.4g Protein; 0.6g Sugars; 0.6g Fiber

Ingredients
1 ½ pounds top loin roasts, sliced into four pieces
2 tablespoons olive oil
1 teaspoon hot paprika
Sea salt and ground black pepper
1 tablespoon Dijon mustard
1 teaspoon garlic, pressed
Directions
Place all ingredients in a lightly greased Air Fryer cooking basket.
Cook the pork at 400 degrees F for 15 minutes, turning it over halfway through the cooking time.
Bon appétit!

Hot and Spicy Center Cut Rib Roast

(Ready in about 55 minutes | Servings 4)
Per serving: 383 Calories; 17.8g Fat; 3.2g Carbs; 49.4g Protein; 1g Sugars; 1.1g Fiber
Ingredients
1 ½ pounds pork center cut rib roast
2 teaspoons butter, melted
1 teaspoon red chili powder
1 teaspoon paprika
1 teaspoon garlic powder
1/2 teaspoon onion powder
Sea salt and ground black pepper, to taste
2 tablespoons tamari sauce
Directions
Toss all ingredients in a lightly greased Air Fryer cooking basket.
Cook the pork at 360 degrees F for 55 minutes, turning it over halfway through the cooking time.
Serve warm and enjoy!

Spicy StLouis-Style Ribs

(Ready in about 40 minutes | Servings 4)
Per serving: 360 Calories; 23.6g Fat; 1.6g Carbs; 33.4g Protein; 0.6g Sugars; 0.2g Fiber
Ingredients
1 ½ pounds St. Louis-style ribs
1 teaspoon hot sauce
1 tablespoon canola oil
Kosher salt and ground black pepper, to taste
2 garlic cloves, minced
Directions
Toss all ingredients in a lightly greased Air Fryer cooking basket.
Cook the pork ribs at 350 degrees F for 35 minutes, turning them over halfway through the cooking time.
Bon appétit!

Ground Pork Dinner Rolls

(Ready in about 20 minutes | Servings 4)
Per serving: 499 Calories; 31.6g Fat; 28.2g Carbs; 24.5g Protein; 2g Sugars; 2.6g Fiber
Ingredients
1 pound ground pork
Sea salt and freshly ground black pepper, to taste
1 teaspoon red pepper flakes, crushed
1/2 cup scallions, chopped
2 garlic cloves, minced
1 tablespoon olive oil
1 tablespoon soy sauce
8 dinner rolls, split
Directions
In a mixing bowl, thoroughly combine the pork, spices, scallions, garlic, olive oil, and soy sauce. Form the mixture into four patties.
Cook the patties at 380 degrees F for about 15 minutes or until cooked through; make sure to turn them over halfway through the cooking time.
Serve the patties in dinner rolls and enjoy!

Mexican-Style Pork Tacos

(Ready in about 1 hour | Servings 4)
Per serving: 538 Calories; 34.2g Fat; 11.3g Carbs; 44.1g Protein; 0.2g Sugars; 1.6g Fiber
Ingredients
2 ancho chiles, seeded and minced
2 garlic cloves, chopped
1 tablespoon olive oil
Kosher salt and freshly ground black pepper, to season
1 teaspoon dried Mexican oregano
1 ½ pounds pork butt
4 corn tortillas, warmed
Directions
Toss all ingredients, except for the tortillas, in a lightly greased Air Fryer cooking basket.
Air fry the pork butt at 360 degrees F for 55 minutes, turning it over halfway through the cooking time.
Using two forks, shred the pork and serve in tortillas with toppings of choice. Serve immediately!

Classic BLT Sandwich

(Ready in about 15 minutes | Servings 3)
Per serving: 401 Calories; 23.3g Fat; 32.3g Carbs; 14.2g Protein; 9.5g Sugars; 6.4g Fiber
Ingredients
6 ounces bacon, thick-cut
2 tablespoons brown sugar
2 teaspoons chipotle chile powder
1 teaspoon cayenne pepper
1 tablespoon Dijon mustard
1 heads lettuce, torn into leaves
2 medium tomatoes, sliced
6 (1/2-inch) slices white bread
Directions
Toss the bacon with the sugar, chipotle chile powder, cayenne pepper, and mustard.
Place the bacon in the Air Fryer cooking basket. Then, cook the bacon at 400 degrees F for approximately 10 minutes, tossing the basket halfway through the cooking time.
Assemble your sandwiches with the bacon, lettuce, and tomato.
Bon appétit!

Classic Italian Sausage Sandwich

(Ready in about 20 minutes | Servings 3)

Per serving: 407 Calories; 14.5g Fat; 31.8g Carbs; 28.8g Protein; 7.6g Sugars; 6.6g Fiber

Ingredients

1 pound sweet Italian sausage
6 white bread slices
2 teaspoons mustard

Directions

Place the sausage in a lightly greased Air fryer cooking basket.
Air fry the sausage at 370 degrees F for approximately 15 minutes, tossing the basket halfway through the cooking time.
Assemble the sandwiches with the bread, mustard, and sausage, and serve immediately.
Bon appétit!

Pork Loin Chops with Onions

(Ready in about 20 minutes | Servings 4)

Per serving: 358 Calories; 18.6g Fat; 8g Carbs; 37.7g Protein; 4.7g Sugars; 1g Fiber

Ingredients

1 ½ pounds pork loin chops, boneless
2 tablespoons olive oil
1/2 teaspoon cayenne pepper
1 teaspoon garlic powder
Sea salt and ground black pepper, to taste
1 onion, cut into wedges

Directions

Place all ingredients in a lightly greased Air Fryer cooking basket.
Cook the pork loin chops at 400 degrees F for 15 minutes, turning them over halfway through the cooking time.
Bon appétit!

Family Favorite Glazed Ham

(Ready in about 1 hour | Servings 4)

Per serving: 368 Calories; 15.3g Fat; 27.8g Carbs; 28.9g Protein; 20.3g Sugars; 3g Fiber

Ingredients

1 ½ pounds smoked and cooked ham
1/4 cup honey
1 small-sized orange, freshly squeezed
1 tablespoon balsamic vinegar
1 tablespoon stone-ground mustard
1/2 teaspoon red pepper flakes, crushed
Freshly ground black pepper, to taste

Directions

Start by preheating your Air Fryer to 400 degrees F for about 13 minutes.
In a mixing bowl, whisk all the remaining ingredients to make the glaze.
Wrap the ham in a piece of aluminum foil and lower it into the Air Fryer cooking basket. Reduce the temperature to 375 degrees F and cook the ham for about 30 minutes.
Remove the foil, turn the temperature to 400 degrees F, and continue to cook an additional 15 minutes, coating the ham with the glaze every 5 minutes.
Bon appétit!

Traditional Cuban Pork Sandwich

(Ready in about 1 hour | Servings 4)

Per serving: 684 Calories; 28.3g Fat; 57.8g Carbs; 45g Protein; 7.7g Sugars; 4.7g Fiber

Ingredients

1 ½ pounds pork butt
1 teaspoon stone-ground mustard
1/2 teaspoon ground cumin
2 cloves garlic, crushed
Kosher salt and freshly ground black pepper, to season
1/2 teaspoon ground allspice
2 tablespoons fresh pineapple juice
2 ounces Swiss cheese, sliced
16 ounces Cuban bread loaf, sliced

Directions

Toss all ingredients , except for the cheese and bread, in a lightly greased Air Fryer cooking basket.
Air fry the pork butt at 360 degrees F for 55 minutes, turning it over halfway through the cooking time.
Using two forks, shred the pork; assemble your sandwiches with cheese and bread. Serve warm and enjoy!

Herb Pork Butt

(Ready in about 55 minutes | Servings 4)

Per serving: 301 Calories; 13g Fat; 1.6g Carbs; 37g Protein; 0.6g Sugars; 0.5g Fiber

Ingredients

1 ½ pounds pork butt
1 teaspoon olive oil
1 teaspoon dried rosemary
1 teaspoon dried thyme
1 teaspoon dried oregano
1 teaspoon dried basil
1 teaspoon cayenne pepper
Sea salt and ground black pepper, to taste

Directions

Toss all ingredients in a lightly greased Air Fryer cooking basket.
Cook the pork at 360 degrees F for 55 minutes, turning it over halfway through the cooking time.
Serve warm and enjoy!

Frankfurter Sausage with Honey and Beer

(Ready in about 20 minutes | Servings 4)

Per serving: 388 Calories; 31.3g Fat; 11.8g Carbs; 13.3g Protein; 8.7g Sugars; 0.1g Fiber

Ingredients

1 pound Frankfurter sausage
1/4 cup ginger ale
2 tablespoons liquid honey
Red pepper flakes, to taste

Directions

Place all ingredients in a lightly greased Air Fryer cooking basket.
Air fry the sausage at 370 degrees F for approximately 15 minutes, tossing the basket halfway through the cooking time.
Bon appétit!

Caribbean-Style Pork Patties

(Ready in about 20 minutes | Servings 4)

Per serving: 433 Calories; 25.6g Fat; 24.7g Carbs; 24.6g Protein; 5g Sugars; 1.4g Fiber

Ingredients

1 pound ground pork
Kosher salt and ground black pepper, to taste
1 tablespoon fresh parsley, chopped
1 tablespoon fresh coriander, chopped
1 teaspoon habanero pepper, sliced
1 tablespoon teriyaki sauce
1 small onion, chopped
1 clove garlic, minced
4 brioche hamburger buns, lightly toasted

Directions

In a mixing bowl, thoroughly combine the pork, spices, habanero pepper, teriyaki sauce, onion, and garlic. Then, roll the mixture into four patties.
Cook the pork patties at 380 degrees F for about 15 minutes or until cooked through; make sure to turn them over halfway through the cooking time.
Serve the patties with the brioche hamburger buns. Enjoy!

Chinese Sticky Ribs

(Ready in about 40 minutes | Servings 4)

Per serving: 470 Calories; 30.2g Fat; 15.6g Carbs; 34.4g Protein; 12.1g Sugars; 2g Fiber

Ingredients

1 tablespoon sesame oil
1 ½ pounds back ribs
1/2 cup tomato sauce
1 tablespoon soy sauce
2 tablespoons agave syrup
2 tablespoons rice wine

Directions

Toss all ingredients in a lightly greased Air Fryer cooking basket.
Cook the pork ribs at 350 degrees F for 35 minutes, turning them over halfway through the cooking time.
Bon appétit!

Pulled Pork Sliders

(Ready in about 55 minutes | Servings 4)

Per serving: 502 Calories; 27.1g Fat; 29.2g Carbs; 33.8g Protein; 3.2g Sugars; 2.6g Fiber

Ingredients

1 pound pork shoulder
1 tablespoon olive oil
2 cloves garlic, minced
1 teaspoon cayenne pepper
1 tablespoon fresh sage, chopped
1 tablespoon fresh thyme, chopped
1 tablespoon brown sugar
2 tablespoons fish sauce
Kosher salt and freshly ground pepper, to taste
8 dinner rolls

Directions

Toss all ingredients, except for the dinner rolls, in a lightly greased Air Fryer cooking basket.
Cook the pork at 360 degrees F for 55 minutes, turning it over halfway through the cooking time.
Serve on dinner rolls and enjoy!

Bacon Veggie Kebabs

(Ready in about 15 minutes | Servings 3)

Per serving: 375 Calories; 30g Fat; 16.6g Carbs; 11.3g Protein; 10.2g Sugars; 4.2g Fiber

Ingredients

1 tablespoon freshly squeezed lemon juice
1 teaspoon fresh ginger, peeled and finely grated
1 tablespoon maple syrup
1/2 pound bacon
1/2 pound squash, diced
1/2 pound eggplant, diced
1 large onion, cut into wedges

Directions

Toss all ingredients in a mixing bowl until well coated on all sides.
Thread the ingredients onto skewers and place them in the Air Fryer cooking basket.
Then, cook the skewers at 400 degrees F for approximately 10 minutes, turning them over halfway through the cooking time.
Serve warm with sauce on the side, if desired. Bon appétit!

Greek Pork Gyros

(Ready in about 55 minutes | Servings 4)

Per serving: 479 Calories; 20.9g Fat; 35.7g Carbs; 34.4g Protein; 1.4g Sugars; 1.9g Fiber

Ingredients

1 pound pork shoulder
1 teaspoon smoked paprika
1/2 teaspoon onion powder
1 teaspoon garlic powder
1/2 teaspoon ground cumin
1/2 teaspoon ground bay leaf
Sea salt and ground black pepper, to taste
4 pitta bread, warmed

Directions

Toss the pork on all sides, top and bottom, with the spices. Place the pork in a lightly greased Air Fryer cooking basket.
Cook the pork at 360 degrees F for 55 minutes, turning it over halfway through the cooking time.
Shred the pork with two forks and serve on warmed pitta bread and some extra toppings of choice. Enjoy!

Traditional Greek Souvlaki

(Ready in about 20 minutes | Servings 4)

Per serving: 395 Calories; 23.9g Fat; 15.3g Carbs; 31g Protein; 8.5g Sugars; 6.3g Fiber

Ingredients

1 tablespoon olive oil
1/2 teaspoon sweet paprika
1 pound pork tenderloin, cubed
1 small lemon, freshly juiced
1 eggplant, diced
2 bell peppers, diced

1/2 pound fennel, diced
Directions
Toss all ingredients in a mixing bowl until well coated on all sides.
Thread the ingredients onto skewers and place them in the Air Fryer cooking basket.
Then, cook the skewers at 400 degrees F for approximately 15 minutes, turning them over halfway through the cooking time.
Bon appétit!

Asian-Style Pork Loin Porterhouse

(Ready in about 20 minutes | Servings 4)
Per serving: 305 Calories; 14.3g Fat; 3.5g Carbs; 37.7g Protein; 1.9g Sugars; 0.3g Fiber
Ingredients
1 ½ pounds pork loin porterhouse, cut into four slices
1 ½ tablespoons sesame oil
1/2 teaspoon Five-spice powder
2 garlic cloves, crushed
1 tablespoon soy sauce
1 tablespoon hoisin sauce
2 tablespoons Shaoxing wine
Directions
Place all ingredients in a lightly greased Air Fryer cooking basket.
Cook the pork loin chops at 400 degrees F for 15 minutes, turning them over halfway through the cooking time.
Bon appétit!

Easy Sriracha Spareribs

(Ready in about 40 minutes | Servings 5)
Per serving: 301 Calories; 10.5g Fat; 2g Carbs; 38.1g Protein; 1g Sugars; 0.5g Fiber
Ingredients
2 pounds spareribs
1/4 cup Sriracha sauce
1 teaspoon paprika
Sea salt and ground black pepper, to taste
Directions
Toss all ingredients in a lightly greased Air Fryer cooking basket.
Cook the pork ribs at 350 degrees F for 35 minutes, turning them over halfway through the cooking time.
Bon appétit!

Crispy Sirloin Chops

(Ready in about 20 minutes | Servings 3)
Per serving: 426 Calories; 27.3g Fat; 4.3g Carbs; 37.4g Protein; 2.2g Sugars; 0.6g Fiber
Ingredients
1 pound sirloin chops
1 egg
2 tablespoons butter, at room temperature
Sea salt and ground black pepper, to taste
3 tablespoons Pecorino cheese, grated
1/2 cup breadcrumbs
1 teaspoon paprika
1 teaspoon garlic powder
Directions
Pat the pork sirloin chops dry with kitchen towels.
In a shallow bowl, whisk the egg until pale and frothy.
In another shallow bowl, thoroughly combine the remaining ingredients. Dip the pork chops into the egg, then the cheese/crumb mixture.
Place the pork sirloin chops in a lightly oiled Air Fryer cooking basket.
Cook the pork sirloin chops at 400 degrees F for 15 minutes, turning them over halfway through the cooking time.
Bon appétit!

Rosemary Garlic Pork Loin Roast

(Ready in about 55 minutes | Servings 4)
Per serving: 380 Calories; 20.9g Fat; 1.5g Carbs; 44.4g Protein; 0.6g Sugars; 0.3g Fiber
Ingredients
1 ½ pounds pork loin roast
2 tablespoons butter, melted
Sea salt and ground black pepper, to taste
1 teaspoon cayenne pepper
1 teaspoon garlic, pressed
1 teaspoon dried rosemary
Directions
Toss all ingredients in a lightly greased Air Fryer cooking basket.
Cook the pork at 360 degrees F for 55 minutes, turning it over halfway through the cooking time.
Serve warm and enjoy!

Holiday Pork Belly

(Ready in about 50 minutes | Servings 5)
Per serving: 475 Calories; 48.1g Fat; 0.8g Carbs; 8.5g Protein; 0.3g Sugars; 0.2g Fiber
Ingredients
1 pound pork belly
1 tablespoon tomato sauce
2 tablespoons rice vinegar
1 teaspoon dried thyme
1 teaspoon dried rosemary
Directions
Toss all ingredients in a lightly greased Air Fryer cooking basket.
Cook the pork belly at 320 degrees F for 20 minutes. Now, turn it over and continue cooking for a further 25 minutes.
Serve warm and enjoy!

Hot Sriracha Burgers

(Ready in about 20 minutes | Servings 5)
Per serving: 645 Calories; 34.1g Fat; 47g Carbs; 35.5g Protein; 5g Sugars; 2.3g Fiber
Ingredients
1 pound ground pork
1/2 pound ground beef
1/2 cup scallions, chopped
1 teaspoon garlic, minced
1 tablespoon Sriracha sauce

5 tablespoons tortilla chips, crushed
2 tablespoons olive oil
Sea salt and ground black pepper, to taste
5 ciabatta rolls

Directions

In a mixing bowl, thoroughly combine the meat, scallions, garlic, Sriracha sauce, tortilla chips, olive oil, salt, and black pepper. Form the mixture into four patties.

Cook the burgers at 380 degrees F for about 15 minutes or until cooked through; make sure to turn them over halfway through the cooking time.

Serve your burgers with ciabatta rolls. Bon appétit!

Paprika Ham Steaks

(Ready in about 20 minutes | Servings 4)

Per serving: 390 Calories; 25.5g Fat; 8.7g Carbs; 30.3g Protein; 8.5g Sugars; 0.2g Fiber

Ingredients

1 pound ham steaks
2 tablespoons butter, at room temperature
1 teaspoon paprika
2 tablespoons agave syrup

Directions

Place the ham in a lightly greased Air Fryer cooking basket.

Mix the butter, paprika, and agave syrup in a small bowl.

Cook the ham steaks at 380 degrees F for about 4 minutes, turn them over and baste them with the butter glaze.

Cook for another 4 minutes, baste the ham steaks, and finally, cook an additional 4 minutes or until cooked through.

Bon appétit!

Old-Fashioned Bacon with Potatoes

(Ready in about 20 minutes | Servings 4)

Per serving: 545 Calories; 44.1g Fat; 20.4g Carbs; 15.5g Protein; 3g Sugars; 2.1g Fiber

Ingredients

1 pound red-skinned potatoes, cut into 1-inch chunks
Kosher salt and ground black pepper, to taste
1 pound bacon, cut into thick slices
1 tablespoon fresh chives, chopped
2 cloves garlic, minced

Directions

Toss all ingredients in the Air Fryer cooking basket.

Then, cook the bacon and potatoes at 400 degrees F for approximately 12 minutes, turning them over halfway through the cooking time.

Serve immediately. Bon appétit!

Sausage with Onions Rings

(Ready in about 20 minutes | Servings 4)

Per serving: 405 Calories; 35.1g Fat; 3.4g Carbs; 16.5g Protein; 13g Sugars; 0.5g Fiber

Ingredients

1 pound pork sausage, smoked
4 ounces onion rings

Directions

Place the sausage in a lightly greased Air fryer cooking basket.

Air fry the sausage at 370 degrees F for approximately 7 minutes, tossing the basket halfway through the cooking time.

Add in the onion rings and continue to cook for 8 minutes more. Bon appétit!

BBQ Pork Butt

(Ready in about 55 minutes | Servings 5)

Per serving: 374 Calories; 25.2g Fat; 2.7g Carbs; 32.3g Protein; 1.4g Sugars; 0.6g Fiber

Ingredients

2 pounds pork butt
1 tablespoon olive oil
Kosher salt and ground black pepper, to taste
1 teaspoon ground cumin
1/2 cup BBQ sauce

Directions

Toss all ingredients in a lightly greased Air Fryer cooking basket.

Cook the pork butt at 360 degrees F for 55 minutes, turning it over halfway through the cooking time.

Serve warm and enjoy!

Rosemary Pork Shoulder Chops

(Ready in about 20 minutes | Servings 4)

Per serving: 354 Calories; 22.3g Fat; 1.5g Carbs; 35.7g Protein; 0.5g Sugars; 0.3g Fiber

Ingredients

1 ½ pounds pork shoulder chops
2 tablespoons olive oil
Kosher salt and ground black pepper, to taste
2 sprigs rosemary, leaves picked and chopped
1 teaspoon garlic, pressed

Directions

Toss all ingredients in a lightly greased Air Fryer cooking basket.

Cook the pork shoulder chops at 400 degrees F for 15 minutes, turning them over halfway through the cooking time.

Bon appétit!

BBQ Pork Ribs

(Ready in about 40 minutes | Servings 4)

Per serving: 440 Calories; 33.3g Fat; 1.8g Carbs; 33.7g Protein; 0.1g Sugars; 0.4g Fiber

Ingredients

1 ½ pound baby back ribs
2 tablespoons olive oil
1 teaspoon smoked paprika
1 teaspoon garlic powder
1 teaspoon onion powder
1/2 teaspoon ground cumin
1 teaspoon mustard powder
1 teaspoon dried thyme
Coarse sea salt and freshly cracked black pepper, to season

Directions

Toss all ingredients in a lightly greased Air Fryer cooking basket.
Cook the pork ribs at 350 degrees F for 35 minutes, turning them over halfway through the cooking time.
Bon appétit!

Summer Pork Skewers

(Ready in about 20 minutes | Servings 4)
Per serving: 344 Calories; 16.3g Fat; 18g Carbs; 32.6g Protein; 10.1g Sugars; 5.3g Fiber
Ingredients
1 pound pork tenderloin, cubed
1 pound bell peppers, diced
1 pound eggplant, diced
1 tablespoon olive oil
1 tablespoon parsley, chopped
1 tablespoon cilantro, chopped
Sea salt and ground black pepper, to taste
Directions
Toss all ingredients in a mixing bowl until well coated on all sides.
Thread the ingredients onto skewers and place them in the Air Fryer cooking basket.
Then, cook the skewers at 400 degrees F for approximately 15 minutes, turning them over halfway through the cooking time.
Bon appétit!

Italian-Style Pork Center Cut

(Ready in about 55 minutes | Servings 5)
Per serving: 356 Calories; 21.7g Fat; 0.1g Carbs; 37.5g Protein; 0.1g Sugars; 0.1g Fiber
Ingredients
2 pounds pork center cut
2 tablespoons olive oil
1 tablespoon Italian herb mix
1 teaspoon red pepper flakes, crushed
Sea salt and freshly ground black pepper, to taste
Directions
Toss all ingredients in a lightly greased Air Fryer cooking basket.
Cook the pork at 360 degrees F for 55 minutes, turning it over halfway through the cooking time.
Serve warm and enjoy!

Pork Sausage with Fennel

(Ready in about 20 minutes | Servings 4)
Per serving: 433 Calories; 35.7g Fat; 9.9g Carbs; 17.8g Protein; 4.5g Sugars; 3.7g Fiber
Ingredients
1 pound pork sausage
1 pound fennel, quartered
1 teaspoon garlic powder
1/2 teaspoon onion powder
2 teaspoons mustard
Directions
Place all ingredients in a lightly greased Air Fryer cooking basket.
Air fry the sausage and fennel at 370 degrees F for approximately 15 minutes, tossing the basket halfway through the cooking time.
Bon appétit!

Decadent Herb Pork Burgers

(Ready in about 20 minutes | Servings 4)
Per serving: 386 Calories; 28.7g Fat; 9.2g Carbs; 22.3g Protein; 1g Sugars; 1.1g Fiber
Ingredients
1 pound ground pork
1 small onion, chopped
1 garlic clove, minced
4 tablespoons tortilla chips, crushed
1 teaspoon fresh sage, minced
1 teaspoon fresh coriander, minced
1 tablespoon fresh parsley, minced
1 egg, beaten
1/2 teaspoon smoked paprika
Sea salt and freshly ground black pepper, to taste
Directions
In a mixing bowl, thoroughly combine all ingredients .
Form the mixture into four patties.
Cook the burgers at 380 degrees F for about 15 minutes or until cooked through; make sure to turn them over halfway through the cooking time.
Bon appétit!

Decadent Pork Butt Roast with Applesauce

(Ready in about 1 hour | Servings 5)
Per serving: 402 Calories; 26.2g Fat; 7.4g Carbs; 32.3g Protein; 5.8g Sugars; 0.7g Fiber
Ingredients
1 tablespoon olive oil
2 tablespoons soy sauce
2 pounds pork butt
Kosher salt and freshly ground black pepper, to taste
2 cloves garlic, smashed
2 sprigs fresh sage, chopped
1 cup applesauce
Directions
Toss all ingredients , except for the applesauce, in a lightly greased Air Fryer cooking basket.
Cook the pork butt at 360 degrees F for 45 minutes, turning it over halfway through the cooking time.
Top the pork butt with the applesauce and continue cooking for a further 10 minutes.
Let it rest for a few minutes before slicing and serving. Bon appétit!

Sticky Bacon with Cauliflower

(Ready in about 15 minutes | Servings 4)
Per serving: 512 Calories; 44.9g Fat; 11.8g Carbs; 16.7g Protein; 6.7g Sugars; 2.7g Fiber
Ingredients
1 pound bacon, cut into thick slices
1 pound cauliflower, cut into florets
1 tablespoon maple syrup
1 teaspoon paprika

Kosher salt and ground black pepper, to taste
2 cloves garlic, minced
Directions
Toss all ingredients in the Air Fryer cooking basket.
Then, cook the bacon and cauliflower at 400 degrees F for approximately 12 minutes, turning them over halfway through the cooking time.
Serve immediately. Bon appétit!

Zingy Glazed Ham

(Ready in about 1 hour | Servings 4)
Per serving: 470 Calories; 30.3g Fat; 1.6g Carbs; 45.7g Protein; 0.4g Sugars; 0.4g Fiber
Ingredients
1 ½ pounds ham
1/4 cup sherry wine
2 tablespoons dark brown sugar
2 tablespoons freshly squeezed lime juice
1 tablespoon stone-ground mustard
A pinch of grated nutmeg
1/2 teaspoon ground cloves
1/4 teaspoon ground cardamom
1/2 teaspoon ground black pepper, to taste
Directions
Start by preheating your Air Fryer to 400 degrees F for about 13 minutes.
In a mixing bowl, whisk all the remaining ingredients to make the glaze.
Wrap the ham in a piece of aluminum foil and lower it into the Air Fryer cooking basket. Reduce the temperature to 375 degrees F and cook the ham for about 30 minutes.
Remove the foil, turn the temperature to 400 degrees F, and continue to cook an additional 15 minutes, coating the ham with the glaze every 5 minutes.
Bon appétit!

Grandma's Sausage Patties

(Ready in about 20 minutes | Servings 4)
Per serving: 392 Calories; 35.7g Fat; 1.5g Carbs; 16.3g Protein; 0.2g Sugars; 0.4g Fiber
Ingredients
1 pound sausage patties
1 tablespoon mustard
1 teaspoon cayenne pepper
1 teaspoon jalapeno pepper, minced
Directions
Place all ingredients in a lightly greased Air Fryer cooking basket.
Air fry the sausage at 370 degrees F for approximately 15 minutes, tossing the basket halfway through the cooking time.
Bon appétit!

Pork Chops with Bell Peppers

(Ready in about 20 minutes | Servings 4)
Per serving: 359 Calories; 22.2g Fat; 2.3g Carbs; 35.7g Protein; 1.1g Sugars; 0.5g Fiber
Ingredients
1 ½ pounds center-cut rib chops
2 bell peppers, seeded and sliced
2 tablespoons olive oil
1/2 teaspoon mustard powder
Kosher salt and freshly ground black pepper, to taste
1 teaspoon fresh rosemary, chopped
1 teaspoon fresh basil, chopped
Directions
Toss all ingredients in a lightly greased Air Fryer cooking basket.
Cook the pork chops and bell peppers at 400 degrees F for 15 minutes, turning them over halfway through the cooking time.
Bon appétit!

Easy Buttery Ribs

(Ready in about 40 minutes | Servings 5)
Per serving: 374 Calories; 23.8g Fat; 1.4g Carbs; 35.4g Protein; 0.6g Sugars; 0.4g Fiber
Ingredients
2 pounds Country-style ribs
Coarse sea salt and ground black pepper, to taste
1 teaspoon smoked paprika
1 teaspoon mustard powder
1 tablespoon butter, melted
1 teaspoon chili sauce
4 tablespoons dry red wine
Directions
Toss all ingredients in a lightly greased Air Fryer cooking basket.
Cook the pork ribs at 350 degrees F for 35 minutes, turning them over halfway through the cooking time.
Bon appétit!

Beer Pork Loin with Crackle

(Ready in about 55 minutes | Servings 5)
Per serving: 315 Calories; 15.2g Fat; 2.1g Carbs; 39.1g Protein; 0.5g Sugars; 0.3g Fiber
Ingredients
4 tablespoons beer
1 tablespoon garlic, crushed
1 teaspoon paprika
Sea salt and ground black pepper, to taste
2 pounds pork loin
Directions
Toss all ingredients in a lightly greased Air Fryer cooking basket.
Cook the pork at 360 degrees F for 55 minutes, turning it over halfway through the cooking time.
Serve warm and enjoy!

Crispy Pork Belly Bites

(Ready in about 20 minutes | Servings 5)
Per serving: 479 Calories; 48.1g Fat; 2.3g Carbs; 8.6g Protein; 1.6g Sugars; 0.1g Fiber
Ingredients
1 pound pork belly, cut into cubes
1 teaspoon coarse sea salt
Freshly ground black pepper, to taste
1 tablespoon granulated sugar
1 teaspoon onion powder

1/2 teaspoon garlic powder
Directions
Toss all ingredients in your Air Fryer cooking basket.
Cook the pork belly at 400 degrees F for about 17 minutes, shaking the basket halfway through the cooking time.
Bon appétit!

Apple and Madeira Glazed Ham

(Ready in about 1 hour | Servings 5)
Per serving: 359 Calories; 15.6g Fat; 23g Carbs; 30.3g Protein; 13.4g Sugars; 3.3g Fiber
Ingredients
2 pounds cooked ham
1 apple, cored and chopped
1/4 cup maple syrup
2 garlic cloves, crushed
1/4 cup Madeira wine
Directions
Start by preheating your Air Fryer to 400 degrees F for about 13 minutes.
In a mixing bowl, whisk all the remaining ingredients to make the glaze.
Wrap the ham in a piece of aluminum foil and lower it onto the Air Fryer cooking basket. Reduce the temperature to 375 degrees F and cook the ham for about 30 minutes.
Remove the foil, turn the temperature to 400 degrees F, and continue to cook an additional 15 minutes, coating the ham with the glaze every 5 minutes.
Bon appétit!

English Muffin Burgers

(Ready in about 20 minutes | Servings 4)
Per serving: 479 Calories; 48.1g Fat; 2.3g Carbs; 8.6g Protein; 1.6g Sugars; 0.1g Fiber
Ingredients
1 pound ground pork
1 egg
1/2 cup seasoned breadcrumbs
1 teaspoon dried oregano
1/2 teaspoon dried basil
Sea salt and ground black pepper, to taste
1 small red onion, chopped
1 teaspoon garlic, minced
1 tablespoon olive oil
4 English muffins
Directions
In a mixing bowl, thoroughly combine the pork, egg, breadcrumbs, spices, onion, garlic, and olive oil. Form the mixture into four patties.
Cook the burgers at 380 degrees F for about 15 minutes or until cooked through; make sure to turn them over halfway through the cooking time.
Serve your burgers with English muffins and enjoy!

Breaded Pork Cutlets

(Ready in about 20 minutes | Servings 4)
Per serving: 480 Calories; 25.1g Fat; 18.2g Carbs; 43.7g Protein; 0.9g Sugars; 1.4g Fiber
Ingredients
1 ½ pounds pork cutlets
Seasoned salt and ground black pepper, to taste
1 cup tortilla chips, crushed
1/2 teaspoon cayenne pepper
2 tablespoons olive oil
Directions
Toss the pork cutlets with the remaining ingredients; place them in a lightly oiled Air Fryer cooking basket.
Cook the pork cutlets at 400 degrees F for 15 minutes, turning them over halfway through the cooking time.
Bon appétit!

Bratwurst with Brussels Sprouts

(Ready in about 20 minutes | Servings 4)
Per serving: 438 Calories; 30.3g Fat; 25g Carbs; 18.7g Protein; 12g Sugars; 5.1g Fiber
Ingredients
1 pound bratwurst
1 pound Brussels sprouts
1 large onion, cut into wedges
1 teaspoon garlic, minced
1 tablespoon mustard
2 tablespoons honey
Directions
Toss all ingredients in a lightly greased Air Fryer cooking basket.
Air fry the sausage at 380 degrees F for approximately 15 minutes, tossing the basket halfway through the cooking time.
Bon appétit!

Dijon Pork Loin

(Ready in about 55 minutes | Servings 4)
Per serving: 302 Calories; 15.3g Fat; 1g Carbs; 36.9g Protein; 0g Sugars; 0.3g Fiber
Ingredients
1 ½ pounds pork top loin
1 tablespoon olive oil
1 tablespoon Dijon mustard
2 cloves garlic, crushed
1 tablespoon parsley
1 tablespoon coriander
1/2 teaspoon red pepper flakes, crushed
Kosher salt and ground black pepper, to taste
Directions
Toss all ingredients in a lightly greased Air Fryer cooking basket.
Cook the pork at 360 degrees F for 55 minutes, turning it over halfway through the cooking time.
Serve warm and enjoy!

Country-Style Ribs

(Ready in about 40 minutes | Servings 5)
Per serving: 371 Calories; 21.6g Fat; 4.4g Carbs; 35.4g Protein; 3.9g Sugars; 0.3g Fiber
Ingredients
2 pounds Country-style ribs
1/4 cup Sriracha sauce

2 tablespoons bourbon
1 tablespoon honey
1 teaspoon stone-ground mustard
Directions
Toss all ingredients in a lightly greased Air Fryer cooking basket.
Cook the pork ribs at 350 degrees F for 35 minutes, turning them over halfway through the cooking time.
Bon appétit!

Orange-Glazed Pork Chops

(Ready in about 20 minutes | Servings 3)
Per serving: 372 Calories; 22.5g Fat; 1.3g Carbs; 38.6g Protein; 1g Sugars; 0.2g Fiber

Ingredients
1 pound rib pork chops
1 ½ tablespoons butter, melted
2 tablespoons orange juice, freshly squeezed
1 teaspoon rosemary, chopped
Sea salt and cayenne pepper, to taste
Directions
Toss all ingredients in a lightly greased Air Fryer cooking basket.
Cook the pork chops at 400 degrees F for 15 minutes, turning them over halfway through the cooking time.
Bon appétit!

FISH & SEAFOOD

Calamari with Garlic and Sherry Wine

(Ready in about 10 minutes | Servings 4)

Per serving: 169 Calories; 7.5g Fat; 6.6g Carbs; 18.3g Protein; 1g Sugars; 0.6g Fiber

Ingredients

1 pound calamari, sliced into rings
2 tablespoons butter, melted
4 garlic cloves, smashed
2 tablespoons sherry wine
2 tablespoons fresh lemon juice
Coarse sea salt and ground black pepper, to taste
1 teaspoon paprika
1 teaspoon dried oregano

Directions

Toss all ingredients in a lightly greased Air Fryer cooking basket.
Cook your calamari at 400 degrees F for 5 minutes, tossing the basket halfway through the cooking time.
Bon appétit!

Lemon Shrimp with Broccoli

(Ready in about 10 minutes | Servings 4)

Per serving: 160 Calories; 4.2g Fat; 6g Carbs; 24.7g Protein; 1.8g Sugars; 1.9g Fiber

Ingredients

1 pound raw shrimp, peeled and deveined
1/2 pound broccoli florets
1 tablespoon olive oil
1 garlic clove, minced
2 tablespoons freshly squeezed lemon juice
Coarse sea salt and ground black pepper, to taste
1 teaspoon paprika

Directions

Toss all ingredients in a lightly greased Air Fryer cooking basket.
Cook the shrimp and broccoli at 400 degrees F for 6 minutes, tossing the basket halfway through the cooking time.
Bon appétit!

Easy Prawn Salad

(Ready in about 10 minutes | Servings 4)

Per serving: 341 Calories; 21.2g Fat; 2.3g Carbs; 34.7g Protein; 1g Sugars; 0.5g Fiber

Ingredients

1 ½ pounds king prawns, peeled and deveined
Coarse sea salt and ground black pepper, to taste
1 tablespoon fresh lemon juice
1 cup mayonnaise
1 teaspoon Dijon mustard
1 tablespoon fresh parsley, roughly chopped
1 teaspoon fresh dill, minced
1 shallot, chopped

Directions

Toss the prawns with the salt and black pepper in a lightly greased Air Fryer cooking basket.
Cook the prawns at 400 degrees F for 6 minutes, tossing the basket halfway through the cooking time.
Add the prawns to a salad bowl; add in the remaining ingredients and stir to combine well.
Bon appétit!

Fried Fish Fingers

(Ready in about 10 minutes | Servings 4)

Per serving: 169 Calories; 7.7g Fat; 3.1g Carbs; 20.6g Protein; 1g Sugars; 0.3g Fiber

Ingredients

2 eggs
1/42 cup all-purpose flour
Sea salt and ground black pepper, to taste
1/2 teaspoon onion powder
1/4 teaspoon garlic powder
1/4 cup plain breadcrumbs
1 ½ tablespoons olive oil
1 pound cod fish fillets, slice into pieces

Directions

In a mixing bowl, thoroughly combine the eggs, flour, and spices. In a separate bowl, thoroughly combine the breadcrumbs and olive oil.
Mix to combine well.
Now, dip the fish pieces into the flour mixture to coat; roll the fish pieces over the breadcrumb mixture until they are well coated on all sides.
Cook the fish fingers at 400 degrees F for 10 minutes, turning them over halfway through the cooking time.
Bon appétit!

English Muffin Tuna Melts

(Ready in about 15 minutes | Servings 4)

Per serving: 528 Calories; 19.9g Fat; 40.4g Carbs; 45.3g Protein; 2.5g Sugars; 3.3g Fiber

Ingredients

1 pound tuna, boneless and chopped
1/2 cup all-purpose flour
1/2 cup breadcrumbs
2 tablespoons buttermilk
2 eggs, whisked
Kosher salt and ground black pepper, to taste
1/2 teaspoon cayenne pepper
1 tablespoon olive oil
4 mozzarella cheese slices
4 English muffins

Directions

Mix all ingredients, except for the cheese and English muffins, in a bowl. Shape the mixture into four patties and place them in a lightly oiled Air Fryer cooking basket.
Cook the fish patties at 400 degrees F for about 14 minutes, turning them over halfway through the cooking time.
Place the cheese slices on the warm patties and serve on hamburger buns and enjoy!

Butter Mahi-Mahi Fillets

(Ready in about 15 minutes | Servings 4)

Per serving: 248 Calories; 16.6g Fat; 1.4g Carbs; 21.3g Protein; 0.2g Sugars; 0.3g Fiber

Ingredients

1 pound mahi-mahi fillets
2 tablespoons butter, at room temperature
2 tablespoons fresh lemon juice
Kosher salt and freshly ground black pepper, to taste
1 teaspoon smoked paprika
1 teaspoon garlic, minced
1 teaspoon dried basil
1 teaspoon dried oregano

Directions

Toss the fish fillets with the remaining ingredients and place them in a lightly oiled Air Fryer cooking basket.
Cook the fish fillets at 400 degrees F for about 14 minutes, turning them over halfway through the cooking time.
Bon appétit!

Classic Fish Tacos

(Ready in about 15 minutes | Servings 4)

Per serving: 414 Calories; 21.9g Fat; 27.4g Carbs; 28.3g Protein; 1.6g Sugars; 6.9g Fiber

Ingredients

1 pound codfish fillets
1 tablespoon olive oil
1 avocado, pitted, peeled and mashed
4 tablespoons mayonnaise
1 teaspoon mustard
1 shallot, chopped
1 habanero pepper, chopped
8 small corn tortillas

Directions

Toss the fish fillets with the olive oil; place them in a lightly oiled Air Fryer cooking basket.
Cook the fish fillets at 400 degrees F for about 14 minutes, turning them over halfway through the cooking time.
Assemble your tacos with the chopped fish and remaining ingredients and serve warm. Bon appétit!

Chili and Paprika Squid

(Ready in about 10 minutes | Servings 5)

Per serving: 205 Calories; 7.7g Fat; 8g Carbs; 24.9g Protein; 1.2g Sugars; 0.6g Fiber

Ingredients

1 ½ pounds squid, cut into pieces
1 chili pepper, chopped
1 small lemon, squeezed
2 tablespoons olive oil
1 tablespoon capers, drained
2 garlic cloves, minced
1 tablespoon coriander, chopped
2 tablespoons parsley, chopped
1 teaspoon sweet paprika
Sea salt and ground black pepper, to taste

Directions

Toss all ingredients in a lightly greased Air Fryer cooking basket.
Cook your squid at 400 degrees F for 5 minutes, tossing the basket halfway through the cooking time.
Bon appétit!

Cilantro Garlic Swordfish

(Ready in about 15 minutes | Servings 4)

Per serving: 295 Calories; 21.7g Fat; 2.8g Carbs; 22.9g Protein; 0.8g Sugars; 0.5g Fiber

Ingredients

1 pound swordfish steaks
4 garlic cloves, peeled
4 tablespoons olive oil
2 tablespoons fresh lemon juice, more for later
1 tablespoon fresh cilantro, roughly chopped
1 teaspoon Spanish paprika
Sea salt and ground black pepper, to taste

Directions

Toss the swordfish steaks with the remaining ingredients and place them in a lightly oiled Air Fryer cooking basket.
Cook the swordfish steaks at 400 degrees F for about 10 minutes, turning them over halfway through the cooking time.
Bon appétit!

Peppercorn Butter Halibut Steaks

(Ready in about 15 minutes | Servings 4)

Per serving: 314 Calories; 27g Fat; 0.3g Carbs; 16.5g Protein; 0.1g Sugars; 0.1g Fiber

Ingredients

1 pound halibut steaks
1/4 cup butter
Sea salt, to taste
2 tablespoons fresh chives, chopped
1 teaspoon garlic, minced
1 teaspoon mixed peppercorns, ground

Directions

Toss the halibut steaks with the rest of the ingredients and place them in a lightly oiled Air Fryer cooking basket.
Cook the halibut steaks at 400 degrees F for about 12 minutes, turning them over halfway through the cooking time.
Bon appétit!

Easy Orange Roughy Fillets

(Ready in about 15 minutes | Servings 4)

Per serving: 144 Calories; 6.7g Fat; 1.6g Carbs; 18.9g Protein; 0.8g Sugars; 0.3g Fiber

Ingredients

1 pound orange roughy fillets
2 tablespoons butter
2 cloves garlic, minced
Sea salt and red pepper flakes, to taste

Directions

Toss the fish fillets with the remaining ingredients and place them in a lightly oiled Air Fryer cooking basket.

Cook the fish fillets at 400 degrees F for about 10 minutes, turning them over halfway through the cooking time.
Bon appétit!

Restaurant-Style Fried Calamari

(Ready in about 10 minutes | Servings 4)
Per serving: 400 Calories; 13.1g Fat; 36.6g Carbs; 39.3g Protein; 0.3g Sugars; 1.6g Fiber
Ingredients
1 cup all-purpose flour
1/2 cup tortilla chips, crushed
1 teaspoon mustard powder
1 tablespoon dried parsley
Sea salt and freshly ground black pepper, to taste
1 teaspoon cayenne pepper
2 tablespoons olive oil
1 pound calamari, sliced into rings
Directions
In a mixing bowl, thoroughly combine the flour, tortilla chips, spices, and olive oil. Mix to combine well.
Now, dip your calamari into the flour mixture to coat.
Cook your calamari at 400 degrees F for 5 minutes, turning them over halfway through the cooking time.
Bon appétit!

Classic Garlic Shrimp

(Ready in about 10 minutes | Servings 4)
Per serving: 181 Calories; 4.3g Fat; 1.1g Carbs; 34.4g Protein; 0.3g Sugars; 0.2g Fiber
Ingredients
1 ½ pounds raw shrimp, peeled and deveined
1 tablespoon olive oil
1 teaspoon garlic, minced
1 teaspoon cayenne pepper
1/2 teaspoon lemon pepper
Sea salt, to taste
Directions
Toss all ingredients in a lightly greased Air Fryer cooking basket.
Cook the shrimp at 400 degrees F for 6 minutes, tossing the basket halfway through the cooking time.
Bon appétit!

Exotic Fried Prawns

(Ready in about 10 minutes | Servings 4)
Per serving: 261 Calories; 8.1g Fat; 12.1g Carbs; 35.4g Protein; 0.3g Sugars; 2g Fiber
Ingredients
1 ½ pounds prawns, peeled and deveined
2 garlic cloves, minced
2 tablespoons fresh chives, chopped
1/2 cup whole-wheat flour
1/2 teaspoon sweet paprika
1 teaspoon hot paprika
Salt and freshly ground black pepper, to taste
2 tablespoons coconut oil
2 tablespoons lemon juice
Directions
Toss all ingredients in a lightly greased Air Fryer cooking basket.
Cook the prawns at 400 degrees F for 9 minutes, tossing the basket halfway through the cooking time.
Bon appétit!

Mom's Famous Fish Sticks

(Ready in about 15 minutes | Servings 4)
Per serving: 196 Calories; 3.5g Fat; 14.2g Carbs; 26.6g Protein; 1.1g Sugars; 0.7g Fiber
Ingredients
1/2 cup all-purpose flour
1 large egg
2 tablespoons buttermilk
1/2 cup crackers, crushed
1 teaspoon garlic powder
Sea salt and ground black pepper, to taste
1/2 teaspoon cayenne pepper
1 pound tilapia fillets, cut into strips
Directions
In a shallow bowl, place the flour. Whisk the egg and buttermilk in a second bowl, and mix the crushed crackers and spices in a third bowl.
Dip the fish strips in the flour mixture, then in the whisked eggs; finally, roll the fish strips over the cracker mixture until they are well coated on all sides.
Arrange the fish sticks in the Air Fryer basket.
Cook the fish sticks at 400 degrees F for about 10 minutes, shaking the basket halfway through the cooking time.
Bon appétit!

Chimichurri Fish Fillets

(Ready in about 15 minutes | Servings 4)
Per serving: 218 Calories; 6.8g Fat; 2.3g Carbs; 34.6g Protein; 0.7g Sugars; 0.3g Fiber
Ingredients
1 tablespoon olive oil, or more to taste
1 ½ pounds mackerel fillets
Sea salt and ground black pepper, taste
2 tablespoons parsley
2 garlic cloves, minced
2 tablespoons fresh lime juice

Directions
Toss the fish fillets with the remaining ingredients and place them in a lightly oiled Air Fryer cooking basket.
Cook the fish fillets at 400 degrees F for about 14 minutes, turning them over halfway through the cooking time.
Bon appétit!

Greek Fish Pita

(Ready in about 15 minutes | Servings 4)
Per serving: 494 Calories; 24.3g Fat; 43.8g Carbs; 28.8g Protein; 3.7g Sugars; 8.3g Fiber
Ingredients
1 pound monkfish fillets
1 tablespoon olive oil

Sea salt and ground black pepper, to taste
Sea salt and ground black pepper, to taste
1 teaspoon cayenne pepper
4 tablespoons coleslaw
1 avocado, pitted, peeled and diced
1 tablespoon fresh parsley, chopped
4 (6-1/2 inch) Greek pitas, warmed

Directions

Toss the fish fillets with the olive oil; place them in a lightly oiled Air Fryer cooking basket.
Cook the fish fillets at 400 degrees F for about 14 minutes, turning them over halfway through the cooking time.
Assemble your pitas with the chopped fish and remaining ingredients and serve warm. Bon appétit!

Easy Fish Nuggets

(Ready in about 15 minutes | Servings 4)

Per serving: 404 Calories; 10.3g Fat; 37.2g Carbs; 39g Protein; 0.7g Sugars; 1.7g Fiber

Ingredients

1 ½ pounds tilapia fillets, cut into 1 1/2-inch pieces
1 tablespoon dried thyme
1 tablespoon dried oregano
1 tablespoon Dijon mustard
2 tablespoons olive oil
1 ½ cups all-purpose flour
Sea salt and ground black pepper, to taste
1/2 teaspoon baking powder

Directions

Pat the fish dry with kitchen towels.
In a mixing bowl, thoroughly combine all remaining ingredients until well mixed. Now, dip the fish pieces into the batter to coat.
Cook the fish nuggets at 400 degrees F for 10 minutes, shaking the basket halfway through the cooking time.
Bon appétit!

Marinated Swordfish Steaks

(Ready in about 15 minutes + marinating time | Servings 4)

Per serving: 230 Calories; 14.3g Fat; 0.8g Carbs; 22.3g Protein; 0.2g Sugars; 0.2g Fiber

Ingredients

1 pound swordfish steaks
2 tablespoons olive oil
2 teaspoons tamari sauce
Salt and freshly ground pepper, to taste
1/4 cup dry red wine
2 sprigs rosemary
1 sprig thyme
1 tablespoon grated lemon rind

Directions

Toss the swordfish steaks with the remaining ingredients in a ceramic dish; cover and let it marinate in your refrigerator for about 2 hours.
Then, discard the marinade and place the fish in a lightly oiled Air Fryer cooking basket.
Cook the swordfish steaks at 400 degrees F for about 10 minutes, turning them over halfway through the cooking time.
Bon appétit!

Old-Fashioned Fish Salad

(Ready in about 15 minutes | Servings 4)

Per serving: 243 Calories; 13.3g Fat; 5.5g Carbs; 24.4g Protein; 2g Sugars; 1.2g Fiber

Ingredients

1 pound salmon fillets
Sea salt and ground black pepper, to taste
2 tablespoons olive oil
2 garlic cloves, minced
1 bell pepper, sliced
1 shallot, chopped
1/2 cup Kalamata olives, pitted and sliced
1/2 lemon, juiced
1 teaspoon Aleppo pepper, minced

Directions

Toss the salmon fillets with the salt, black pepper, and olive oil; place them in a lightly oiled Air Fryer cooking basket.
Cook the salmon fillets at 380 degrees F for about 12 minutes, turning them over halfway through the cooking time.
Chop the salmon fillets using two forks and add them to a salad bowl; add in the remaining ingredients and toss to combine.
Bon appétit!

Coconut Sea Bass with Tomato

(Ready in about 20 minutes | Servings 4)

Per serving: 237 Calories; 3.6g Fat; 15.4g Carbs; 33.3g Protein; 1.8g Sugars; 1.2g Fiber

Ingredients

1 ½ pounds sea bass fillet
2 tablespoons lemon juice
2 garlic cloves, minced
1/2 cup coconut, shredded
1/2 cup all-purpose flour
Coarse sea salt and ground black pepper, to taste
2 tomatoes, sliced

Directions

Toss the fish fillets with the lemon juice, garlic, coconut, flour, salt, and black pepper; place them in a lightly oiled Air Fryer cooking basket.
Cook the fish fillets at 400 degrees F for about 8 minutes.
Turn them over and top with the tomatoes. Continue to cook for a further 8 minutes.
Bon appétit!

Honey Garlic Trout

(Ready in about 15 minutes | Servings 4)

Per serving: 238 Calories; 10.9g Fat; 10.3g Carbs; 23.6g Protein; 9.2g Sugars; 0.3g Fiber

Ingredients

1 pound trout, cut into sticks
1 tablespoon olive oil

2 tablespoons liquid honey
2 teaspoons apple cider vinegar
2 cloves garlic, minced
Sea salt and ground black pepper, to taste
1/2 teaspoon cayenne pepper
Directions
Toss all ingredients in a lightly greased Air Fryer cooking basket.
Cook your fish at 390 degrees F for 12 minutes, tossing the basket halfway through the cooking time.
Bon appétit!

Classic Chimichurri Squid

(Ready in about 10 minutes | Servings 4)
Per serving: 311 Calories; 16.3g Fat; 8.3g Carbs; 31.3g Protein; 0.7g Sugars; 0.6g Fiber
Ingredients
1 ½ pounds small squid tubes
Sea salt and ground black pepper, to taste
1 teaspoon paprika
1/2 cup parsley, minced
2 cloves garlic, minced
1/4 cup olive oil
Directions
Toss the squid, salt, black pepper, and paprika in a lightly greased Air Fryer cooking basket.
Cook your squid at 400 degrees F for 5 minutes, tossing the basket halfway through the cooking time.
Bon appétit!

Beer-Battered Calamari

(Ready in about 10 minutes | Servings 4)
Per serving: 397 Calories; 5.5g Fat; 55.5g Carbs; 24.8g Protein; 0.7g Sugars; 2g Fiber
Ingredients
2 cups all-purpose flour
1 cup beer
Sea salt and ground black pepper, to taste
2 teaspoons garlic powder
1 teaspoon dried parsley flakes
1 tablespoon olive oil
1 pound calamari rings
Directions
In a mixing bowl, thoroughly combine the flour, beer, spices, and olive oil. Mix to combine well.
Now, dip your calamari into the flour mixture to coat.
Cook your calamari at 400 degrees F for 5 minutes, turning them over halfway through the cooking time.
Bon appétit!

Restaurant-Style Fried Shrimp

(Ready in about 10 minutes | Servings 4)
Per serving: 358 Calories; 9.8g Fat; 31.5g Carbs; 29.1g Protein; 3.7g Sugars; 5g Fiber
Ingredients
1/2 cup flour
Sea salt and lemon pepper, to taste
2 large eggs
1 cup seasoned breadcrumbs
2 tablespoons olive oil
1 pound shrimp, peeled and deveined
Directions
In a shallow bowl, mix the flour, salt, and lemon pepper. Beat the eggs in a second bowl, and place the breadcrumbs in a third bowl.
Dip the shrimp in the flour mixture, then in the whisked eggs; finally, roll the shrimp over the breadcrumbs until they are well coated on all sides.
Arrange the shrimp in the Air Fryer basket. Drizzle the olive oil over the shrimp.
Cook the shrimp at 400 degrees F for about 10 minutes, shaking the basket halfway through the cooking time.
Bon appétit!

Cod Fish Patties

(Ready in about 15 minutes | Servings 4)
Per serving: 308 Calories; 10.2g Fat; 23.5g Carbs; 27.3g Protein; 3.3g Sugars; 1.5g Fiber
Ingredients
1 pound cod fish, boneless and chopped
1/2 cup breadcrumbs
2 medium eggs
1 teaspoon Dijon mustard
2 garlic cloves, minced
Sea salt and ground black pepper, to taste
1/2 teaspoon onion powder
1 teaspoon hot paprika
1 tablespoon olive oil
4 hamburger buns
Directions
Mix all ingredients , except for the hamburger buns, in a bowl. Shape the mixture into four patties and place them in a lightly oiled Air Fryer cooking basket.
Cook the fish patties at 400 degrees F for about 14 minutes, turning them over halfway through the cooking time.
Serve on hamburger buns and enjoy!

Parmesan Monkfish Fillets

(Ready in about 15 minutes | Servings 4)
Per serving: 168 Calories; 8.9g Fat; 2.2g Carbs; 18.2g Protein; 0.7g Sugars; 0.2g Fiber
Ingredients
1 pound monkfish fillets
Coarse sea salt and ground black pepper, to taste
2 tablespoons butter
2 tablespoons lemon juice
4 tablespoon Parmesan cheese, grated
Directions
Toss the fish fillets with the remaining ingredients, except for the Parmesan cheese; place them in a lightly oiled Air Fryer cooking basket.
Cook the fish fillets at 400 degrees F for about 14 minutes, turning them over halfway through the cooking time.
Top the fish fillets with the grated Parmesan cheese and serve immediately. Bon appétit!

Asian Barramundi with Mustard Crust

(Ready in about 15 minutes | Servings 4)
Per serving: 194 Calories; 4.3g Fat; 11.2g Carbs; 22.6g Protein; 2.4g Sugars; 2.6g Fiber
Ingredients
1 pound Barramundi fillets
Sea salt and ground Szechuan pepper, to taste
1 tablespoon sesame oil
2 tablespoons rice wine vinegar
1/2 cup seasoned breadcrumbs
1 tablespoon grain mustard
Directions
Toss the fish with the remaining ingredients; place them in a lightly oiled Air Fryer cooking basket.
Cook the fish at 400 degrees F for about 12 minutes, turning them over halfway through the cooking time.
Bon appétit!

Crispy Salmon Sticks

(Ready in about 15 minutes | Servings 4)
Per serving: 308 Calories; 9.6g Fat; 23.3g Carbs; 27.3g Protein; 2.5g Sugars; 3.1g Fiber
Ingredients
1 egg, beaten
1/2 cup all-purpose flour
Sea salt and ground black pepper, to taste
1 teaspoon hot paprika
1/2 cup seasoned breadcrumbs
1 tablespoon olive oil
1 pound salmon strips
Directions
In a mixing bowl, thoroughly combine the egg, flour, and spices. In a separate bowl, thoroughly combine the breadcrumbs and olive oil.
Mix to combine well.
Now, dip the salmon strips into the flour mixture to coat; roll the fish pieces over the breadcrumb mixture until they are well coated on all sides.
Cook the salmon strips at 400 degrees F for 10 minutes, turning them over halfway through the cooking time.
Bon appétit!

Prawns with Sherry Wine

(Ready in about 10 minutes | Servings 4)
Per serving: 182 Calories; 4.3g Fat; 1.6g Carbs; 34.5g Protein; 0.7g Sugars; 0.3g Fiber
Ingredients
1 ½ pounds tiger prawns, peeled and deveined
1 tablespoon coconut oil
1 teaspoon garlic, crushed
1 teaspoon Old Bay seasoning
Coarse sea salt and ground black pepper, to taste
1/4 cup sherry wine
1 teaspoon Dijon mustard
Directions
Toss all ingredients in a lightly greased Air Fryer cooking basket.
Cook the prawns at 400 degrees F for 9 minutes, tossing the basket halfway through the cooking time.
Bon appétit!

Mint and Lemon Swordfish Steaks

(Ready in about 15 minutes | Servings 4)
Per serving: 229 Calories; 14.3g Fat; 1.4g Carbs; 22.4g Protein; 0.3g Sugars; 0.3g Fiber
Ingredients
1 pound swordfish steaks
2 tablespoons olive oil
2 tablespoons fresh mint leaves, chopped
3 tablespoons fresh lemon juice
1 teaspoon garlic powder
1/2 teaspoon shallot powder
Sea salt and freshly ground black pepper, to taste
Directions
Toss the swordfish steaks with the remaining ingredients and place them in a lightly oiled Air Fryer cooking basket.
Cook the swordfish steaks at 400 degrees F for about 10 minutes, turning them over halfway through the cooking time.
Bon appétit!

Fish Croquettes with English Muffins

(Ready in about 15 minutes | Servings 4)
Per serving: 404 Calories; 20.4g Fat; 28.4g Carbs; 26.6g Protein; 2.1g Sugars; 3.3g Fiber
Ingredients
1 pound mackerel fillet, boneless and chopped
1 tablespoon olive oil
1/2 onion, chopped
2 garlic cloves, crushed
1 teaspoon hot paprika
1 tablespoon fresh cilantro, chopped
2 tablespoons fresh parsley, chopped
Sea salt and ground black pepper, to taste
4 English muffins, toasted
Directions
Mix all ingredients , except for the English muffins, in a bowl. Shape the mixture into four patties and place them in a lightly oiled Air Fryer cooking basket.
Cook the fish patties at 400 degrees F for about 14 minutes, turning them over halfway through the cooking time.
Serve on English muffins and enjoy!

Authentic Mediterranean Calamari

(Ready in about 10 minutes | Servings 4)
Per serving: 187 Calories; 8.3g Fat; 5.6g Carbs; 18g Protein; 0.8g Sugars; 0.3g Fiber
Ingredients
1 pound calamari, sliced into rings

2 garlic cloves, minced
1 teaspoon red pepper flakes
2 tablespoons dry white wine
2 tablespoons olive oil
2 tablespoons fresh lemon juice
1 teaspoon basil, chopped
1 teaspoon dill, chopped
1 teaspoon parsley, chopped
Coarse sea salt and freshly cracked black pepper, to taste

Directions

Toss all ingredients in a lightly greased Air Fryer cooking basket.
Cook your calamari at 400 degrees F for 5 minutes, tossing the basket halfway through the cooking time.
Bon appétit!

Smoked Paprika Pollock Fishcakes

(Ready in about 15 minutes | Servings 4)

Per serving: 476 Calories; 29.1g Fat; 34.3g Carbs; 19g Protein; 17.4g Sugars; 2g Fiber

Ingredients

1 pound pollock, chopped
1 teaspoon chili sauce
Sea salt and ground black pepper, to taste
4 tablespoons all-purpose
1 teaspoon smoked paprika
2 tablespoons olive oil
4 ciabatta buns

Directions

Mix all ingredients , except for the ciabatta buns, in a bowl. Shape the mixture into four patties and place them in a lightly oiled Air Fryer cooking basket.
Cook the fish patties at 400 degrees F for about 14 minutes, turning them over halfway through the cooking time.
Serve on hamburger buns and enjoy!

Cheesy Italian Squid

(Ready in about 10 minutes | Servings 4)

Per serving: 267 Calories; 11.3g Fat; 9.3g Carbs; 29.8g Protein; 2g Sugars; 0.4g Fiber

Ingredients

1 ½ pounds small squid tubes
2 tablespoons butter, melted
1 chili pepper, chopped
2 garlic cloves, minced
1 teaspoon red pepper flakes
Sea salt and ground black pepper, to taste
1/4 cup dry white wine
2 tablespoons fresh lemon juice
1 teaspoon Mediterranean herb mix
2 tablespoons Parmigiano-Reggiano cheese, grated

Directions

Toss all ingredients , except for the Parmigiano-Reggiano cheese, in a lightly greased Air Fryer cooking basket.
Cook your squid at 400 degrees F for 5 minutes, tossing the basket halfway through the cooking time.
Top the warm squid with the cheese. Bon appétit!

Crunchy Fried Shrimp

(Ready in about 15 minutes | Servings 4)

Per serving: 299 Calories; 7.1g Fat; 15.7g Carbs; 42.8g Protein; 0.8g Sugars; 0.7g Fiber

Ingredients

1 ½ pounds shrimp, cleaned and deveined
1/2 cup all-purpose flour
1/2 teaspoon shallot powder
1/2 teaspoon garlic powder
1 teaspoon red pepper flakes, crushed
Sea salt and ground black pepper, to taste
2 large eggs
1 cup crackers, crushed
1/2 cup Parmesan cheese, grated

Directions

In a shallow bowl, mix the flour and spices. Beat the eggs in the second bowl, and mix the crackers and cheese in the third bowl.
Dip the shrimp in the flour mixture, then in the whisked eggs; finally, roll the shrimp over the cracker/cheese mixture until they are well coated on all sides.
Arrange the shrimp in a well-greased Air Fryer cooking basket.
Cook the shrimp at 400 degrees F for about 10 minutes, shaking the basket halfway through the cooking time.
Bon appétit!

Fisherman's Famous Sea Bass

(Ready in about 15 minutes | Servings 3)

Per serving: 294 Calories; 13.1g Fat; 10.7g Carbs; 31.8g Protein; 0.9g Sugars; 0.9g Fiber

Ingredients

2 tablespoons butter, room temperature
1 pound sea bass such
1/4 cup dry white wine
1/4 cup all-purpose flour
Sea salt and ground black pepper, to taste
1 teaspoon mustard seeds
1 teaspoon fennel seeds
2 cloves garlic, minced

Directions

Toss the fish with the remaining ingredients; place them in a lightly oiled Air Fryer cooking basket.
Cook the fish at 400 degrees F for about 10 minutes, turning them over halfway through the cooking time.

Bon appétit!

Herb Salmon Fillets

(Ready in about 15 minutes | Servings 4)

Per serving: 293 Calories; 14.7g Fat; 3.7g Carbs; 36g Protein; 0.9g Sugars; 0.7g Fiber

Ingredients

1 ½ pounds salmon fillets
2 sprigs fresh rosemary
1 tablespoon fresh basil
1 tablespoon fresh thyme
1 tablespoon fresh dill
1 small lemon, juiced
2 tablespoons olive oil
Sea salt and ground black pepper, to taste
1 teaspoon stone-ground mustard
2 cloves garlic, chopped

Directions

Toss the salmon with the remaining ingredients; place them in a lightly oiled Air Fryer cooking basket.
Cook the salmon fillets at 380 degrees F for about 12 minutes, turning them over halfway through the cooking time.
Serve immediately and enjoy!

Chili Fried Calamari

(Ready in about 10 minutes | Servings 4)

Per serving: 316 Calories; 9.9g Fat; 30.1g Carbs; 24.4g Protein; 1.7g Sugars; 1.2g Fiber

Ingredients

1/2 cup milk
1 cup all-purpose flour
2 tablespoons olive oil
1 teaspoon turmeric powder
Sea salt flakes and ground black, to taste
1 teaspoon paprika
1 red chili, minced
1 pound calamari, cut into rings

Directions

In a mixing bowl, thoroughly combine the milk, flour, olive oil, turmeric powder, salt, black pepper, paprika, and red chili. Mix to combine well.
Now, dip your calamari into the flour mixture to coat.
Cook your calamari at 400 degrees F for 5 minutes, turning them over halfway through the cooking time.
Bon appétit!

Dad's Spicy Burgers

(Ready in about 15 minutes | Servings 4)

Per serving: 508 Calories; 23.7g Fat; 31.3g Carbs; 42.4g Protein; 2.4g Sugars; 2.6g Fiber

Ingredients

1 pound tilapia fish fillets, chopped
1/2 cup breadcrumbs
4 tablespoons shallots, chopped
2 garlic cloves, minced
1 tablespoon olive oil
8 dinner rolls
8 slices Provolone cheese

Directions

Mix all ingredients , except for the dinner rolls and cheese, in a bowl. Shape the mixture into four patties and place them in a lightly oiled Air Fryer cooking basket.
Cook the fish patties at 400 degrees F for about 14 minutes, turning them over halfway through the cooking time.
Serve with the cheese and dinner rolls. Enjoy!

Shrimp Salad Sandwich

(Ready in about 10 minutes | Servings 4)

Per serving: 422 Calories; 24.1g Fat; 23.2g Carbs; 27.5g Protein; 3.1g Sugars; 1.5g Fiber

Ingredients

1 pound shrimp, peeled and chilled
1 teaspoon olive oil
1 stalks celery, sliced
1 English cucumber, sliced
1 shallot, sliced
1 tablespoon fresh dill, roughly chopped
1 tablespoon fresh parsley, roughly chopped
1 tablespoon fresh lime juice
1 tablespoon apple cider vinegar
1/2 cup mayonnaise
1 teaspoon Creole seasoning mix
1 ½ teaspoons Dijon mustard
Coarse sea salt and lemon pepper, to taste
4 hoagie rolls

Directions

Toss the shrimp and olive oil in the Air Fryer cooking basket.
Cook the shrimp at 400 degrees F for 6 minutes, tossing the basket halfway through the cooking time.
Place the shrimp in a mixing bowl along with the remaining ingredients; toss to combine and serve on the prepared hoagie rolls.
Bon appétit!

Italian-Style Sea Bass

(Ready in about 15 minutes | Servings 4)

Per serving: 205 Calories; 10.5g Fat; 2.9g Carbs; 22.8g Protein; 0.8g Sugars; 0.7g Fiber

Ingredients

1 pound sea bass
2 garlic cloves, minced
2 tablespoons olive oil
1 tablespoon Italian seasoning mix
Sea salt and ground black pepper, to taste

1/4 cup dry white wine

Directions

Toss the fish with the remaining ingredients; place them in a lightly oiled Air Fryer cooking basket.

Cook the fish at 400 degrees F for about 10 minutes, turning them over halfway through the cooking time.

Bon appétit!

Fried Mustard Calamari

(Ready in about 10 minutes | Servings 4)

Per serving: 398 Calories; 9g Fat; 52g Carbs; 24.5g Protein; 0.8g Sugars; 2g Fiber

Ingredients

2 cups flour

Sea salt and ground black pepper, to taste

1 teaspoon garlic, minced

1 tablespoon mustard

2 tablespoons olive oil

1 pound calamari, sliced into rings

Directions

In a mixing bowl, thoroughly combine the flour, salt, black pepper, garlic, mustard, and, and olive oil. Mix to combine well.

Now, dip your calamari into the flour mixture to coat.

Cook your calamari at 400 degrees F for 5 minutes, turning them over halfway through the cooking time.

Bon appétit!

Italian Fish Fingers

(Ready in about 15 minutes | Servings 4)

Per serving: 218 Calories; 6.4g Fat; 14.6g Carbs; 23.8g Protein; 0.8g Sugars; 0.9g Fiber

Ingredients

1/2 cup all-purpose flour

Sea salt and ground black pepper

1 teaspoon cayenne pepper

1/2 teaspoon onion powder

1 tablespoon Italian parsley, chopped

1 teaspoon garlic powder

1 egg, whisked

1/2 cup Pecorino Romano cheese, grated

1 pound monkfish, sliced into strips

Directions

In a shallow bowl, mix the flour, spices, egg, and cheese. Dip the fish strips in the batter until they are well coated on all sides.

Arrange the fish strips in the Air Fryer cooking basket.

Cook the fish strips at 400 degrees F for about 10 minutes, shaking the basket halfway through the cooking time.

Bon appétit!

Spicy Fish Croquettes

(Ready in about 15 minutes | Servings 4)

Per serving: 258 Calories; 13.7g Fat; 11.3g Carbs; 18.8g Protein; 1.6g Sugars; 0.8g Fiber

Ingredients

1 pound catfish, skinless, boneless and chopped

2 tablespoons olive oil

2 cloves garlic, minced

1 small onion, minced

1/4 cup all-purpose flour

Sea salt and ground black pepper, to taste

1/2 cup breadcrumbs

Directions

Mix all ingredients in a bowl. Shape the mixture into bite-sized balls and place them in a lightly oiled Air Fryer cooking basket.

Cook the fish croquettes at 400 degrees F for about 14 minutes, shaking the basket halfway through the cooking time.

Bon appétit!

Southern-Style Shrimp

(Ready in about 15 minutes | Servings 4)

Per serving: 381 Calories; 1.4g Fat; 45.2g Carbs; 39.8g Protein; 5.2g Sugars; 5.4g Fiber

Ingredients

1 cup all-purpose flour

1 teaspoon Old Bay seasoning

Sea salt and lemon pepper, to taste

1/2 cup buttermilk

1 cup seasoned breadcrumbs

1 ½ pounds shrimp, peeled and deveined

Directions

In a shallow bowl, mix the flour, spices, and buttermilk. Place the seasoned breadcrumbs in the second bowl.

Dip the shrimp in the flour mixture, then in the breadcrumbs until they are well coated on all sides.

Arrange the shrimp in a well-greased Air Fryer cooking basket.

Cook the shrimp at 400 degrees F for about 10 minutes, shaking the basket halfway through the cooking time.

Bon appétit!

Mediterranean-Pita Wraps

(Ready in about 15 minutes | Servings 4)

Per serving: 366 Calories; 16.3g Fat; 16.4g Carbs; 38.1g Protein; 2.9g Sugars; 3.7g Fiber

Ingredients

1 pound mackerel fish fillets

2 tablespoons olive oil

1 tablespoon Mediterranean seasoning mix

1/2 teaspoon chili powder

Sea salt and freshly ground black pepper, to taste

2 ounces Feta cheese, crumbled
4 (6-1/2 inch) tortillas
Directions
Toss the fish fillets with the olive oil; place them in a lightly oiled Air Fryer cooking basket.
Cook the fish fillets at 400 degrees F for about 14 minutes, turning them over halfway through the cooking time.
Assemble your pitas with the chopped fish and remaining ingredients and serve warm. Bon appétit!

Butter Cilantro Shrimp

(Ready in about 10 minutes | Servings 4)
Per serving: 160 Calories; 6.3g Fat; 0.6g Carbs; 23.1g Protein; 0.1g Sugars; 0.2g Fiber
Ingredients
1 pound jumbo shrimp
2 tablespoons butter, at room temperature
Coarse sea salt and lemon pepper, to taste
2 tablespoons fresh cilantro, chopped
2 tablespoons fresh chives, chopped
2 garlic cloves, crushed
Directions
Toss all ingredients in a lightly greased Air Fryer cooking basket.
Cook the shrimp at 400 degrees F for 8 minutes, tossing the basket halfway through the cooking time.
Bon appétit!

Rosemary Sea Scallops

(Ready in about 10 minutes | Servings 4)
Per serving: 318 Calories; 15.1g Fat; 11.1g Carbs; 32.7g Protein; 0.6g Sugars; 0.4g Fiber
Ingredients
1 ½ pounds sea scallops
4 tablespoons butter, melted
1 tablespoon garlic, minced
Sea salt and ground black pepper, to season
2 rosemary sprigs, leaves picked and chopped
4 tablespoons dry white wine
Directions
Toss all ingredients in a lightly greased Air Fryer cooking basket.
Cook the scallops at 400 degrees F for 7 minutes, tossing the basket halfway through the cooking time.
Bon appétit!

Sausage-Stuffed Squid

(Ready in about 10 minutes | Servings 4)
Per serving: 280 Calories; 13.7g Fat; 11.2g Carbs; 26.3g Protein; 1.8g Sugars; 1.5g Fiber
Ingredients
2 tablespoons olive oil, divided, or as needed
1 small onion, chopped
2 cloves garlic, minced
1 tablespoon fresh parsley, chopped
1 small Italian pepper, chopped
Sea salt and ground black pepper, to taste
4 ounces beef sausage, crumbled
1 pound squid tubes, cleaned
Directions
In a mixing bowl, thoroughly combine the olive oil, onion, garlic, parsley, Italian pepper, salt, black pepper, and sausage.
Stuff the squid tubes with the sausage filling and secure them with toothpicks. Place them in a lightly oiled Air Fryer cooking basket.
Cook the stuffed squid tubes at 400 degrees F for 5 minutes, turning them over halfway through the cooking time.
Bon appétit!

Perfect Haddock Fishcakes

(Ready in about 15 minutes | Servings 4)
Per serving: 400 Calories; 11.7g Fat; 39g Carbs; 33.3g Protein; 3.8g Sugars; 1.7g Fiber
Ingredients
1 pound haddock, boneless and
1/4 cup all-purpose flour
2 eggs
1/2 cup parmesan cheese, grated
1/2 cup breadcrumbs
4 brioche buns
Directions
Mix all ingredients, except for the brioche buns, in a bowl. Shape the mixture into four patties and place them in a lightly oiled Air Fryer cooking basket.
Cook the fish patties at 400 degrees F for about 14 minutes, turning them over halfway through the cooking time.
Serve on hamburger buns and enjoy!

Creamed Shrimp Salad

(Ready in about 10 minutes | Servings 4)
Per serving: 282 Calories; 14.1g Fat; 3g Carbs; 36.3g Protein; 1.1g Sugars; 1g Fiber
Ingredients
1 ½ pounds shrimp, peeled and deveined
1 tablespoon olive oil
Sea salt and freshly ground black pepper, to taste
1 teaspoon fresh dill, chopped
1 teaspoon fresh basil, chopped
1 tablespoon fresh parsley, chopped
2 tablespoons chives, chopped
1 bell pepper, seeded and chopped
1 celery stalk, trimmed and chopped
1/2 cup mayonnaise
1 teaspoon stone-ground mustard

1 tablespoon fresh lime juice

Directions

Toss the shrimp and olive oil in the Air Fryer cooking basket.

Cook the shrimp at 400 degrees F for 6 minutes, tossing the basket halfway through the cooking time.

Place the shrimp in a salad bowl; add in the remaining ingredients and gently stir to combine. Serve well-chilled.

Bon appétit!

Mediterranean Herb Calamari (Kalamarakia Tiganita)

(Ready in about 10 minutes | Servings 4)

Per serving: 293 Calories; 15.3g Fat; 19.2g Carbs; 19.1g Protein; 2g Sugars; 1g Fiber

Ingredients

1 pound calamari, sliced into rings
Sea salt and ground black pepper, to taste
1 teaspoon cayenne pepper
1 teaspoon garlic powder
2 tablespoons lemon juice
2 tablespoons olive oil

Directions

Toss all ingredients in a lightly greased Air Fryer cooking basket.

Cook your calamari at 400 degrees F for 5 minutes, tossing the basket halfway through the cooking time.

Bon appétit!

Sea Scallop Salad

(Ready in about 10 minutes | Servings 4)

Per serving: 243 Calories; 10.2g Fat; 3.3g Carbs; 32.1g Protein; 1.8g Sugars; 0.5g Fiber

Ingredients

1 ½ pounds sea scallops
Sea salt and ground black pepper, to taste
2 tablespoons olive oil
1 tablespoon balsamic vinegar
2 garlic cloves, minced
2 teaspoons fresh tarragon, minced
1 teaspoon Dijon mustard
1 cup mixed baby greens
1 small tomato, diced

Directions

Toss the scallops, salt, and black pepper in a lightly greased Air Fryer cooking basket.

Cook the scallops at 400 degrees F for 7 minutes, tossing the basket halfway through the cooking time.

Toss the scallops with the remaining ingredients and serve at room temperature or well-chilled.

Bon appétit!

Classic Fish Burgers

(Ready in about 15 minutes | Servings 4)

Per serving: 368 Calories; 20.7g Fat; 23.3g Carbs; 20.9g Protein; 3.4g Sugars; 1.4g Fiber

Ingredients

1 pound halibut, chopped
2 garlic cloves, crushed
4 tablespoons scallions, chopped
Sea salt and ground black pepper, to taste
1 teaspoon smoked paprika
A pinch of grated nutmeg
1 tablespoon olive oil
4 hamburger buns

Directions

Mix all ingredients , except for the hamburger buns, in a bowl. Shape the mixture into four patties and place them in a lightly oiled Air Fryer cooking basket.

Cook the fish patties at 400 degrees F for about 14 minutes, turning them over halfway through the cooking time.

Serve on hamburger buns and enjoy!

Decadent Coconut Shrimp

(Ready in about 10 minutes | Servings 4)

Per serving: 366 Calories; 16.3g Fat; 16.4g Carbs; 38.1g Protein; 2.9g Sugars; 3.7g Fiber

Ingredients

1/2 cup whole wheat flour
1 cup coconut, shredded
1/4 cup buttermilk
2 tablespoons olive oil
2 garlic cloves, crushed
1 tablespoon fresh lemon juice
Sea salt and red pepper flakes, to taste
1 ½ pounds shrimp, peeled and deveined

Directions

Mix the flour, coconut, buttermilk, olive oil, garlic, lemon juice, salt, and red pepper in a mixing bowl.

Dip the shrimp in the batter and place them in a well-greased Air Fryer cooking basket.

Cook the shrimp at 400 degrees F for 9 minutes, tossing the basket halfway through the cooking time.

Bon appétit!

Tuna Salad with a Twist

(Ready in about 15 minutes | Servings 4)

Per serving: 187 Calories; 5.7g Fat; 5.3g Carbs; 27.5g Protein; 2.3g Sugars; 1.3g Fiber

Ingredients

1 pound fresh tuna steak
Sea salt and ground black pepper, to taste
2 tablespoons fresh lemon juice
1 small onion, thinly sliced
1 carrot, julienned
2 cups baby spinach

2 tablespoons parsley, roughly chopped

Directions

Toss the fish with the salt and black pepper; place your tuna in a lightly oiled Air Fryer cooking basket.

Cook your tuna at 400 degrees F for about 10 minutes, turning it over halfway through the cooking time.

Chop your tuna with two forks and add in the remaining ingredients; stir to combine and serve well-chilled.

Bon appétit!

Tangy Butter Scallops

(Ready in about 10 minutes | Servings 4)

Per serving: 157 Calories; 7.8g Fat; 5.8g Carbs; 15.4g Protein; 0.8g Sugars; 0.2g Fiber

Ingredients

1 pound sea scallops
2 tablespoons butter, room temperature
2 tablespoons lemon juice
2 garlic cloves, crushed
Salt and fresh ground black pepper to taste
1/4 cup dry white wine

Directions

Toss all ingredients in a lightly greased Air Fryer cooking basket.

Cook the scallops at 400 degrees F for 7 minutes, tossing the basket halfway through the cooking time.

Bon appétit!

Lobster with Butter and Spring Onions

(Ready in about 10 minutes | Servings 4)

Per serving: 199 Calories; 12.4g Fat; 2.3g Carbs; 19.3g Protein; 0.8g Sugars; 0.4g Fiber

Ingredients

1 pound lobster tails
4 tablespoons butter, room temperature
2 garlic cloves, minced
Coarse sea salt and freshly cracked black pepper, to taste
4 tablespoons springs onions
1 tablespoon fresh lime juice

Directions

Butterfly the lobster tails by cutting through the shell and place them in a lightly oiled Air Fryer basket.

In a mixing bowl, thoroughly combine the remaining ingredients.

Now, spread 1/2 of the butter mixture over the top of the lobster meat. Air fry the lobster tails at 380 degrees F for 4 minutes.

After that, spread another 1/2 of the butter mixture on top; continue to cook for a further 4 minutes.

Bon appétit!

Butter and Parsley Calamari

(Ready in about 10 minutes | Servings 4)

Per serving: 263 Calories; 8.9g Fat; 7.8g Carbs; 35.4g Protein; 0.1g Sugars; 0.2g Fiber

Ingredients

1 pound calamari, sliced into rings
2 tablespoons butter
2 tablespoons parsley, chopped
2 garlic cloves, minced
1 teaspoon cayenne pepper
Sea salt and freshly ground black pepper, to taste

Directions

Toss all ingredients in a lightly greased Air Fryer cooking basket.

Cook your calamari at 400 degrees F for 5 minutes, tossing the basket halfway through the cooking time.

Bon appétit!

RICE & GRAINS

Cinnamon Banana Muffins

(Ready in about 20 minutes | Servings 4)

Per serving: 236 Calories; 13g Fat; 26.6g Carbs; 3.7g Protein; 10g Sugars; 2g Fiber

Ingredients

1 large egg, whisked
1 ripe banana, peeled and mashed
1/4 cup butter, melted
1/4 cup agave nectar
1/2 cup all-purpose flour
1/4 almond flour
1 teaspoon baking powder
1/4 cup brown sugar
1/2 teaspoon vanilla essence
1 teaspoon cinnamon powder
1/4 teaspoon ground cloves

Directions

Start by preheating your Air Fryer to 320 degrees F.
Mix all ingredients in a bowl.
Scrape the batter into silicone baking molds; place them in the Air Fryer basket.
Bake your muffins for about 15 minutes or until a tester comes out dry and clean. Allow the muffins to cool before unmolding and serving.

Bourbon Ciabatta Bread Pudding

(Ready in about 35 minutes | Servings 5)

Per serving: 217 Calories; 7.3g Fat; 34.6g Carbs; 5.1g Protein; 26.5g Sugars; 1g Fiber

Ingredients

1 ½ cups ciabatta bread, cubed
2 eggs, whisked
1/2 cup double cream
1/2 cup milk
1/2 teaspoon vanilla extract
1 tablespoon bourbon
1/4 cup honey
1/2 cup golden raisins

Directions

Place the ciabatta bread in a lightly greased baking pan.
In a mixing bowl, thoroughly combine the eggs, double cream, milk, vanilla, bourbon, and honey.
Pour the egg/cream mixture over the bread cubes.
Fold in the raisins and set aside for 15 minutes to soak.
Bake your bread pudding at 350 degrees F for about 20 minutes or until the custard is set but still a little wobbly.
Serve at room temperature. Bon appétit!

Classic Baked Oatmeal

(Ready in about 15 minutes | Servings 4)

Per serving: 277 Calories; 5.8g Fat; 44.8g Carbs; 9.9g Protein; 22.2g Sugars; 4.1g Fiber

Ingredients

1 cup old-fashioned oats
1/4 cup agave syrup
1 cup milk
1 egg, whisked
1 cup apple, chopped
1/2 teaspoon baking powder
1/2 teaspoon ground cinnamon
A pinch of grated nutmeg
A pinch of salt

Directions

Thoroughly combine all ingredients in a mixing bowl.
Spoon the mixture into four lightly greased ramekins.
Then, place the ramekins in the Air Fryer cooking basket.
Bake your oatmeal at 380 degrees F for about 12 minutes.
Bon appétit!

Easiest Quinoa Patties Ever

(Ready in about 20 minutes | Servings 4)

Per serving: 227 Calories; 11.8g Fat; 19.8g Carbs; 10g Protein; 2g Sugars; 2.4g Fiber

Ingredients

1 ½ cups quinoa, cooked
1/2 cup bread crumbs
1/2 cup Pecorino cheese, grated
2 eggs, beaten
2 garlic cloves, minced
1/2 small onion, chopped
1 small bell pepper, seeded and chopped
1 tablespoon olive oil
2 tablespoons fresh Mediterranean herbs, finely chopped
Sea salt and ground black pepper, to taste

Directions

Start by preheating your Air Fryer to 380 degrees F.
Mix all ingredients until everything is well combined.
Form the mixture into patties.
Air fry the patties for about 15 minutes or until cooked through. Turn them over halfway through the cooking time.
Bon appétit!

Easy Cornbread Bites

(Ready in about 25 minutes | Servings 6)

Per serving: 243 Calories; 11.4g Fat; 31.6g Carbs; 4.5g Protein; 12.8g Sugars; 0.8g Fiber

Ingredients

1/2 cup all-purpose flour
1/2 cup yellow cornmeal
1 ½ teaspoons baking powder
4 tablespoons honey
A pinch of sea salt
A pinch of grated nutmeg
4 tablespoons coconut oil, room temperature
2 eggs, whisked
1/2 cup milk

Directions
Start by preheating your Air Fryer to 360 degrees F.
Mix all ingredients until everything is well incorporated. Scrape the batter into baking molds and place them in the Air Fryer basket.
Bake your mini cornbread for about 22 minutes or until a tester comes out dry and clean.
Allow your mini cornbread to cool before unmolding and serving. Bon appétit!

Cheesy Cauliflower Risotto

(Ready in about 15 minutes | Servings 4)
Per serving: 218 Calories; 11g Fat; 24.6g Carbs; 5g Protein; 1.8g Sugars; 2g Fiber
Ingredients
2 cups rice, cooked
2 tablespoons olive oil
1/2 cup cauliflower, chopped
1/2 cup vegetable broth
4 tablespoons mozzarella cheese, shredded
Directions
Start by preheating your Air Fryer to 360 degrees F.
Thoroughly combine all ingredients in a lightly greased baking pan.
Lower the pan into the Air Fryer cooking basket.
Cook for about 10 minutes or until cooked through.
Bon appétit!

Classic Polenta Rounds

(Ready in about 20 minutes | Servings 4)
Per serving: 168 Calories; 7.8g Fat; 22.6g Carbs; 2.1g Protein; 0.2g Sugars; 2.2g Fiber
Ingredients
1 cup polenta
Sea salt, to taste
1 teaspoon dried oregano
2 tablespoons olive oil
Directions
Cook the polenta according to the package directions. Season with the salt and oregano to taste.
Pour the polenta into a large baking sheet. Let it cool and firm up; cut the polenta into rounds. Drizzle the olive oil over them.
Cook the polenta rounds at 350 degrees F for about 15 minutes, turning them halfway through the cooking time.
Bon appétit!

Chinese Spring Rolls

(Ready in about 20 minutes | Servings 6)
Per serving: 139 Calories; 3.8g Fat; 22g Carbs; 3.9g Protein; 2.5g Sugars; 1.5g Fiber
Ingredients
1 tablespoon sesame oil
2 garlic cloves, minced
1 cup carrots, chopped
1/2 cup bamboo shoots, thinly sliced
1 tablespoon Hoisin sauce
1 tablespoon soy sauce
6 spring roll wrappers
Directions
Heat the oil in a wok over medium-high heat; cook the garlic for about 30 seconds.
Then, sauté the carrots and bamboo for 4 to 5 minutes.
Add in the Hoisin sauce and soy sauce and mix to combine well.
Divide the filling between the spring roll wrappers and roll them up tightly; seal the wrapper with water.
Place the spring rolls into the Air Fryer cooking basket. Cook the spring rolls for 6 minutes; turn them over and cook for 5 minutes longer.
Bon appétit!

Autumn Walnut Porridge

(Ready in about 15 minutes | Servings 4)
Per serving: 249 Calories; 10.1g Fat; 33.6g Carbs; 8.3g Protein; 9.2g Sugars; 4.8g Fiber
Ingredients
1/2 cup rolled oats
1/2 cup rye flakes
1 cup milk
1 cup applesauce, unsweetened
1/2 cup walnuts, chopped
A pinch of coarse sea salt
A pinch of freshly grated nutmeg
Directions
Thoroughly combine all ingredients in a mixing bowl.
Spoon the mixture into a lightly greased casserole dish.
Lower the dish into the Air Fryer cooking basket.
Bake your oatmeal at 380 degrees F for about 12 minutes.
Bon appétit!

Mixed Berry Breakfast Muffins

(Ready in about 20 minutes | Servings 6)
Per serving: 202 Calories; 10g Fat; 25.5g Carbs; 3g Protein; 12.8g Sugars; 1.2g Fiber
Ingredients
3/4 cup all-purpose flour
1/4 cup honey
1/2 teaspoon ground cinnamon
1/4 teaspoon ground cloves
1/4 cup buttermilk
1 egg
4 tablespoons olive oil
1 teaspoon vanilla extract
1/2 cup fresh mixed berries
Directions
Start by preheating your Air Fryer to 320 degrees F.
Mix all ingredients in a bowl. Scrape the batter into silicone baking molds; place them in the Air Fryer basket.
Bake your muffins for about 15 minutes or until a tester comes out dry and clean.
Allow the muffins to cool before unmolding and serving. Bon appétit!

Perfect Millet Patties

(Ready in about 20 minutes | Servings 4)
Per serving: 180 Calories; 7.6g Fat; 22.5g Carbs; 3.3g Protein; 0.8g Sugars; 1.5g Fiber
Ingredients
2 cups millet, cooked
2 tablespoons olive oil
1 small onion, chopped
2 garlic cloves, minced
1 tablespoon celery leaves, chopped
1 tablespoon parsley leaves, chopped
Sea salt and ground black pepper, to taste
Directions
Start by preheating your Air Fryer to 380 degrees F.
Mix all ingredients until everything is well combined.
Form the mixture into patties.
Air fry the patties for about 15 minutes or until cooked through. Turn them over halfway through the cooking time.
Bon appétit!

Dried Berry Bread Pudding

(Ready in about 35 minutes | Servings 6)
Per serving: 152 Calories; 3.3g Fat; 26.1g Carbs; 4.3g Protein; 18.5g Sugars; 0.8g Fiber
Ingredients
2 cups sweet raisin bread, cubed
2 eggs, whisked
1 cup milk
1/2 teaspoon vanilla extract
1/4 cup agave syrup
1/4 cup dried cherries
1/4 cup dried cranberries
Directions
Place the bread cubes in a lightly greased baking pan.
In a mixing bowl, thoroughly combine the remaining ingredients.
Pour the egg/milk mixture over the bread cubes; set aside for 15 minutes to soak.
Bake your bread pudding at 350 degrees F for about 20 minutes or until the custard is set but still a little wobbly.
Serve at room temperature. Bon appétit!

Mushroom and Rice Bake

(Ready in about 15 minutes | Servings 4)
Per serving: 192 Calories; 6.4g Fat; 28.1g Carbs; 6.3g Protein; 3.3g Sugars; 1.4g Fiber
Ingredients
1 pound brown mushrooms, chopped
1 small onion, peeled and chopped
2 tablespoons butter, room temperature
2 garlic cloves, minced
Sea salt and ground black pepper, to taste
1 cup vegetable broth
1 ½ cups brown rice, cooked
Directions
Start by preheating your Air Fryer to 360 degrees F.
Thoroughly combine all ingredients in a lightly greased baking pan.
Lower the pan into the Air Fryer cooking basket.
Cook for about 10 minutes or until cooked through.
Bon appétit!

Classic Corn Koftas

(Ready in about 20 minutes | Servings 5)
Per serving: 159 Calories; 6.7g Fat; 21.3g Carbs; 4.3g Protein; 1.9g Sugars; 1.3g Fiber
Ingredients
6 ounces canned corn kernels
1/2 small-sized onion, peeled and chopped
2 cloves garlic, minced
2 tablespoons fresh parsley, chopped
2 tablespoons fresh mint, chopped
2 tablespoons butter, melted
2 eggs, beaten
1/2 cup rice flour
1 teaspoon baking powder
Sea salt and ground black pepper, to taste
1 teaspoon turmeric powder
Directions
Start by preheating your Air Fryer to 380 degrees F.
Mix all ingredients until everything is well combined.
Form the mixture into balls.
Air fry the balls for about 15 minutes or until cooked through, tossing the basket halfway through the cooking time.
Bon appétit!

Classic British Scones

(Ready in about 20 minutes | Servings 6)
Per serving: 177 Calories; 1.7g Fat; 34.5g Carbs; 4.3g Protein; 18.7g Sugars; 0.9g Fiber
Ingredients
1 cup all-purpose flour
1 teaspoon baking powder
1/4 teaspoon salt
1/4 teaspoon grated nutmeg
1/2 cup brown sugar
2 egg, beaten
1/4 cup buttermilk
1/2 teaspoon vanilla extract
6 tablespoons raisins, soaked for 15 minutes
Directions
Start by preheating your Air Fryer to 360 degrees F.
Mix all ingredients until everything is well incorporated. Spoon the batter into baking cups; lower the cups into the Air Fryer basket.
Bake your scones for about 17 minutes or until a tester comes out dry and clean.
Bon appétit!

Mini Cornbread Loaves

(Ready in about 25 minutes | Servings 6)
Per serving: 210 Calories; 10g Fat; 25.6g Carbs; 4.5g Protein; 6.7g Sugars; 0.8g Fiber
Ingredients
1/2 cup all-purpose flour
1/2 cup yellow cornmeal
1 ½ teaspoons baking powder

A pinch of kosher salt
A pinch of grated nutmeg
4 tablespoons butter, melted
1/2 cup milk
2 eggs, whisked
2 tablespoons agave syrup
Directions
Start by preheating your Air Fryer to 360 degrees F. Mix all ingredients until everything is well incorporated. Scrape the batter into baking molds and place them in the Air Fryer basket.
Bake your mini cornbread loaves for about 22 minutes or until a tester comes out dry and clean. Allow your mini cornbread loaves to cool before unmolding and serving. Bon appétit!

Decadent Bread Pudding

(Ready in about 35 minutes | Servings 5)
Per serving: 317 Calories; 14.3g Fat; 44g Carbs; 6.1g Protein; 18.2g Sugars; 1g Fiber
Ingredients
8 slices bread, cubed
1 cup coconut milk
1/4 cup coconut oil
1 egg, beaten
1/4 cup honey
1/2 teaspoon ground cinnamon
1/4 teaspoon ground cloves
A pinch of kosher salt
1/2 cup prunes, pitted and chopped
Directions
Place the bread cubes in a lightly greased baking pan.
In a mixing bowl, thoroughly combine the milk, coconut oil, egg, honey, cinnamon, cloves, and salt. Pour the custard mixture over the bread cubes. Fold in the prunes and set aside for 15 minutes to soak.
Bake the bread pudding at 350 degrees F for about 20 minutes or until the custard is set but still a little wobbly.
Bon appétit!

Breakfast Banana Oatmeal

(Ready in about 15 minutes | Servings 4)
Per serving: 217 Calories; 4.7g Fat; 35.4g Carbs; 8.8g Protein; 6.7g Sugars; 5.1g Fiber
Ingredients
1 cup old-fashioned oats
1 cup coconut milk
1 cup water
1 banana, mashed
1/2 teaspoon vanilla extract
1/2 teaspoon ground cinnamon
A pinch of grated nutmeg
A pinch of sea salt
Directions
Thoroughly combine all ingredients in a mixing bowl. Spoon the mixture into lightly greased mugs.
Then, place the mugs in the Air Fryer cooking basket.
Bake your oatmeal at 380 degrees F for about 12 minutes.
Bon appétit!

Old-Fashioned Granola

(Ready in about 20 minutes | Servings 6)
Per serving: 332 Calories; 21.1g Fat; 33.4g Carbs; 6.8g Protein; 17g Sugars; 4.1g Fiber
Ingredients
1/2 cup rolled oats
1/4 cup wheat germ, toasted
1/2 cup dried cranberries
1/4 cup pumpkin seeds
1/4 cup sunflower seeds
1/4 cup pecans, chopped
1/4 cup walnuts, chopped
1/2 teaspoon vanilla extract
1/4 cup agave syrup
4 tablespoons coconut oil
1 teaspoon pumpkin pie spice mix
Directions
Start by preheating your Air Fryer to 350 degrees F. Thoroughly combine all ingredients in a lightly greased baking pan.
Then, place the pan in the Air Fryer cooking basket.
Bake your granola for about 15 minutes, stirring every 5 minutes.
Store at room temperature in an airtight container for up to three weeks.
Bon appétit!

Apple Oat Muffins

(Ready in about 20 minutes | Servings 6)
Per serving: 290 Calories; 12g Fat; 42.1g Carbs; 5.3g Protein; 24.8g Sugars; 2.2g Fiber
Ingredients
1/2 cups self-rising flour
1/2 cup rolled oats
1/2 cup agave syrup
1/4 teaspoon grated nutmeg
1/2 teaspoon cinnamon powder
A pinch of coarse salt
1/2 cup milk
1/4 cup coconut oil, room temperature
2 eggs
1 teaspoon coconut extract
1 cup apples, cored and chopped
Directions
Start by preheating your Air Fryer to 320 degrees F.
Mix all ingredients in a bowl.
Scrape the batter into silicone baking molds; place them in the Air Fryer basket.
Bake your muffins for about 15 minutes or until a tester comes out dry and clean. Allow the muffins to cool before unmolding and serving.

Crispy Chicken Wontons

(Ready in about 20 minutes | Servings 6)
Per serving: 193 Calories; 6.8g Fat; 22.3g Carbs; 10.5g Protein; 2.1g Sugars; 1.2g Fiber
Ingredients
1 tablespoon sesame oil

1 teaspoon garlic, pressed
1 teaspoon fresh ginger, peeled and grated
1/2 pound ground chicken
1 small onion, chopped
1 cup green cabbage, shredded
2 tablespoons soy sauce
2 tablespoons rice wine
6 wonton wrappers

Directions

Heat the oil in a wok over medium-high heat; cook the garlic and ginger for about 30 seconds.
Then, sauté the chicken, onion, and cabbage for approximately 5 minutes.
Remove from the heat. Add in the soy sauce and rice wine; stir to combine well.
Divide the filling between wonton wrappers and roll them up tightly; seal the wrappers with water.
Lower the wonton wrappers into the Air Fryer cooking basket. Cook the wonton wrappers for 6 minutes; turn them over and cook for 5 minutes longer.
Bon appétit!

Country Scallion Pilaf

(Ready in about 15 minutes | Servings 4)

Per serving: 168 Calories; 7.1g Fat; 19.6g Carbs; 3.7g Protein; 1.2g Sugars; 2g Fiber

Ingredients

1 ½ cups cooked multigrain rice
1 cup vegetable broth
1/2 cup scallions, thinly sliced
1 tablespoon fresh parsley, chopped
1 tablespoon fresh cilantro, chopped
2 tablespoons olive oil
Sea salt and cayenne pepper, to taste
1 teaspoon garlic powder

Directions

Start by preheating your Air Fryer to 360 degrees F.
Thoroughly combine all ingredients in a lightly greased baking pan.
Lower the pan into the Air Fryer cooking basket. Cook for about 10 minutes or until cooked through.
Bon appétit!

Almond Bread Pudding

(Ready in about 35 minutes | Servings 6)

Per serving: 196 Calories; 9.2g Fat; 22g Carbs; 7.3g Protein; 14.8g Sugars; 2g Fiber

Ingredients

2 cups brioche bread, cubed
1 cup almond milk
2 eggs, whisked
1/4 teaspoon ground cinnamon
1/4 teaspoon ground cardamom
1/2 teaspoon vanilla extract
1/4 cup honey
1/2 cup almonds, chopped

Directions

Place the bread cubes in a lightly greased baking pan.
In a mixing bowl, thoroughly combine the remaining ingredients.
Pour the custard mixture over the bread cubes; set aside for 15 minutes to soak.
Bake your bread pudding at 350 degrees F for about 20 minutes or until the custard is set but still a little wobbly.
Serve at room temperature. Bon appétit!

Italian Arancini with a Twist

(Ready in about 20 minutes | Servings 4)

Per serving: 223 Calories; 7.5g Fat; 27.2g Carbs; 11.6g Protein; 17.8g Sugars; 2.5g Fiber

Ingredients

2 cups quinoa, cooked
2 eggs, whisked
1 small onion, chopped
2 garlic cloves, minced
1 cup broccoli, chopped
1/2 cup breadcrumbs
1/2 cup Parmesan cheese, grated
1 tablespoon fresh Italian herbs, chopped
Sea salt and ground black pepper, to taste

Directions

Start by preheating your Air Fryer to 380 degrees F.
Mix all ingredients until everything is well combined.
Form the mixture into patties.
Air fry the patties for about 15 minutes or until cooked through. Turn them over halfway through the cooking time.
Bon appétit!

Easy Corn Fritters

(Ready in about 20 minutes | Servings 4)

Per serving: 265 Calories; 14.5g Fat; 28.2g Carbs; 8.1g Protein; 1.8g Sugars; 4.2g Fiber

Ingredients

1 cup corn kernels, canned and creamed
1 cup whole-wheat flour
1 teaspoon baking powder
2 eggs, whisked
1/2 cup heavy cream
2 tablespoons butter

Directions

Start by preheating your Air Fryer to 380 degrees F.
Mix all ingredients until everything is well combined.
Form the mixture into patties.
Cook your fritters for about 15 minutes or until cooked through. Turn them over halfway through the cooking time.
Bon appétit!

Italian Mac and Cheese

(Ready in about 20 minutes | Servings 4)

Per serving: 319 Calories; 2.8g Fat; 45.2g Carbs; 27.1g Protein; 5.8g Sugars; 3.2g Fiber

Ingredients

2 cups macaroni
1 cup milk
2 cups mozzarella cheese, grated

1/2 teaspoon Italian seasoning
Sea salt and ground black pepper, to taste
1/2 teaspoon garlic powder
1 teaspoon dry mustard

Directions

Cook the macaroni according to the package directions.
Drain the macaroni and place them in a lightly greased baking pan.
Fold in the remaining ingredients and stir to combine.
Bake your mac and cheese in the preheated Air Fryer at 360 degrees F for about 15 minutes. Serve garnished with fresh Italian herbs, if desired.
Bon appétit!

Crescent Danish Rolls with Cheese

(Ready in about 15 minutes | Servings 4)

Per serving: 314 Calories; 20g Fat; 26.9g Carbs; 6.6g Protein; 7.3g Sugars; 1.5g Fiber

Ingredients

1 can (8-ounce) refrigerated crescent rolls
4 ounces cream cheese, room temperature

Directions

Separate the dough into rectangles. Spread each rectangle with cream cheese and roll them up.
Place the rolls in the Air Fryer cooking basket.
Bake the rolls at 300 degrees F for about 5 minutes; turn them over and cook for another 5 minutes.
Bon appétit!

Traditional French Toast

(Ready in about 15 minutes | Servings 3)

Per serving: 194 Calories; 12.4g Fat; 12.6g Carbs; 6.8g Protein; 3.3g Sugars; 0.8g Fiber

Ingredients

2 eggs
1/2 cup milk
2 tablespoons butter, room temperature
1 teaspoon vanilla extract
1/4 teaspoon grated nutmeg
1/2 teaspoon cinnamon powder
3 slices challah bread

Directions

In a mixing bowl, thoroughly combine the eggs, milk, butter, vanilla, nutmeg, and cinnamon.
Then dip each piece of bread into the egg mixture; place the bread slices in a lightly greased baking pan.
Air fry the bread slices at 330 degrees F for about 4 minutes; turn them over and cook for a further 3 to 4 minutes. Enjoy!

Indian Pakoda Fritters

(Ready in about 20 minutes | Servings 4)

Per serving: 213 Calories; 7.3g Fat; 32.2g Carbs; 2.6g Protein; 0.6g Sugars; 1.2g Fiber

Ingredients

1/2 cup rice flour
1/2 cup Ragi
1/2 teaspoon baking powder
1 cup methi, chopped
1 green chilli, finely chopped
1 teaspoon ginger-garlic paste
2 tablespoons sesame oil
Sea salt and ground black pepper, to taste

Directions

Start by preheating your Air Fryer to 380 degrees F.
Mix all ingredients until everything is well combined.
Form the mixture into patties.
Air fry the patties for about 15 minutes or until cooked through. Turn them over halfway through the cooking time.
Bon appétit!

Chocolate Chip Muffins

(Ready in about 20 minutes | Servings 6)

Per serving: 250 Calories; 16.2g Fat; 25.1g Carbs; 4.2g Protein; 14.4g Sugars; 2g Fiber

Ingredients

1/2 cup all-purpose flour
1/3 cup almond flour
1 teaspoon baking powder
A pinch of sea salt
A pinch of grated nutmeg
1 egg
1/4 cup honey
1/4 cup milk
1 teaspoon vanilla extract
4 tablespoons coconut oil
1/2 cup dark chocolate chips

Directions

Start by preheating your Air Fryer to 320 degrees F.
Mix all ingredients in a bowl. Scrape the batter into silicone baking molds; place them in the Air Fryer basket.
Bake your muffins for about 15 minutes or until a tester comes out dry and clean.
Allow the muffins to cool before unmolding and serving. Bon appétit!

Bread Pudding with Figs

(Ready in about 35 minutes | Servings 5)

Per serving: 212 Calories; 4.4g Fat; 36.6g Carbs; 6.9g Protein; 20.5g Sugars; 2.1g Fiber

Ingredients

8 slices bread, cubed
1 cup milk
2 eggs, beaten
1/4 cup brown sugar
2 ounces dried figs, chopped
A pinch of sea salt
1/2 teaspoon ground cinnamon
1/2 teaspoon vanilla extract

Directions

Place the bread in a lightly greased baking pan.
In a mixing bowl, thoroughly combine the remaining ingredients.
Pour the milk/egg mixture over the bread cubes. Set aside for 15 minutes to soak.

Bake your bread pudding at 350 degrees F for about 20 minutes or until the custard is set but still a little wobbly.
Serve at room temperature. Bon appétit!

Vanilla Oatmeal with Almonds

(Ready in about 15 minutes | Servings 4)
Per serving: 334 Calories; 11.4g Fat; 49g Carbs; 11.4g Protein; 21g Sugars; 5.9g Fiber
Ingredients
1 cup rolled oats
1 cup water
1 cup milk
1 teaspoon vanilla paste
A pinch of kosher salt
1/2 teaspoon ground cloves
4 tablespoons honey
1/2 cup almonds, slivered
Directions
Thoroughly combine all ingredients in a mixing bowl.
Spoon the mixture into lightly greased ramekins.
Then, place the ramekins in the Air Fryer cooking basket.
Bake your oatmeal at 380 degrees F for about 12 minutes. Serve warm or at room temperature.
Bon appétit!

Chocolate Chip Granola

(Ready in about 20 minutes | Servings 8)
Per serving: 334 Calories; 11.4g Fat; 49g Carbs; 11.4g Protein; 21g Sugars; 5.9g Fiber
Ingredients
1/2 cup old-fashioned oats
1/4 cup coconut flakes, unsweetened
1/4 cup quinoa flakes
1/4 cup almonds, slivered
1/4 cup hazelnuts, chopped
1/4 cup chia seeds
1 teaspoon ground cinnamon
A pinch of grated nutmeg
A pinch of sea salt
2 tablespoons coconut oil
1/4 cup maple syrup
1 teaspoon vanilla extract
1/2 cup chocolate chips
Directions
Start by preheating your Air Fryer to 350 degrees F.
Thoroughly combine all ingredients in a lightly greased baking pan.
Then, place the pan in the Air Fryer cooking basket.
Bake your granola for about 15 minutes, stirring every 5 minutes.
Store at room temperature in an airtight container for up to three weeks.
Bon appétit!

Curried Indian Rice

(Ready in about 15 minutes | Servings 4)
Per serving: 402 Calories; 6.6g Fat; 77.1g Carbs; 7.9g Protein; 0.4g Sugars; 3.1g Fiber
Ingredients
2 cups jasmine rice, cooked
1 cup vegetable broth
1 teaspoon garlic powder
1/2 cup scallions, chopped
2 tablespoons butter, room temperature
Kosher salt and red pepper, to taste
Directions
Start by preheating your Air Fryer to 360 degrees F.
Thoroughly combine all ingredients in a lightly greased baking pan.
Lower the pan into the Air Fryer cooking basket.
Cook for about 10 minutes or until cooked through.
Bon appétit!

Doughnut Bread Pudding

(Ready in about 35 minutes | Servings 6)
Per serving: 284 Calories; 10.8g Fat; 41.8g Carbs; 5.5g Protein; 30.1g Sugars; 0.5g Fiber
Ingredients
2 cups doughnuts, diced
2 eggs, whisked
1 cup milk
1 cup half-and-half
4 tablespoons honey
1 teaspoon vanilla extract
A pinch of salt
A pinch of grated nutmeg
Directions
Place the doughnuts in a lightly greased baking pan.
In a mixing bowl, thoroughly combine the remaining ingredients.
Pour the custard mixture over the doughnuts. Set aside for 15 minutes to soak.
Bake your bread pudding at 350 degrees F for about 20 minutes or until the custard is set but still a little wobbly.
Serve at room temperature. Bon appétit!

Baked Basmati Rice

(Ready in about 15 minutes | Servings 4)
Per serving: 228 Calories; 11g Fat; 27.6g Carbs; 3.5g Protein; 2.8g Sugars; 2.7g Fiber
Ingredients
3 tablespoons olive oil
3 cloves garlic, chopped
1 large onion, peeled and chopped
1 sprigs fresh curry leaves, chopped
2 cups basmati rice, cooked
1 teaspoon cayenne pepper
Kosher salt and ground black pepper, to taste
Directions
Start by preheating your Air Fryer to 360 degrees F.
Thoroughly combine all ingredients in a lightly greased baking pan. Pour 1 cup of boiling water over the rice.
Lower the pan into the Air Fryer cooking basket.
Cook for about 10 minutes or until cooked through.
Bon appétit!

Hot and Spicy Mac and Cheese

(Ready in about 20 minutes | Servings 4)

Per serving: 293 Calories; 11.3g Fat; 26.7g Carbs; 21.2g Protein; 2g Sugars; 2.3g Fiber

Ingredients

1 cups macaroni
1 cup cream of onion soup
2 tablespoons butter
4 ounces Ricotta cheese
6 ounces mozzarella cheese, crumbled
Kosher salt and ground white pepper, to taste
1/2 teaspoon cumin, ground
1 teaspoon dry mustard
1 teaspoon red chili powder

Directions

Cook the macaroni according to the package directions.
Drain the macaroni and place them in a lightly greased baking pan.
Fold in the remaining ingredients and stir to combine.
Bake your mac and cheese in the preheated Air Fryer at 360 degrees F for about 15 minutes. Serve garnished with fresh Italian herbs, if desired.
Bon appétit!

Blueberry Crescent Rolls

(Ready in about 15 minutes | Servings 6)

Per serving: 343 Calories; 16.3g Fat; 44.3g Carbs; 5.6g Protein; 29g Sugars; 1.6g Fiber

Ingredients

1 (8-ounce) can refrigerated crescent dinner rolls
6 ounces cream cheese, room temperature
4 tablespoons granulated sugar
1 teaspoon lemon zest, grated
1 cup fresh blueberries
1 cup powdered sugar
1/4 teaspoon ground cinnamon

Directions

Separate the dough into rectangles. Mix the remaining ingredients until well combined.
Spread each rectangle with the cheese mixture; roll them up tightly.
Place the rolls in the Air Fryer cooking basket.
Bake the rolls at 300 degrees F for about 5 minutes; turn them over and bake for a further 5 minutes.
Bon appétit!

Decadent Porridge with Apricots

(Ready in about 15 minutes | Servings 4)

Per serving: 407 Calories; 13.4g Fat; 66g Carbs; 7.4g Protein; 29.1g Sugars; 5.2g Fiber

Ingredients

1/2 cup old fashioned oats
1/2 cup quinoa flakes
1/4 cup almonds, chopped
1/4 cup pecans, chopped
2 cups orange juice
4 tablespoons honey
2 tablespoons coconut oil
4 tablespoons dried apricots, chopped

Directions

Thoroughly combine all ingredients in a mixing bowl.
Spoon the mixture into lightly greased mugs.
Then, place the mugs in the Air Fryer cooking basket.
Bake your porridge at 380 degrees F for about 12 minutes.
Serve immediately. Bon appétit!

Greek-Style Muffins

(Ready in about 20 minutes | Servings 6)

Per serving: 172 Calories; 1.2g Fat; 35.1g Carbs; 5.1g Protein; 15.4g Sugars; 1.6g Fiber

Ingredients

1 cup all-purpose flour
1 teaspoon baking powder
1/2 brown sugar
1 Greek yogurt
1/2 cup prunes, pitted and chopped
1 egg, beaten
1 teaspoon vanilla essence

Directions

Start by preheating your Air Fryer to 330 degrees F.
Mix all ingredients until well-combined; then, divide the batter evenly between silicone baking molds; place them in the Air Fryer cooking basket.
Bake your muffins for about 15 minutes or until a tester comes out dry and clean.
Allow the muffins to cool before unmolding and serving. Bon appétit!

Perfect Indian Biryani

(Ready in about 15 minutes | Servings 4)

Per serving: 188 Calories; 6.6g Fat; 24.1g Carbs; 2.9g Protein; 0.7g Sugars; 2.1g Fiber

Ingredients

2 cups jasmine rice, cooked
1 cup water
1 teaspoon ginger-garlic paste
2 tablespoons shallots, chopped
1/2 teaspoon ground cinnamon
2 tablespoons butter
1/2 teaspoon cumin seeds
1 teaspoon garam masala
1/2 teaspoon turmeric powder

Directions

Start by preheating your Air Fryer to 360 degrees F.
Thoroughly combine all ingredients in a lightly greased baking pan.
Lower the pan into the Air Fryer cooking basket.
Cook for about 10 minutes or until cooked through.
Bon appétit!

Autumn Oatmeal Cups

(Ready in about 20 minutes | Servings 4)

Per serving: 412 Calories; 13.9g Fat; 64.1g Carbs; 11.1g Protein; 33g Sugars; 6.2g Fiber

Ingredients

1 cup full-fat milk
1 cup applesauce, unsweetened
1 egg, beaten

1/2 cup pure maple syrup
1 cup old-fashioned oats
1 teaspoon baking powder
1 teaspoon pure vanilla extract
1/2 teaspoon ground cinnamon
1/4 teaspoon freshly grated nutmeg
A pinch of kosher salt
1/2 cup pecans, chopped
Directions
Thoroughly combine all ingredients in a mixing bowl.
Spoon the mixture into lightly greased mugs.
Then, place the mugs in the Air Fryer cooking basket.
Bake your oatmeal at 380 degrees F for about 12 minutes.
Bon appétit!

Grandma's Pumpkin Porridge

(Ready in about 15 minutes | Servings 5)
Per serving: 412 Calories; 13.9g Fat; 64.1g Carbs; 11.1g Protein; 33g Sugars; 6.2g Fiber
Ingredients
1/2 cup old-fashioned oats
1/2 cup quinoa flakes
1/4 cup pecans, chopped
2 tablespoons chia seeds, ground
2 tablespoons flax seeds, ground
1 teaspoon vanilla essence
2 ounces dark chocolate chips
1/2 cup canned pumpkin
1/2 cup almond milk
Directions
Thoroughly combine all ingredients in a mixing bowl.
Spoon the mixture into a lightly greased baking pan.
Then, place the baking pan in the Air Fryer cooking basket. Bake your porridge at 380 degrees F for about 12 minutes.
Serve immediately. Bon appétit!

Aromatic Rice Pudding

(Ready in about 20 minutes | Servings 4)
Per serving: 319 Calories; 10.7g Fat; 51.8g Carbs; 5.6g Protein; 30g Sugars; 2.4g Fiber
Ingredients
2 cups brown rice, cooked
1 ½ cups coconut milk
1/4 cup agave syrup
1 teaspoon vanilla
2 tablespoons coconut oil
2 tablespoons rose water
4 tablespoons dried apricots, chopped
A pinch of sea salt
Directions
Thoroughly combine all ingredients in a lightly greased baking pan.
Lower the pan into the Air Fryer cooking basket.
Cook for about 15 minutes or until cooked through.
Bon appétit!

Traditional Chawal ke Pakore

(Ready in about 20 minutes | Servings 4)
Per serving: 268 Calories; 11.5g Fat; 34.4g Carbs; 6.6g Protein; 0.8g Sugars; 1.5g Fiber
Ingredients
1 cup rice flour
1/2 onion, chopped
2 garlic cloves, minced
2 tablespoons butter, room temperature
1 teaspoon paprika
1 teaspoon cumin powder
1/2 cup Paneer cheese, crumbled
Directions
Start by preheating your Air Fryer to 380 degrees F.
Mix all ingredients until everything is well combined.
Form the mixture into patties.
Air fry the patties for about 15 minutes or until cooked through. Turn them over halfway through the cooking time.
Bon appétit!

Cheesy Rice Casserole

(Ready in about 15 minutes | Servings 4)
Per serving: 332 Calories; 14.1g Fat; 38.1g Carbs; 12g Protein; 7.4g Sugars; 2.9g Fiber
Ingredients
1 small shallot, minced
2 garlic cloves, minced
2 tablespoons olive oil
1/2 teaspoon paprika
2 eggs, whisked
1 cup half-and-half
1 cup cheddar cheese, shredded
2 cups cooked brown rice
1 tablespoon Italian parsley leaves, chopped
1 cup cream of celery soup
Sea salt and freshly ground black pepper, to taste
Directions
Start by preheating your Air Fryer to 360 degrees F.
Thoroughly combine all ingredients in a lightly greased baking pan. Lower the pan into the Air Fryer cooking basket.
Cook for about 10 minutes or until cooked through.
Bon appétit!

Bourbon Vanilla French Toast

(Ready in about 15 minutes | Servings 4)
Per serving: 188 Calories; 12.7g Fat; 11.4g Carbs; 6.7g Protein; 2.4g Sugars; 0.7g Fiber
Ingredients
2 eggs, beaten
1/4 cup milk
2 tablespoons coconut oil, room temperature
1/2 teaspoon bourbon vanilla extract
1/2 teaspoon ground cinnamon
4 slices bread
Directions
In a mixing bowl, thoroughly combine the eggs, milk, coconut oil, vanilla, and cinnamon.
Then dip each piece of bread into the egg mixture; place the bread slices in a lightly greased baking pan.

Air Fryer the bread slices at 330 degrees F for about 4 minutes; turn them over and cook for a further 3 to 4 minutes. Enjoy!

Mini Monkey Breads

(Ready in about 15 minutes | Servings 5)

Per serving: 322 Calories; 16.1g Fat; 38.9g Carbs; 5.6g Protein; 21g Sugars; 2.1g Fiber

Ingredients

1 (8-ounces) can crescent rolls
1 teaspoon ground cinnamon
4 ounces cream cheese, room temperature
1/4 cup sugar
2 tablespoons full-fat milk
1/2 cup apple pie filling, canned

Directions

Separate the dough into rectangles. Mix the remaining ingredients until well combined.
Spread each rectangle with the cinnamon/cheese mixture; roll them up tightly.
Place the rolls in the Air Fryer cooking basket.
Bake the rolls at 300 degrees F for about 5 minutes; turn them over and bake for a further 5 minutes.
Bon appétit!

Traditional Chinese Rice

(Ready in about 15 minutes | Servings 4)

Per serving: 252 Calories; 10.5g Fat; 32.1g Carbs; 6.8g Protein; 4.4g Sugars; 4.8g Fiber

Ingredients

2 cups multigrain rice, cooked
1 small onion, finely chopped
1 teaspoon garlic, minced
2 tablespoons sesame oil
1 egg, whisked
2 tablespoons soy sauce
1 carrot, chopped
1 cup green peas
Sea salt and red chili flakes, to taste

Directions

Start by preheating your Air Fryer to 360 degrees F.
Thoroughly combine all ingredients in a lightly greased baking pan.
Lower the pan into the Air Fryer cooking basket.
Cook for about 10 minutes or until cooked through.
Bon appétit!

Breakfast Mocha Muffins

(Ready in about 20 minutes | Servings 6)

Per serving: 189 Calories; 5.3g Fat; 32.6g Carbs; 5.1g Protein; 19.4g Sugars; 3.1g Fiber

Ingredients

1/2 cup coconut flour
1/2 cup all-purpose flour
1/2 cup cocoa powder
1/2 cup brown sugar
1/2 teaspoon baking powder
A pinch of sea salt
A pinch of grated nutmeg
1 tablespoon instant coffee granules
1/2 cup milk
2 eggs, whisked
1/2 teaspoon vanilla extract

Directions

Start by preheating your Air Fryer to 330 degrees F.
Mix all ingredients until well-combined; then, divide the batter evenly between silicone baking molds; place them in the Air Fryer cooking basket.
Bake your muffins for about 15 minutes or until a tester comes out dry and clean.
Allow the muffins to cool before unmolding and serving. Bon appétit!

Porridge with Sultanas

(Ready in about 15 minutes | Servings 5)

Per serving: 263 Calories; 12.3g Fat; 30.3g Carbs; 8.6g Protein; 5.1g Sugars; 3.7g Fiber

Ingredients

1/2 cup old-fashioned oats
1/2 cup millet, rinsed and drained
2 tablespoons flax seeds, ground
1/2 cup Sultanas
2 cups coconut milk
2 tablespoons coconut oil
A pinch of salt
A pinch of ground cloves

Directions

Thoroughly combine all ingredients in a mixing bowl.
Spoon the mixture into a lightly greased baking pan.
Then, place the baking pan in the Air Fryer cooking basket. Bake your porridge at 380 degrees F for about 12 minutes.
Serve immediately. Bon appétit!

Easy Chia Oatmeal

(Ready in about 15 minutes | Servings 4)

Per serving: 315 Calories; 6.3g Fat; 57g Carbs; 9.6g Protein; 28.4g Sugars; 6.5g Fiber

Ingredients

1 cup old-fashioned oats
1 teaspoon baking powder
1/2 teaspoon cinnamon
A pinch of sea salt
A pinch of grated nutmeg
1 cup coconut milk
1 cup pineapple juice
1/4 cup agave syrup
2 tablespoons ground chia seeds
1 teaspoon vanilla extract

Directions

Thoroughly combine all ingredients in a mixing bowl.
Spoon the mixture into lightly greased mugs.
Then, place the mugs in the Air Fryer cooking basket.
Bake your oatmeal at 380 degrees F for about 12 minutes.
Bon appétit!

Brioche Pudding with A Twist

(Ready in about 35 minutes | Servings 6)

Per serving: 219 Calories; 13.3g Fat; 16.7g Carbs; 7.5g Protein; 9.8g Sugars; 1.5g Fiber

Ingredients

2 cups Brioche bread, cubed
1/2 teaspoon cinnamon powder
4 tablespoons brown sugar
2 eggs, whisked
2 tablespoons coconut oil
1 cup eggnog
1/2 cup almonds, chopped

Directions

Place the bread cubes in a lightly greased baking pan.
In a mixing bowl, thoroughly combine the remaining ingredients.
Pour the custard mixture over the bread cubes. Set aside for 15 minutes to soak.
Bake the bread pudding at 350 degrees F for about 20 minutes or until the custard is set but still a little wobbly.
Bon appétit!

Traditional Indian Bhajji

(Ready in about 20 minutes | Servings 4)

Per serving: 238 Calories; 7.1g Fat; 38.4g Carbs; 5g Protein; 1.8g Sugars; 2.5g Fiber

Ingredients

1 cup rice flour
4 tablespoons chickpea flour
1/2 teaspoon sweet paprika
1 teaspoon chili powder
Sea salt and ground black pepper, to taste
1/2 cup green cabbage, shredded
1 teaspoon onion powder
1 teaspoon garlic powder
2 tablespoons butter
1/2 cup vegetable broth

Directions

Start by preheating your Air Fryer to 380 degrees F.
Mix all ingredients until everything is well combined.
Form the mixture into patties.
Air fry the patties for about 15 minutes or until cooked through. Turn them over halfway through the cooking time.
Bon appétit!

Mediterranean-Style Biscuits

(Ready in about 20 minutes | Servings 6)

Per serving: 180 Calories; 9.2g Fat; 18.8g Carbs; 2.7g Protein; 0.1g Sugars; 0.6g Fiber

Ingredients

1 cup all-purpose flour
1 teaspoon baking powder
4 tablespoons olive oil
1/2 cup sour cream
A pinch of sea salt
1 teaspoon Mediterranean seasoning mix

Directions

Start by preheating your Air Fryer to 360 degrees F.
Mix all ingredients until well combined. Use a 2-inch biscuit cutter and cut out biscuits. Place the biscuits on a lightly greased baking pan.
Lower the pan into the Air Fryer basket.
Bake your biscuits for about 15 minutes or until a tester comes out dry and clean. Bon appétit!

Easy Rice Pudding

(Ready in about 20 minutes | Servings 4)

Per serving: 218 Calories; 5.2g Fat; 35.6g Carbs; 6.7g Protein; 22.1g Sugars; 1.4g Fiber

Ingredients

1 cup pudding rice
3 tablespoons honey
2 cups milk
1 cup half-and-half
1 teaspoon vanilla extract
1/2 teaspoon ground cinnamon

Directions

Thoroughly combine all ingredients in a lightly greased baking pan.
Lower the pan into the Air Fryer cooking basket.
Cook for about 15 minutes or until cooked through.
Bon appétit!

Cornbread French Toast Casserole

(Ready in about 20 minutes | Servings 6)

Per serving: 268 Calories; 14.5g Fat; 26g Carbs; 5.8g Protein; 11g Sugars; 0.8g Fiber

Ingredients

3 eggs
2 tablespoons coconut oil, room temperature
1/2 cup heavy cream
1 teaspoon vanilla
1/2 cup brown sugar
1/2 teaspoon ground cinnamon
A pinch of grated nutmeg
A pinch of salt
6 slices sweet cornbread

Directions

In a mixing bowl, thoroughly combine the eggs, coconut oil, heavy cream, vanilla, sugar, cinnamon, nutmeg, and salt.
Then, place the cornbread slices in a lightly greased baking pan. Pour the custard mixture over the cornbread slices.
Bake your casserole at 330 degrees F for about 12 minutes. Enjoy!

Risotto ala Carbonara

(Ready in about 15 minutes | Servings 4)

Per serving: 430 Calories; 31.2g Fat; 27.2g Carbs; 10.1g Protein; 1.3g Sugars; 1.9g Fiber

Ingredients

2 cups Arborio rice, cooked
2 tablespoons sesame oil
1 shallot, chopped
1/2 cup white Italian wine
1/2 cup heavy cream

Coarse sea salt and freshly ground black pepper, to taste
4 tablespoons pancetta, chopped
1 cup Parmesan cheese, preferably freshly grated
1 tablespoon fresh Italian parsley, chopped

Directions

Start by preheating your Air Fryer to 360 degrees F.
Thoroughly combine all ingredients in a lightly greased baking pan.
Lower the pan into the Air Fryer cooking basket. Cook for about 10 minutes or until cooked through. Bon appétit!

Three-Grain Porridge

(Ready in about 15 minutes | Servings 5)

Per serving: 336 Calories; 6.3g Fat; 63.1g Carbs; 12.3g Protein; 20.7g Sugars; 6.6g Fiber

Ingredients

1/2 cup rolled oats
1/2 cup quinoa flakes
1/2 cup rye flakes
1 cup coconut milk
1 cup orange juice
2 eggs, whisked
4 tablespoons honey
1/2 teaspoon ground cinnamon

Directions

Thoroughly combine all ingredients in a mixing bowl. Spoon the mixture into a lightly greased baking pan. Then, place the baking pan in the Air Fryer cooking basket. Bake your porridge at 380 degrees F for about 12 minutes.
Serve immediately. Bon appétit!

Cheesy Cornbread Muffins

(Ready in about 25 minutes | Servings 4)

Per serving: 319 Calories; 18.2g Fat; 32.1g Carbs; 7.9g Protein; 1.7g Sugars; 2.6g Fiber

Ingredients

1 cup self-rising cornmeal
4 ounces canned creamed corn
1/2 cup Colby cheese, shredded
1/4 cup milk
1/4 cup butter, room temperature

Directions

Start by preheating your Air Fryer to 360 degrees F.
Mix all ingredients until everything is well incorporated. Scrape the batter into baking molds and place them in the Air Fryer basket.
Bake your cornbread muffins for about 22 minutes or until a tester comes out dry and clean.
Allow your cornbread muffins to cool before unmolding and serving. Bon appétit!

SNACKS & APPETIZERS

Herb Sweet Potato Chips

(Ready in about 20 minutes | Servings 3)

Per serving: 97 Calories; 2.6g Fat; 17.1g Carbs; 1.4g Protein; 3.6g Sugars; 2.6g Fiber

Ingredients

2 large-sized sweet potatoes, peeled and cut into thin slices
2 teaspoons butter, melted
Sea salt and ground black pepper, to taste
1/2 teaspoon dried oregano
1/2 teaspoon dried basil
1/2 teaspoon dried rosemary

Directions

Start by preheating your Air Fryer to 360 degrees F.
Toss the sweet potato with the remaining ingredients and place them in the Air Fryer cooking basket.
Air fry the sweet potato chips for 14 minutes, tossing halfway through the cooking time and working in batches.
Enjoy!

Classic Onion Rings

(Ready in about 10 minutes | Servings 4)

Per serving: 243 Calories; 2.8g Fat; 44.7g Carbs; 8.5g Protein; 2.5g Sugars; 2.3g Fiber

Ingredients

1 cup all-purpose flour
Sea salt and black pepper, to taste
1 teaspoon red pepper flakes, crushed
1/2 teaspoon cumin powder
1 egg
1 cup breadcrumbs
1 medium yellow onion, sliced

Directions

Start by preheating your Air Fryer to 380 degrees F.
In a shallow bowl, mix the flour, salt, black pepper, red pepper flakes, and cumin powder.
Whisk the egg in another shallow bowl. Place the breadcrumbs in a separate bowl.
Dip the onion rings in the flour, then in the eggs, then in the breadcrumbs. Place the onion rings in the Air Fryer basket.
Cook the onion rings for about 8 minutes or until golden brown and cooked through.
Bon appétit!

Hot and Spicy Tortilla Chips

(Ready in about 10 minutes | Servings 4)

Per serving: 148 Calories; 4.8g Fat; 24.7g Carbs; 3.1g Protein; 0.5g Sugars; 3.4g Fiber

Ingredients

9 corn tortillas, cut into wedges
1 tablespoon olive oil
1 teaspoon hot paprika
Sea salt and ground black pepper, to taste

Directions

Toss the tortilla wedges with the remaining ingredients.
Cook your tortilla chips at 360 degrees F for about 5 minutes or until crispy. Work in batches.
Enjoy!

Favorite Jalapeno Poppers

(Ready in about 10 minutes | Servings 4)

Per serving: 300 Calories; 24.4g Fat; 6.3g Carbs; 13.1g Protein; 4.3g Sugars; 0.8g Fiber

Ingredients

4 ounces Cottage cheese, crumbled
4 ounces cheddar cheese, shredded
1 teaspoon mustard seeds
8 jalapenos, seeded and sliced in half lengthwise
8 slices bacon, sliced in half lengthwise

Directions

Thoroughly combine the cheese and mustard seeds.
Spoon the mixture into the jalapeno halves.
Wrap each jalapeno with half a slice of bacon and secure with toothpicks
Air fry the jalapeno poppers at 370 degrees for about 7 minutes or until golden brown.
Bon appétit!

Easy Chicken Wings

(Ready in about 20 minutes | Servings 3)

Per serving: 284 Calories; 21.4g Fat; 0.3g Carbs; 21.1g Protein; 0.3g Sugars; 0.3g Fiber

Ingredients

3/4 pound chicken wings
1 tablespoon olive oil
1 teaspoon mustard seeds
1 teaspoon cayenne pepper
1 teaspoon garlic powder
Sea salt and ground black pepper, to taste

Directions

Toss the chicken wings with the remaining ingredients.
Cook the chicken wings at 380 degrees F for 18 minutes, turning them over halfway through the cooking time.
Bon appétit!

Crispy Cauliflower Florets

(Ready in about 20 minutes | Servings 4)

Per serving: 178 Calories; 4.1g Fat; 27.3g Carbs; 9.1g Protein; 4.6g Sugars; 4.1g Fiber

Ingredients

2 eggs, whisked
1 cup breadcrumbs
Sea salt and ground black pepper, to taste
1 teaspoon cayenne pepper
1 teaspoon chili powder
1/2 teaspoon onion powder
1/2 teaspoon cumin powder
1/2 teaspoon garlic powder

1 pound cauliflower florets

Directions

Mix the eggs, breadcrumbs, and spices until well combined. Dip the cauliflower florets in the batter.

Cook the cauliflower florets at 350 degrees F for about 15 minutes, turning them over halfway through the cooking time.

Bon appétit!

Spicy and Sticky Brussels Sprouts

(Ready in about 15 minutes | Servings 4)

Per serving: 149 Calories; 7.3g Fat; 20.3g Carbs; 9.1g Protein; 11.6g Sugars; 4.9g Fiber

Ingredients

1 pound Brussels sprouts, trimmed
2 tablespoons sesame oil
2 tablespoons agave syrup
2 tablespoons rice wine
1 teaspoon chili flakes
1 teaspoon garlic powder
1/2 teaspoon paprika
Sea salt and ground black pepper, to taste

Directions

Toss the Brussels sprouts with the remaining ingredients; then, arrange the Brussels sprouts in the Air Fryer cooking basket.

Cook the Brussels sprouts at 380 degrees F for 10 minutes, shaking the basket halfway through the cooking time.

Serve warm and enjoy!

Glazed Baby Carrots

(Ready in about 20 minutes | Servings 3)

Per serving: 162 Calories; 9.3g Fat; 21.1g Carbs; 0.9g Protein; 17g Sugars; 3.4g Fiber

Ingredients

3/4 pound baby carrots, halved lengthwise
2 tablespoons coconut oil
1/2 teaspoon cumin powder
2 tablespoons honey
2 tablespoons white wine

Directions

Toss the carrots with the remaining ingredients; then, arrange the carrots in the Air Fryer cooking basket.

Cook the carrots at 380 degrees F for 15 minutes, shaking the basket halfway through the cooking time.

Bon appétit!

Mediterranean Potato Chips

(Ready in about 20 minutes | Servings 3)

Per serving: 262 Calories; 9.2g Fat; 42.1g Carbs; 4.9g Protein; 1.9g Sugars; 5.4g Fiber

Ingredients

2 large-sized potatoes, thinly sliced
2 tablespoons olive oil
1 teaspoon Mediterranean herb mix
1 teaspoon cayenne pepper
Coarse sea salt and ground black pepper, to taste

Directions

Start by preheating your Air Fryer to 360 degrees F.

Toss the potatoes with the remaining ingredients and place them in the Air Fryer cooking basket.

Air fry the potato chips for 16 minutes, shaking the basket halfway through the cooking time and working in batches.

Enjoy!

Classic Broccoli Florets

(Ready in about 15 minutes | Servings 4)

Per serving: 102 Calories; 6.9g Fat; 8.3g Carbs; 3.5g Protein; 2.6g Sugars; 3g Fiber

Ingredients

1 pound broccoli florets
2 tablespoons butter, room temperature
1/4 teaspoon mustard seeds
1 tablespoon soy sauce
Sea salt and freshly ground black pepper, to taste

Directions

Toss all the ingredients in a lightly oiled Air Fryer basket.

Cook the broccoli florets at 370 degrees F for about 10 minutes, shaking the basket halfway through the cooking time.

Bon appétit!

Cinnamon Apple Chips

(Ready in about 15 minutes | Servings 4)

Per serving: 47 Calories; 0.1g Fat; 12.3g Carbs; 0.2g Protein; 9.4g Sugars; 2.2g Fiber

Ingredients

2 large sweet, crisp apples, cored and sliced
1 teaspoon ground cinnamon
1/2 teaspoon grated nutmeg
A pinch of salt

Directions

Start by preheating your Air Fryer to 390 degrees F.

Toss the apple slices with the remaining ingredients and arrange them in a single layer in the Air Fryer cooking basket.

Cook the apple chips for about 9 minutes at 390 degrees F, shaking the basket halfway through the cooking time. Work in batches.

Bon appétit!

Crispy Sweet Potato Fries

(Ready in about 20 minutes | Servings 3)

Per serving: 79 Calories; 3.6g Fat; 18.5g Carbs; 1.6g Protein; 3.7g Sugars; 2.6g Fiber

Ingredients

2 large-sized sweet potatoes, peeled and cut into 1/4-inch sticks
2 teaspoons olive oil
1 teaspoon garlic powder
1 tablespoon Mediterranean herb mix
Kosher salt and freshly ground black pepper, to taste

Directions

Start by preheating your Air Fryer to 360 degrees F.

Toss the sweet potato with the remaining ingredients and place them in the Air Fryer cooking basket.

Air fry the sweet potato sticks for 15 minutes, tossing halfway through the cooking time and working in batches.
Enjoy!

Sticky Pork Ribs

(Ready in about 40 minutes | Servings 4)
Per serving: 412 Calories; 18.8g Fat; 10.8g Carbs; 47.6g Protein; 9.3g Sugars; 0.7g Fiber
Ingredients
2 pounds pork ribs
2 tablespoons honey
2 tablespoons butter
1 teaspoon sweet paprika
1 teaspoon hot paprika
1 teaspoon granulated garlic
Sea salt and ground black pepper, to taste
1 teaspoon brown mustard
1 teaspoon ground cumin
Directions
Toss all ingredients in a lightly greased Air Fryer cooking basket.
Cook the pork ribs at 350 degrees F for 35 minutes, turning them over halfway through the cooking time.
Bon appétit!

Autumn Pumpkin Chips

(Ready in about 20 minutes | Servings 4)
Per serving: 97 Calories; 7g Fat; 9.3g Carbs; 1.6g Protein; 3.7g Sugars; 1g Fiber
Ingredients
1 pound pumpkin, peeled and sliced
2 tablespoons coconut oil
1 teaspoon ground allspice
1/2 teaspoon chili powder
1/2 teaspoon garlic powder
1/2 teaspoon ground cumin
Sea salt and ground black pepper, to taste
Directions
Toss the pumpkin with the remaining ingredients until well coated on all sides.
Cook for about 13 minutes, tossing the basket one or twice.
Bon appétit!

Crispy Fried Green Beans

(Ready in about 10 minutes | Servings 4)
Per serving: 180 Calories; 6.4g Fat; 21.4g Carbs; 9.6g Protein; 1.3g Sugars; 2.8g Fiber
Ingredients
1/2 cup flour
2 eggs, beaten
1/2 cup bread crumbs
1/2 cup Parmesan cheese, grated
1/2 teaspoon onion powder
1/4 teaspoon cumin powder
1/2 teaspoon garlic powder
1 pound fresh green beans
Directions
In a shallow bowl, thoroughly combine the flour and eggs; mix to combine well.
Then, in another bowl, mix the remaining ingredients.
Dip the green beans in the egg mixture, then, in the breadcrumb mixture.
Air fry the green beans at 390 degrees F for about 6 minutes, tossing the basket halfway through the cooking time.
Enjoy!

Fried Green Tomatoes

(Ready in about 20 minutes | Servings 4)
Per serving: 215 Calories; 10.4g Fat; 23.1g Carbs; 7.6g Protein; 2.8g Sugars; 1.8g Fiber
Ingredients
1/2 cup all-purpose flour
Sea salt and ground black pepper, to taste
1 teaspoon garlic powder
1 teaspoon cayenne pepper
2 eggs
1/2 cup milk
2 tablespoons olive oil
1 cup breadcrumbs
1 pound green tomatoes, sliced
Directions
Start by preheating your Air Fryer to 390 degrees F.
In a shallow bowl, mix the flour, salt, black pepper, garlic powder, and cayenne pepper.
Whisk the egg and milk in another shallow bowl. Mix the olive oil and breadcrumbs in a separate bowl.
Dip the green tomatoes in the flour, then in the eggs, then in the breadcrumbs. Place the green tomatoes in the Air Fryer basket.
Cook the green tomatoes for about 15 minutes or until golden brown and cooked through.
Serve with toothpicks. Bon appétit!

Lemon Garlic Eggplant Chips

(Ready in about 20 minutes | Servings 4)
Per serving: 95 Calories; 7g Fat; 8.4g Carbs; 1.5g Protein; 4.7g Sugars; 3.6g Fiber
Ingredients
1 pound eggplant, sliced
2 tablespoons olive oil
1 teaspoon garlic, minced
Sea salt and ground black pepper, to taste
2 tablespoons lemon juice, freshly squeezed
Directions
Toss the eggplant pieces with the remaining ingredients until they are well coated on all sides.
Arrange the eggplant in the Air Fryer basket.
Cook the eggplant at 400 degrees F for about 15 minutes, shaking the basket halfway through the cooking time.
Bon appétit!

Cheesy Zucchini Chips

(Ready in about 15 minutes | Servings 4)
Per serving: 133 Calories; 7g Fat; 8.1g Carbs; 10.5g Protein; 0.5g Sugars; 1.4g Fiber

Ingredients
1 pound zucchini, sliced
1 cup Pecorino Romano cheese, grated
Sea salt and cayenne pepper, to taste
Directions
Start by preheating your Air Fryer to 390 degrees F.
Toss the zucchini slices with the remaining ingredients and arrange them in a single layer in the Air Fryer cooking basket.
Cook the zucchini slices for about 10 minutes at 390 degrees F, shaking the basket halfway through the cooking time. Work in batches.
Bon appétit!

Herb Tomato Chips

(Ready in about 20 minutes | Servings 2)
Per serving: 145 Calories; 13.7g Fat; 6g Carbs; 1.3g Protein; 3.5g Sugars; 1.7g Fiber
Ingredients
1 beefsteak tomato, thinly sliced
2 tablespoons extra-virgin olive oil
Coarse sea salt and fresh ground pepper, to taste
1 teaspoon dried basil
1 teaspoon dried thyme
1 teaspoon dried rosemary
Directions
Toss the tomato slices with the remaining ingredients until they are well coated on all sides.
Arrange the tomato slices in the Air Fryer cooking basket.
Cook the tomato slices at 360 degrees F for about 10 minutes. Turn the temperature to 330 degrees F and continue to cook for a further 5 minutes.
Bon appétit!

Paprika Potato Chips

(Ready in about 20 minutes | Servings 3)
Per serving: 198 Calories; 9.2g Fat; 26.5g Carbs; 3.1g Protein; 1.2g Sugars; 3.6g Fiber
Ingredients
1 pound potatoes, thinly sliced
2 tablespoons olive oil
1 teaspoon paprika
Coarse salt and cayenne pepper, to taste
Directions
Start by preheating your Air Fryer to 360 degrees F.
Toss the potatoes with the remaining ingredients and place them in the Air Fryer cooking basket.
Air fry the potato chips for 16 minutes, shaking the basket halfway through the cooking time and work in batches.
Enjoy!

Roasted Mixed Nuts

(Ready in about 10 minutes | Servings 4)
Per serving: 210 Calories; 19.2g Fat; 6.2g Carbs; 6.7g Protein; 1.5g Sugars; 3.5g Fiber
Ingredients
1/4 cup almonds
1/2 cup hazelnuts
1/4 cup peanuts
Directions
Preheat your Air Fryer to 330 degrees F.
Air fry the nuts for 6 minutes, shaking the basket halfway through the cooking time and working in batches.
Enjoy!

Ham and Cheese Stuffed Serrano Peppers

(Ready in about 10 minutes | Servings 4)
Per serving: 169 Calories; 11.1g Fat; 1.7g Carbs; 13.6g Protein; 1.1g Sugars; 0.6g Fiber
Ingredients
8 Serrano peppers
4 ounces ham cubes
4 ounces goat cheese, crumbled
Directions
Stuff the peppers with ham and cheese; transfer them to a lightly oiled Air Fryer basket.
Air fry the peppers at 370 degrees for about 7 minutes or until golden brown.
Bon appétit!

Cheese Bacon-Stuffed Mushrooms

(Ready in about 10 minutes | Servings 4)
Per serving: 225 Calories; 14.8g Fat; 7.2g Carbs; 17.6g Protein; 3.2g Sugars; 1.4g Fiber
Ingredients
1 tablespoon butter
6 ounces Pecorino Romano cheese, grated
2 tablespoons chives, chopped
1 tablespoon minced garlic
1/2 teaspoon cayenne pepper
Sea salt and ground black pepper, to taste
1 pound button mushrooms, stems removed
Directions
In a mixing bowl, thoroughly combine the butter, cheese, chives, garlic, cayenne pepper, salt, and black pepper.
Divide the filling between your mushrooms. Arrange the mushrooms in the Air Fryer basket.
Cook your mushrooms at 400 degrees F for about 7 minutes, shaking the basket halfway through the cooking time.
Bon appétit!

Green Bean Fries

(Ready in about 10 minutes | Servings 4)
Per serving: 181 Calories; 8.8g Fat; 17g Carbs; 11.1g Protein; 4.1g Sugars; 3.5g Fiber
Ingredients
1 pound green beans
4 tablespoons all-purpose flour
2 eggs, whisked
1/2 cup breadcrumbs
1/2 cup grated parmesan cheese
1 teaspoon cayenne pepper
1/2 teaspoon mustard seeds
1 teaspoon garlic powder
Sea salt and ground black pepper, to taste

Directions

In a shallow bowl, thoroughly combine the flour and eggs; mix to combine well.

Then, in another bowl, mix the remaining ingredients.

Dip the green beans in the egg mixture, then, in the breadcrumb mixture.

Air fry the green beans at 390 degrees F for about 6 minutes, tossing the basket halfway through the cooking time.

Enjoy!

Hot and Spicy Drumettes

(Ready in about 20 minutes | Servings 5)

Per serving: 404 Calories; 25.8g Fat; 3.7g Carbs; 37.5g Protein; 0.5g Sugars; 1.3g Fiber

Ingredients

2 pounds chicken drumettes
1 teaspoon ancho chile pepper
1 teaspoon smoked paprika
1 teaspoon onion powder
1 teaspoon garlic powder
Kosher salt and ground black pepper, to taste
1/4 tsp black pepper
2 tablespoons olive oil

Directions

Toss the chicken drumettes with the remaining ingredients.

Cook the chicken drumettes at 380 degrees F for 18 minutes, turning them over halfway through the cooking time.

Bon appétit!

Cheesy Cauliflower Wings

(Ready in about 20 minutes | Servings 4)

Per serving: 358 Calories; 16.3g Fat; 37.3g Carbs; 14.9g Protein; 4.5g Sugars; 3.6g Fiber

Ingredients

1/2 cup milk
1 cup all-purpose flour
1 teaspoon garlic powder
1 teaspoon onion powder
1 teaspoon hot paprika
Sea salt and ground black pepper, to taste
2 tablespoons olive oil
1 pound cauliflower florets
4 ounces parmesan cheese, preferably freshly grated

Directions

In a mixing bowl, thoroughly combine the milk, flour, spices, and olive oil.

Dip the cauliflower florets in the flour mixture.

Cook the cauliflower florets at 350 degrees F for about 10 minutes, turning them over halfway through the cooking time.

Top the cauliflower florets with cheese and continue to cook an additional 5 minutes.

Bon appétit!

Cheesy Broccoli Bites

(Ready in about 15 minutes | Servings 4)

Per serving: 156 Calories; 10.6g Fat; 10.5g Carbs; 6.5g Protein; 2.4g Sugars; 3.1g Fiber

Ingredients

1 pound broccoli florets
1 teaspoon granulated garlic
1 tablespoon onion flakes, dried
1 teaspoon red pepper flakes, crushed
2 tablespoons olive oil
1/2 cup Pecorino Romano cheese, grated

Directions

Toss all ingredients in a lightly oiled Air Fryer basket.

Cook the broccoli florets at 370 degrees F for about 10 minutes, shaking the basket halfway through the cooking time.

Enjoy!

Cheddar Garlic Brussels Sprouts

(Ready in about 15 minutes | Servings 4)

Per serving: 127 Calories; 7.3g Fat; 11.9g Carbs; 5.8g Protein; 3.5g Sugars; 4.3g Fiber

Ingredients

1 pound Brussels sprouts, trimmed
2 tablespoons butter, melted
Sea salt and freshly ground black pepper, to taste
1 teaspoon garlic, minced
2 tablespoons red wine vinegar
2 ounces cheddar cheese, shredded

Directions

Toss the Brussels sprouts with the remaining ingredients; then, arrange the Brussels sprouts in the Air Fryer cooking basket.

Cook the Brussels sprouts at 380 degrees F for 10 minutes, shaking the basket halfway through the cooking time.

Serve warm and enjoy!

Spicy Spare Ribs

(Ready in about 40 minutes | Servings 4)

Per serving: 442 Calories; 33g Fat; 4.7g Carbs; 32.3g Protein; 1.9g Sugars; 0.5g Fiber

Ingredients

1 ½ pounds spare ribs
Kosher salt and ground black pepper, to taste
2 teaspoons brown sugar
1 teaspoon paprika
1 teaspoon chile powder
1 teaspoon garlic powder

Directions

Toss all the ingredients in a lightly greased Air Fryer cooking basket.

Cook the pork ribs at 350 degrees F for 35 minutes, turning them over halfway through the cooking time.

Bon appétit!

Butter Roasted Baby Carrots

(Ready in about 20 minutes | Servings 4)

Per serving: 104 Calories; 6.3g Fat; 12.4g Carbs; 1.8g Protein; 6g Sugars; 3.7g Fiber

Ingredients

1 pound baby carrots
2 tablespoons butter
Kosher salt and ground white pepper, to taste
1 teaspoon paprika
1 teaspoon dried oregano

Directions

Toss the carrots with the remaining ingredients; then, arrange the carrots in the Air Fryer cooking basket.
Cook the carrots at 380 degrees F for 15 minutes, shaking the basket halfway through the cooking time.
Bon appétit!

Sticky Chicken Wings

(Ready in about 20 minutes | Servings 5)

Per serving: 344 Calories; 13g Fat; 15.3g Carbs; 40.5g Protein; 14.4g Sugars; 1g Fiber

Ingredients

2 pounds chicken wings
1/4 cup agave syrup
2 tablespoons soy sauce
2 tablespoons scallions, chopped
2 tablespoons olive oil
1 teaspoon ginger, peeled and grated
2 cloves garlic, minced
Sea salt and ground black pepper, to taste

Directions

Toss the chicken wings with the remaining ingredients.
Cook the chicken wings at 380 degrees F for 18 minutes, turning them over halfway through the cooking time.
Bon appétit!

Classic Yam Chips

(Ready in about 20 minutes | Servings 2)

Per serving: 141 Calories; 6.6g Fat; 20.5g Carbs; 1.5g Protein; 0.3g Sugars; 3.1g Fiber

Ingredients

1 large-sized yam, peeled and cut into 1/4-inch sticks
1 tablespoon olive oil
Kosher salt and red pepper, to taste

Directions

Start by preheating your Air Fryer to 360 degrees F.
Toss the yam with the remaining ingredients and place them in the Air Fryer cooking basket.
Air fry the yam sticks for 15 minutes, tossing halfway through the cooking time and working in batches.
Enjoy!

Potato Chips with a Twist

(Ready in about 20 minutes | Servings 3)

Per serving: 281 Calories; 10.1g Fat; 43.5g Carbs; 1.5g Protein; 1.9g Sugars; 5.1g Fiber

Ingredients

2 large-sized potatoes, peeled and thinly sliced
2 tablespoons olive oil
1 teaspoon Sichuan peppercorns
1 teaspoon garlic powder
1/2 teaspoon Chinese five-spice powder
Sea salt, to taste

Directions

Start by preheating your Air Fryer to 360 degrees F.
Toss the potatoes with the remaining ingredients and place them in the Air Fryer cooking basket.
Air fry the potato chips for 16 minutes, shaking the basket halfway through the cooking time and working in batches.
Enjoy!

Crispy Zucchini Fries

(Ready in about 15 minutes | Servings 4)

Per serving: 281 Calories; 10.1g Fat; 43.5g Carbs; 1.5g Protein; 1.9g Sugars; 5.1g Fiber

Ingredients

1 pound zucchini, cut into sticks
1 egg, whisked
1/4 cup parmesan cheese, grated
1/2 cup breadcrumbs
1 teaspoon garlic powder
1/2 teaspoon onion powder
Sea salt and ground black pepper, to taste

Directions

Start by preheating your Air Fryer to 390 degrees F.
Toss the zucchini sticks with the remaining ingredients and arrange them in a single layer in the Air Fryer cooking basket.
Cook the zucchini sticks for about 10 minutes at 390 degrees F, shaking the basket halfway through the cooking time. Work in batches.
Bon appétit!

Sriracha Chicken Wings

(Ready in about 20 minutes | Servings 4)

Per serving: 403 Calories; 19.4g Fat; 3.3g Carbs; 50.1g Protein; 1.3g Sugars; 0.7g Fiber

Ingredients

2 pounds chicken wings
1 tablespoon white vinegar
Sea salt and ground black pepper, to taste
1 teaspoon cayenne pepper

1 teaspoon garlic powder
1/2 teaspoon onion powder
4 tablespoons butter, room temperature
1/4 cup Sriracha sauce

Directions

Toss the chicken wings with the remaining ingredients.
Cook the chicken wings at 380 degrees F for 18 minutes, turning them over halfway through the cooking time.
Bon appétit!

Wax Bean Fries

(Ready in about 10 minutes | Servings 4)

Per serving: 69 Calories; 2.4g Fat; 8.7g Carbs; 2.2g Protein; 3.7g Sugars; 3.2g Fiber

Ingredients

1 pound fresh wax beans, trimmed
2 teaspoons olive oil
1/2 teaspoon onion powder
1 teaspoon garlic powder
1/2 teaspoon cumin powder
Sea salt and ground black pepper, to taste

Directions

Toss the wax beans with the remaining ingredients.
Air fry the wax beans at 390 degrees F for about 6 minutes, tossing the basket halfway through the cooking time.
Enjoy!

Balsamic Eggplant Fries

(Ready in about 20 minutes | Servings 3)

Per serving: 124 Calories; 9.2g Fat; 10.1g Carbs; 1.5g Protein; 6.4g Sugars; 3.8g Fiber

Ingredients

3/4 pound eggplant
Sea salt and ground black pepper, to taste
1/2 teaspoon paprika
2 tablespoons olive oil
2 tablespoons balsamic vinegar

Directions

Toss the eggplant pieces with the remaining ingredients until they are well coated on all sides.
Arrange the eggplant in the Air Fryer basket.
Cook the eggplant at 400 degrees F for about 15 minutes, shaking the basket halfway through the cooking time.
Bon appétit!

Cheesy Tomato Chips

(Ready in about 20 minutes | Servings 3)

Per serving: 154 Calories; 13.3g Fat; 5.1g Carbs; 4.1g Protein; 3.1g Sugars; 1g Fiber

Ingredients

1 large-sized beefsteak tomatoes
2 tablespoons olive oil
1/2 teaspoon paprika
Sea salt, to taste
1 teaspoon garlic powder
1 tablespoon fresh cilantro, chopped
4 tablespoons Pecorino cheese, grated

Directions

Toss the tomato slices with the olive oil and spices until they are well coated on all sides.
Arrange the tomato slices in the Air Fryer cooking basket.
Cook the tomato slices at 360 degrees F for about 10 minutes. Turn the temperature to 330 degrees F and top the tomato slices with the cheese; now, continue to cook for a further 5 minutes.
Bon appétit!

Hot Spicy Nuts

(Ready in about 10 minutes | Servings 4)

Per serving: 264 Calories; 24.3g Fat; 8.8g Carbs; 7.6g Protein; 2.2g Sugars; 4.7g Fiber

Ingredients

1 egg white lightly beaten
1/2 cup pecan halves
1/2 cup almonds
1/2 cup walnuts
Sea salt and cayenne pepper, to taste
1 teaspoon chili powder
1/2 teaspoon ground cinnamon
1/2 teaspoon ground allspice

Directions

Preheat your Air Fryer to 330 degrees F.
Mix the nuts with the rest of the ingredients and place them in the Air Fryer cooking basket.
Air fry the nuts for 6 minutes, shaking the basket halfway through the cooking time and working in batches.
Enjoy!

Golden Beet Chips

(Ready in about 35 minutes | Servings 2)

Per serving: 188 Calories; 13.6g Fat; 15.1g Carbs; 2.7g Protein; 9g Sugars; 4.2g Fiber

Ingredients

1/2 pound golden beets, peeled and thinly sliced
Kosher salt and ground black pepper, to taste
1 teaspoon paprika
2 tablespoons olive oil
1/2 teaspoon garlic powder
1 teaspoon ground turmeric

Directions

Start by preheating your Air Fryer to 330 degrees F.

Toss the beets with the remaining ingredients and place them in the Air Fryer cooking basket.
Air fry your chips for 30 minutes, shaking the basket occasionally and working in batches.
Enjoy!

Cheese and Herb Stuffed Mushrooms

(Ready in about 10 minutes | Servings 4)

Per serving: 150 Calories; 10.7g Fat; 7.9g Carbs; 7.5g Protein; 2.5g Sugars; 1.3g Fiber

Ingredients

2 tablespoons olive oil
1/2 cup breadcrumbs
1/2 cup Parmesan cheese, grated
1 teaspoon garlic, minced
1 tablespoon fresh parsley, chopped
1 tablespoon fresh chives, chopped
Sea salt and freshly ground black pepper, to taste
1 pound button mushrooms, stems removed

Directions

In a mixing bowl, thoroughly combine the olive oil, breadcrumbs, Parmesan cheese, garlic, parsley, chives, salt, and black pepper.
Divide the filling between your mushrooms. Arrange the mushrooms in the Air Fryer basket.
Cook your mushrooms at 400 degrees F for about 7 minutes, shaking the basket halfway through the cooking time.
Bon appétit!

Classic Kale Chips

(Ready in about 10 minutes | Servings 4)

Per serving: 45 Calories; 3.5g Fat; 3g Carbs; 1.1g Protein; 0.9g Sugars; 0.8g Fiber

Ingredients

4 cups kale, torn into pieces
1 tablespoon sesame oil
1 teaspoon garlic powder
Sea salt and ground black pepper, to taste

Directions

Start by preheating your Air Fryer to 360 degrees F.
Toss the kale leaves with the remaining ingredients and place them in the Air Fryer cooking basket.
Air fry your chips for 8 minutes, shaking the basket occasionally and working in batches.
Enjoy!

Mini Bacon-Wrapped Sausages

(Ready in about 20 minutes | Servings 4)

Per serving: 540 Calories; 46.5g Fat; 8.9g Carbs; 21g Protein; 6.6g Sugars; 0.6g Fiber

Ingredients

1 pound mini sausages
2 tablespoons tamari sauce
2 tablespoons maple syrup
1 teaspoon chili powder
Ground black pepper, to taste
4 ounces bacon, thinly slices

Directions

Toss the mini sausages with the tamari sauce, maple syrup, chili powder, and black pepper.
Wrap the mini sausages with the bacon.
Place the sausages in a lightly oiled Air Fryer cooking basket.
Cook the sausages at 380 degrees F for 15 minutes, tossing the basket halfway through the cooking time.
Serve warm and enjoy!

Pigs in a Blanket

(Ready in about 10 minutes | Servings 6)

Per serving: 164 Calories; 6.2g Fat; 24.1g Carbs; 3.1g Protein; 3.2g Sugars; 1.5g Fiber

Ingredients

6 ounces crescent rolls, refrigerated
1 tablespoon mustard
10 ounces mini hot dogs

Directions

Separate the dough into triangles. Cut them lengthwise into 3 small triangles. Spread each triangle with mustard.
Place a mini hot dog on the shortest side of each triangle and roll it up.
Place the rolls in the Air Fryer cooking basket.
Bake the rolls at 320 degrees F for about 8 minutes, turning them over halfway through the cooking time.
Bon appétit!

Cheddar Cheese Cauliflower Bites

(Ready in about 15 minutes | Servings 4)

Per serving: 208 Calories; 12.2g Fat; 17.1g Carbs; 7.9g Protein; 3.9g Sugars; 3.1g Fiber

Ingredients

1 pound cauliflower, grated
1/2 cup cheddar cheese, shredded
1 ounce butter, room temperature
Sea salt and ground black pepper, to taste
1/2 cup tortilla chips, crushed
2 eggs whisked

Directions

Thoroughly combine all the ingredients in a mixing bowl. Shape the mixture into bite-sized balls.
Cook the cauliflower balls at 350 degrees F for about 13 minutes, turning them over halfway through the cooking time.
Bon appétit!

Sticky Pancetta-Wrapped Shrimp

(Ready in about 10 minutes | Servings 4)

Per serving: 118 Calories; 7.9g Fat; 7.1g Carbs; 4.5g Protein; 6.2g Sugars; 0.2g Fiber

Ingredients

12 shrimp, peeled and deveined
3 slices pancetta, cut into strips
2 tablespoons maple syrup
1 tablespoon Dijon mustard

Directions

Wrap the shrimp in the pancetta strips and toss them with the maple syrup and mustard.
Place the shrimp in a lightly greased Air Fryer cooking basket.
Cook the shrimp at 400 degrees F for 6 minutes, tossing the basket halfway through the cooking time.
Bon appétit!

Apple Pie Mini Rolls

(Ready in about 15 minutes | Servings 4)

Per serving: 344 Calories; 21.2g Fat; 33.4g Carbs; 6.3g Protein; 17g Sugars; 2.2g Fiber

Ingredients

6 ounces refrigerated crescent rolls
1 apple, peeled, cored, and grated
6 ounces cream cheese, crumbled
1/4 cup brown sugar
1 teaspoon apple pie spice

Directions

Separate the dough into rectangles. Mix the remaining ingredients until well combined.
Spread each rectangle with the cheese mixture; roll them up tightly. Place the rolls in the Air Fryer cooking basket.
Bake the rolls at 320 degrees F for about 5 minutes; turn them over and bake for a further 5 minutes.
Bon appétit!

Spicy Kale Crisps

(Ready in about 10 minutes | Servings 4)

Per serving: 48 Calories; 3.6g Fat; 3.6g Carbs; 1.2g Protein; 1g Sugars; 1.2g Fiber

Ingredients

5 cups kale leaves, torn into pieces, stems removed
1 tablespoon olive oil
1 teaspoon chili powder
Sea salt and ground black pepper, to taste
2 garlic cloves, minced

Directions

Start by preheating your Air Fryer to 360 degrees F.
Toss the kale leaves with the remaining ingredients and place them in the Air Fryer cooking basket.
Air fry the kale crisps for 8 minutes, shaking the basket occasionally and working in batches.
Enjoy!

Mediterranean-Style Beet Chips

(Ready in about 35 minutes | Servings 4)

Per serving: 89 Calories; 3.6g Fat; 12.4g Carbs; 2.2g Protein; 8g Sugars; 3.3g Fiber

Ingredients

1 pound red and yellow beets, peeled and sliced
1 tablespoon olive oil
Coarse sea salt and ground black pepper, to taste
1 teaspoon dried rosemary
1 teaspoon dried parsley flakes
1 teaspoon garlic
2 tablespoons scallions, chopped

Directions

Start by preheating your Air Fryer to 330 degrees F.
Toss the beets with the remaining ingredients and place them in the Air Fryer cooking basket.
Air fry your chips for 30 minutes, shaking the basket occasionally and working in batches.
Enjoy!

Southern-Fried Sweet Onion Rings

(Ready in about 10 minutes | Servings 4)

Per serving: 366 Calories; 9.3g Fat; 59g Carbs; 9.7g Protein; 9.3g Sugars; 4.1g Fiber

Ingredients

1/2 cup beer
1 cup plain flour
1 teaspoon baking powder
1 teaspoon cayenne pepper
Sea salt and ground black pepper, to taste
2 eggs, whisked
1 cup tortilla chips, crushed
2 sweet onions

Directions

Start by preheating your Air Fryer to 380 degrees F.
In a shallow bowl, mix the beer, flour, baking powder, cayenne pepper, salt, and black pepper.
Whisk the egg in another shallow bowl. Place the crushed tortilla chips in a separate bowl.
Dip the onion rings in the flour mixture, then in the eggs, then in the tortilla chips. Place the onion rings in the Air Fryer basket.
Cook the onion rings for about 8 minutes or until golden brown and cooked through.
Bon appétit!

Mexican-Style Tortilla Chips

(Ready in about 10 minutes | Servings 4)

Per serving: 88 Calories; 4.2g Fat; 11.7g Carbs; 1.5g Protein; 0.4g Sugars; 1.8g Fiber

Ingredients

4 corn tortillas, cut into wedges
1 tablespoon olive oil
1 tablespoon Mexican oregano

2 tablespoons lime juice
1 teaspoon chili powder
1 teaspoon ground cumin
Sea salt, to taste

Directions

Toss the tortilla wedges with the remaining ingredients.
Cook your tortilla chips at 360 degrees F for about 5 minutes or until crispy, working in batches.
Enjoy!

Gruyere Cheese-Stuffed Poblanos

(Ready in about 10 minutes | Servings 4)

Per serving: 242 Calories; 17.4g Fat; 10.4g Carbs; 13.2g Protein; 4.6g Sugars; 2.1g Fiber

Ingredients

8 poblano peppers, seeded and halved
4 ounces Gruyere cheese
4 ounces bacon, chopped

Directions

Stuff the peppers with the cheese and bacon; transfer them to a lightly oiled Air Fryer basket.
Air fry the peppers at 370 degrees for about 7 minutes or until golden brown.
Bon appétit!

Paprika Carrot Bites

(Ready in about 20 minutes | Servings 4)

Per serving: 113 Calories; 7.2g Fat; 12.4g Carbs; 1.2g Protein; 6g Sugars; 3.6g Fiber

Ingredients

1 pound carrots, cut into slices
2 tablespoons coconut oil
1 teaspoon paprika
1/2 teaspoon garlic powder
1/2 teaspoon dried oregano
1/2 teaspoon dried parsley flakes
Sea salt and ground black pepper, to taste

Directions

Toss the carrots with the remaining ingredients; then, arrange the carrots in the Air Fryer cooking basket.
Cook the carrots at 380 degrees F for 15 minutes, shaking the basket halfway through the cooking time.
Bon appétit!

Greek-Style Potato Wedges

(Ready in about 40 minutes | Servings 4)

Per serving: 153 Calories; 7g Fat; 21.2g Carbs; 2.6g Protein; 1.5g Sugars; 2.6g Fiber

Ingredients

1 pound potatoes, cut into wedges
2 tablespoons olive oil
Sea salt and ground black pepper, to taste
1 teaspoon paprika
1 teaspoon dried parsley flakes
1 teaspoon Greek seasoning mix

Directions

Start by preheating your Air Fryer to 400 degrees F.
Toss the potatoes with the remaining ingredients and place them in the Air Fryer cooking basket.
Air fry the potato wedges for 35 minutes, shaking the basket halfway through the cooking time.
Enjoy!

Asian Spare Ribs

(Ready in about 40 minutes | Servings 4)

Per serving: 153 Calories; 7g Fat; 21.2g Carbs; 2.6g Protein; 1.5g Sugars; 2.6g Fiber

Ingredients

2 pounds spare ribs
1/4 cup soy sauce
1/4 cup rice vinegar
1/4 cup sesame oil
2 garlic cloves, minced

Directions

Toss all ingredients in a lightly greased Air Fryer cooking basket.
Cook the ribs at 350 degrees F for 35 minutes, turning them over halfway through the cooking time.
Bon appétit!

Korean-Style Drumettes

(Ready in about 20 minutes | Servings 4)

Per serving: 304 Calories; 12.8g Fat; 22.4g Carbs; 24.5g Protein; 20.5g Sugars; 0.7g Fiber

Ingredients

1 pound chicken drumettes
4 tablespoons soy sauce
1/4 cup rice vinegar
4 tablespoons honey
2 tablespoons sesame oil
1 teaspoon Gochugaru, Korean chili powder
2 tablespoons scallions, chopped
2 garlic cloves, minced

Directions

Toss the chicken drumettes with the remaining ingredients.
Cook the chicken drumettes at 380 degrees F for 18 minutes, turning them over halfway through the cooking time.
Bon appétit!

Mozzarella Eggplant Chips

(Ready in about 20 minutes | Servings 4)

Per serving: 129 Calories; 6g Fat; 9.3g Carbs; 10.4g Protein; 5.1g Sugars; 4.3g Fiber

Ingredients

1 pound eggplant, cut into slices

2 tablespoons butter, melted
1/2 teaspoon smoked paprika
1 teaspoon Italian seasoning
Sea salt and ground black pepper, to taste
1 cup mozzarella cheese, shredded

Directions

Toss the eggplant with the butter and spices. Arrange the eggplant slices in the Air Fryer basket.

Cook the eggplant at 400 degrees F for about 15 minutes, shaking the basket halfway through the cooking time.

Bon appétit!

Hot Zucchini Fries

(Ready in about 15 minutes | Servings 4)

Per serving: 227 Calories; 17.6g Fat; 9.3g Carbs; 10.8g Protein; 1.2g Sugars; 3.1g Fiber

Ingredients

1 pound zucchini, cut into sticks
1/2 cup Parmesan cheese
1/2 cup almond flour
1 egg, whisked
2 tablespoons olive oil
1 teaspoon hot paprika
Sea salt and ground black pepper, to taste

Directions

Start by preheating your Air Fryer to 390 degrees F.

Toss the zucchini sticks with the remaining ingredients and arrange them in a single layer in the Air Fryer cooking basket.

Cook the zucchini sticks for about 10 minutes at 390 degrees F, shaking the basket halfway through the cooking time. Work in batches.

Bon appétit!

Red Beet Chips

(Ready in about 35 minutes | Servings 4)

Per serving: 79 Calories; 3.6g Fat; 10.4g Carbs; 1.8g Protein; 7.2g Sugars; 3.2g Fiber

Ingredients

1 pound red beets, peeled and cut into 1/8-inch slices
1 tablespoon olive oil
1 teaspoon cayenne pepper
Sea salt and ground black pepper, to taste

Directions

Start by preheating your Air Fryer to 330 degrees F.

Toss the beets with the remaining ingredients and place them in the Air Fryer cooking basket.

Air fry your chips for 30 minutes, shaking the basket occasionally and working in batches.

Enjoy!

Ginger and Honey Wings

(Ready in about 20 minutes | Servings 4)

Per serving: 404 Calories; 13.4g Fat; 18.3g Carbs; 50.1g Protein; 18.3g Sugars; 0.3g Fiber

Ingredients

2 pounds chicken wings
1/4 cup honey
2 tablespoons fish sauce
2 garlic cloves, crushed
1 teaspoon ginger, peeled and grated
2 tablespoons butter, melted
Sea salt and ground black pepper, to taste

Directions

Toss the chicken wings with the remaining ingredients.

Cook the chicken wings at 380 degrees F for 18 minutes, turning them over halfway through the cooking time.

Bon appétit!

VEGAN

Old-Fashioned Falafel

(Ready in about 20 minutes | Servings 4)

Per serving: 214 Calories; 12.4g Fat; 20.8g Carbs; 4.5g Protein; 18.3g Sugars; 5.7g Fiber

Ingredients

1 (15-ounce) cans chickpeas, rinsed and drained
1/4 cup fresh cilantro, chopped
2 cloves garlic, minced
1 onion, minced
2 tablespoons tahini
1 teaspoon smoked paprika
2 tablespoons fresh lemon juice
Sea salt and ground black pepper, to taste
2 tablespoons olive oil

Directions

Pulse all the ingredients in your food processor until everything is well incorporated.
Shape the mixture into balls and place them in a lightly greased Air Fryer cooking basket.
Cook the falafel at 380 degrees F for about 15 minutes, shaking the basket occasionally to ensure even cooking.
Serve in pita bread with toppings of your choice. Enjoy!

Breaded Zucchini Slices

(Ready in about 15 minutes | Servings 4)

Per serving: 106 Calories; 8.5g Fat; 5.8g Carbs; 3.7g Protein; 0.8g Sugars; 2.7g Fiber

Ingredients

1 pound zucchini, sliced
1 tablespoon chia seeds, ground
1/2 cup crackers, crushed
2 tablespoons olive oil
1 teaspoon cayenne pepper
Kosher salt and ground black pepper, to taste

Directions

Start by preheating your Air Fryer to 390 degrees F.
Mix the remaining ingredients; dip the zucchini slices in the batter mixture, then, arrange them in a single layer in the Air Fryer cooking basket.
Cook the zucchini slices for about 10 minutes at 390 degrees F, shaking the basket halfway through the cooking time. Work in batches.
Bon appétit!

Lentil Stuffed Eggplant

(Ready in about 15 minutes | Servings 2)

Per serving: 336 Calories; 14.5g Fat; 44.5g Carbs; 12.3g Protein; 16g Sugars; 16.7g Fiber

Ingredients

1 medium eggplants, halved
2 tablespoons olive oil
1 onion, minced
2 garlic cloves, minced
2 tablespoons tomato paste
6 ounces red lentils, canned and drained
Sea salt and ground black pepper, to taste

Directions

Toss the eggplants with the oil; place them in the Air Fryer cooking basket.
Mix the remaining ingredients to make the filling.
Spoon the filling into the eggplant halves.
Cook the stuffed eggplants at 400 degrees F for about 15 minutes.
Serve warm and enjoy!

Fried Celery Sticks

(Ready in about 15 minutes | Servings 4)

Per serving: 176 Calories; 8.4g Fat; 21.5g Carbs; 3.9g Protein; 2.6g Sugars; 1.7g Fiber

Ingredients

4 stalks celery, cleaned and cut into matchsticks
Sea salt and ground black pepper, to taste
1 cup bread crumbs
2 tablespoons avocado oil

Directions

Toss the celery with the remaining ingredients; place them in the Air Fryer cooking basket.
Cook the celery sticks at 400 degrees F for about 15 minutes, shaking the basket occasionally to ensure even cooking.
Serve warm and enjoy!

Italian Herb Potatoes

(Ready in about 25 minutes | Servings 4)

Per serving: 149 Calories; 6.8g Fat; 20.3g Carbs; 2.3g Protein; 0.9g Sugars; 2.6g Fiber

Ingredients

1 pound potatoes, peeled and cut into wedges
2 tablespoons olive oil
1 teaspoon granulated garlic
1 tablespoon Italian herb mix
1 teaspoon cayenne pepper
Kosher salt and freshly ground black pepper, to taste

Directions

Toss the potatoes with the remaining ingredients until well coated on all sides. Arrange the potatoes in the Air Fryer basket.
Cook the potatoes at 400 degrees F for about 20 minutes, shaking the basket halfway through the cooking time.
Bon appétit!

Basic Fried Cucumber

(Ready in about 20 minutes | Servings 4)

Per serving: 144 Calories; 7.2g Fat; 17.5g Carbs; 1.9g Protein; 1.6g Sugars; 1.5g Fiber

Ingredients

2 cucumbers, sliced
2 tablespoons olive oil
1/2 cup cornmeal
Sea salt and ground black pepper, to taste

Directions

Toss the cucumbers with the remaining ingredients; place them in the Air Fryer cooking basket.

Cook the cucumbers at 400 degrees F for about 15 minutes, shaking the basket occasionally to ensure even cooking.

Serve warm and enjoy!

Chinese-Style Bok Choy

(Ready in about 10 minutes | Servings 4)

Per serving: 78 Calories; 7g Fat; 2.9g Carbs; 1.9g Protein; 1g Sugars; 1.3g Fiber

Ingredients

1 pound baby Bok choy, separate leaves
2 tablespoons sesame oil
2 garlic cloves, minced
1 teaspoon Five-spice powder

Directions

Toss the Bok choy with the remaining ingredients until well coated on all sides.

Cook the Bok choy at 350 degrees F for 6 minutes, shaking the basket halfway through the cooking time.

Bon appétit!

Fried Broccoli Florets

(Ready in about 10 minutes | Servings 4)

Per serving: 258 Calories; 21g Fat; 15.2g Carbs; 3.6g Protein; 2.1g Sugars; 3.3g Fiber

Ingredients

1 pound broccoli florets
1/2 cup mayonnaise
1/4 cup parsley leaves, minced
1/4 cup coriander leaves, minced
4 tablespoons cornstarch
Sea salt and ground black pepper, to taste

Directions

Toss the broccoli florets with the remaining ingredients until well coated.

Arrange the broccoli florets in the Air Fryer basket.

Cook the broccoli florets at 395 degrees F for 6 minutes, shaking the basket halfway through the cooking time.

Bon appétit!

Roasted Cauliflower Florets

(Ready in about 20 minutes | Servings 3)

Per serving: 75 Calories; 3.5g Fat; 9.2g Carbs; 3.3g Protein; 3.7g Sugars; 3.5g Fiber

Ingredients

1 pound cauliflower florets
2 teaspoons olive oil
1/2 teaspoon turmeric powder
1/2 teaspoon smoked paprika
Sea salt and ground black pepper

Directions

Toss the cauliflower florets with the remaining ingredients.

Cook the cauliflower florets at 350 degrees F for about 15 minutes, turning them over halfway through the cooking time.

Bon appétit!

Moroccan Carrot Bites

(Ready in about 20 minutes | Servings 3)

Per serving: 125 Calories; 9.3g Fat; 10.5g Carbs; 1.1g Protein; 5.3g Sugars; 3.2g Fiber

Ingredients

3/4 pound carrots, peeled and sliced
2 tablespoons coconut oil
1 tablespoon Moroccan spice mix
Sea salt and ground black pepper, to taste

Directions

Toss the carrots with the remaining ingredients; then, arrange the carrots in the Air Fryer cooking basket.

Cook the carrots at 380 degrees F for 15 minutes, shaking the basket halfway through the cooking time.

Bon appétit!

Moroccan-Style Sweet Potatoes

(Ready in about 40 minutes | Servings 4)

Per serving: 155 Calories; 6.9g Fat; 20.5g Carbs; 2.3g Protein; 0.9g Sugars; 2.2g Fiber

Ingredients

1 pound sweet potatoes, peeled and cut into cubes
2 tablespoons olive oil, melted
Sea salt and ground black pepper, to taste
1 teaspoon granulated garlic
1 teaspoon ginger powder
1/2 teaspoon ground chili powder
1 teaspoon paprika
1/2 teaspoon ground allspice

Directions

Toss the sweet potatoes with the remaining ingredients.

Cook the sweet potatoes at 380 degrees F for 35 minutes, shaking the basket halfway through the cooking time.

Taste and adjust the seasonings. Bon appétit!

Classic Parsnip Fries

(Ready in about 20 minutes | Servings 4)

Per serving: 138 Calories; 5.5g Fat; 21.5g Carbs; 1.6g Protein; 6g Sugars; 5.2g Fiber

Ingredients

1 pound parsnip, trimmed and sliced
2 tablespoons vegan mayonnaise
1/2 teaspoon cayenne pepper
1/2 teaspoon dried oregano
Kosher salt and ground black pepper, to taste

Directions

Toss the parsnip with the remaining ingredients; place them in the Air Fryer cooking basket.

Cook the parsnip slices at 400 degrees F for about 15 minutes, shaking the basket occasionally to ensure even cooking.

Serve warm and enjoy!

Hot Spicy Falafel

(Ready in about 20 minutes | Servings 4)

Per serving: 175 Calories; 8.4g Fat; 19.4g Carbs; 6g Protein; 3.6g Sugars; 5.4g Fiber

Ingredients

1 ½ cups chickpeas, canned or boiled
1 shallot, diced
2 cloves garlic, minced
2 tablespoons olive oil
1/4 cup parsley leaves, chopped
1 teaspoon red chili powder
1/2 teaspoon cumin powder
1/2 teaspoon mustard powder
1 teaspoon cayenne pepper
Sea salt and ground black pepper, to taste

Directions

Pulse all the ingredients in your food processor until everything is well incorporated.
Shape the mixture into balls and place them in a lightly greased Air Fryer cooking basket.
Cook the falafel at 380 degrees F for about 15 minutes, shaking the basket occasionally to ensure even cooking.
Serve in pita bread with toppings of your choice. Enjoy!

Spicy Roasted Cabbage

(Ready in about 10 minutes | Servings 4)

Per serving: 96 Calories; 6.9g Fat; 8.5g Carbs; 1.7g Protein; 4.3g Sugars; 2.4g Fiber

Ingredients

1 pound cabbage, cut into wedges
1 teaspoon garlic, minced
2 tablespoons olive oil
1 teaspoon red pepper flakes
Sea salt and ground black pepper, to taste

Directions

Toss the cabbage wedges with the remaining ingredients.
Cook the cabbage wedges at 350 degrees F for 7 minutes, shaking the basket halfway through the cooking time.
Taste and adjust the seasonings. Bon appétit!

Roasted Beets with Tofu

(Ready in about 35 minutes | Servings 2)

Per serving: 136 Calories; 6.7g Fat; 14.5g Carbs; 5.7g Protein; 9g Sugars; 4.2g Fiber

Ingredients

1/2 pound red beets, peeled and sliced
2 tablespoons mayonnaise
Sea salt and ground black pepper, to taste
1/2 teaspoon cumin powder
1 tablespoon Dijon mustard
2 ounces tofu cheese, crumbled

Directions

Toss the red beets with the mayo, salt, black pepper, cumin powder, and Dijon mustard until well coated on all sides.
Air fry the red beets at 390 degrees F for about 30 minutes, tossing the basket every 10 minutes to ensure even cooking.
Top the roasted beets with tofu cheese and enjoy!

Parsley and Garlic Roasted Peppers

(Ready in about 20 minutes | Servings 2)

Per serving: 220 Calories; 14.3g Fat; 24.5g Carbs; 3.7g Protein; 0.5g Sugars; 3.5g Fiber

Ingredients

4 bell peppers, seeded and halved lengthwise
2 tablespoons olive oil
1 tablespoon fresh parsley, chopped
2 cloves garlic, minced
Sea salt and ground black pepper, to taste

Directions

Toss the peppers with the remaining ingredients; place them in the Air Fryer cooking basket.
Cook the peppers at 400 degrees F for about 15 minutes, shaking the basket halfway through the cooking time.
Taste, adjust the seasonings and serve at room temperature. Bon appétit!

Favorite Homemade Sausage

(Ready in about 20 minutes | Servings 4)

Per serving: 218 Calories; 8.4g Fat; 28.5g Carbs; 8.8g Protein; 2.4g Sugars; 6.5g Fiber

Ingredients

1 cup canned red beans, drained and rinsed
1/2 cup oats
1/4 cup walnuts
1 small onion, peeled and quartered
2 garlic cloves
1 red bell pepper, chopped
2 chia eggs (2 tablespoons ground chia seeds + 4 tablespoons water
1 tablespoon marinara sauce
1/2 teaspoon ground cumin
1/2 teaspoon mustard seeds
1 tablespoon olive oil
Sea salt and ground black pepper, to taste

Directions

Pulse all the ingredients in your food processor until everything is well incorporated.
Shape the mixture into four sausages and place them in a lightly greased Air Fryer basket.
Cook the sausage at 390 degrees F for about 15 minutes, shaking the basket halfway through the cooking time.
Bon appétit!

Asian-Style Sticky Mushrooms

(Ready in about 15 minutes | Servings 3)

Per serving: 140 Calories; 10.4g Fat; 10.5g Carbs; 3.3g Protein; 8.5g Sugars; 1.1g Fiber

Ingredients

10 ounces button mushrooms
2 tablespoons olive oil
1 teaspoon granulated garlic

2 tablespoons rice vinegar
1 tablespoon agave syrup
1 tablespoon soy sauce
Directions
Toss your mushrooms with the remaining ingredients. Arrange them on a lightly greased Air Fryer basket.
Air fry the mushrooms at 375 degrees F for about 10 minutes, shaking the basket halfway through the cooking time.
Enjoy!

Peppery Polenta Bites

(Ready in about 20 minutes | Servings 4)
Per serving: 242 Calories; 10.9g Fat; 32.5g Carbs; 3.1g Protein; 1.2g Sugars; 1.8g Fiber
Ingredients
1 pound prepared polenta
2 tablespoons olive oil
1 bell peppers, seeded and sliced
Directions
Cut the polenta into pieces. Drizzle the olive oil over them and top each piece with the peppers.
Cook the polenta bites at 350 degrees F for about 15 minutes.
Bon appétit!

Herbed Baby Potatoes

(Ready in about 25 minutes | Servings 3)
Per serving: 202 Calories; 9g Fat; 27.5g Carbs; 3.2g Protein; 1.2g Sugars; 3.8g Fiber
Ingredients
1 pound baby potatoes
2 tablespoons olive oil
1 teaspoon dried thyme
1 teaspoon dried rosemary
1 teaspoon dried basil
1 teaspoon dried oregano
1 teaspoon dried parsley flakes
1 teaspoon garlic, minced
Sea salt and ground black pepper, to taste
1 teaspoon cayenne pepper
Directions
Toss the potatoes with the remaining ingredients until well coated on all sides.
Arrange the potatoes in the Air Fryer basket.
Cook the potatoes at 400 degrees F for about 20 minutes, shaking the basket halfway through the cooking time.
Bon appétit!

Mom's Famous Chickpea Burgers

(Ready in about 20 minutes | Servings 4)
Per serving: 295 Calories; 14g Fat; 33.4g Carbs; 10.6g Protein; 6.6g Sugars; 10g Fiber
Ingredients
16 ounces canned chickpeas, drained and rinsed
1/4 cup flaxseeds, ground
2 garlic cloves, minced
1 medium-sized onion, chopped
2 tablespoons fresh lemon juice
2 tablespoons olive oil
1/2 teaspoon ground cumin
1/4 teaspoon ground allspice
Sea salt and ground black pepper, to taste
Directions
Pulse all ingredients in your food processor until everything is well incorporated.
Toss the beets with the remaining ingredients and place them in the Air Fryer cooking basket.
Cook the burgers at 380 degrees F for about 15 minutes, turning them over halfway through the cooking time.
Bon appétit!

Zucchini alla Poverella

(Ready in about 15 minutes | Servings 4)
Per serving: 99 Calories; 7.5g Fat; 6.6g Carbs; 3.4g Protein; 1.8g Sugars; 1.7g Fiber
Ingredients
1 pound zucchini, sliced
1 teaspoon granulated garlic
2 tablespoons olive oil
Sea salt and ground black pepper, to taste
1 teaspoon Italian seasoning
2 tablespoons white balsamic vinegar
Directions
Start by preheating your Air Fryer to 390 degrees F.
Toss the zucchini slices with the remaining ingredients and place them in the Air Fryer cooking basket.
Cook the zucchini slices for about 10 minutes at 390 degrees F, shaking the basket halfway through the cooking time. Work in batches.
Bon appétit!

Sticky Carrot Sticks

(Ready in about 20 minutes | Servings 4)
Per serving: 149 Calories; 7.3g Fat; 21.2g Carbs; 1.4g Protein; 14.2g Sugars; 3.6g Fiber
Ingredients
1 pound carrots, trimmed and cut into sticks
2 tablespoons agave syrup
1/2 teaspoon ground cinnamon
Himalayan salt and cayenne pepper, to taste
2 tablespoons avocado oil
1 teaspoon garlic powder
1 teaspoon dried parsley flakes
Directions
Toss the carrots with the remaining ingredients; then, arrange the carrots in the Air Fryer cooking basket.
Cook the carrots at 380 degrees F for 15 minutes, shaking the basket halfway through the cooking time.
Bon appétit!

Garlic Cauliflower Florets

(Ready in about 20 minutes | Servings 4)
Per serving: 94 Calories; 7.1g Fat; 7g Carbs; 2.4g Protein; 2.2g Sugars; 2.5g Fiber
Ingredients

1 pound cauliflower florets
2 tablespoon olive oil
1 teaspoon garlic, minced
1/2 teaspoon cayenne pepper
Sea salt and ground black pepper, to taste

Directions

Toss the cauliflower florets with the remaining ingredients.
Cook the cauliflower florets at 350 degrees F for about 15 minutes, tossing the basket halfway through the cooking time.
Bon appétit!

Tofu and Corn Stuffed Peppers

(Ready in about 20 minutes | Servings 2)

Per serving: 184 Calories; 5.7g Fat; 25.7g Carbs; 12.4g Protein; 3.9g Sugars; 4.9g Fiber

Ingredients

2 bell peppers, seeded and halved
4 ounces firm tofu, crumbled
4 tablespoons canned sweetcorn
1 tomato, crushed
Sea salt and ground black pepper, to taste
1 teaspoon garlic, minced
1 teaspoon smoked paprika

Directions

Arrange the peppers in the Air Fryer cooking basket.
Mix the remaining ingredients until well combined.
Dived the filling between the peppers.
Cook the peppers at 400 degrees F for about 15 minutes.
Bon appétit!

French Potatoes with Tofu Cheese

(Ready in about 25 minutes | Servings 3)

Per serving: 344 Calories; 18.7g Fat; 40.3g Carbs; 5.7g Protein; 1.3g Sugars; 3.9g Fiber

Ingredients

1 pound French fingerling potatoes, halved lengthwise
2 tablespoons olive oil
2 cloves garlic, pressed
1 tablespoon fresh parsley, chopped
1 tablespoon fresh coriander, chopped
1 tablespoon fresh chives, chopped
Sea salt and ground black pepper, to taste
2 ounces tofu cheese, crumbled

Directions

Toss the potatoes with the remaining ingredients, except for the tofu cheese, until well coated on all sides.
Arrange the potatoes in the Air Fryer basket.
Cook the potatoes at 400 degrees F for about 15 minutes, shaking the basket halfway through the cooking time.
Top with the tofu cheese and continue cooking an additional 5 minutes.
Bon appétit!

Asian-Style Sriracha Tofu

(Ready in about 25 minutes + marinating time | Servings 3)

Per serving: 164 Calories; 12.2g Fat; 3.9g Carbs; 11.7g Protein; 1.6g Sugars; 0.9g Fiber

Ingredients

12 ounces extra-firm tofu, cubed
1 tablespoon soy sauce
1 tablespoon sesame oil
1 teaspoon sriracha
1 teaspoon shallot powder
1 teaspoon garlic, minced

Directions

Toss the tofu with the remaining ingredients. Let it marinate for 30 minutes.
Place the tofu cubes in the Air Fryer cooking basket, discarding the marinade.
Cook the tofu cubes at 360 degrees F for 10 minutes; shake the basket and continue to cook for 12 minutes more. Bon appétit!

Classic Stuffed Mushrooms

(Ready in about 15 minutes | Servings 4)

Per serving: 144 Calories; 11.3g Fat; 8.1g Carbs; 4.4g Protein; 2.3g Sugars; 1.8g Fiber

Ingredients

1/4 cup crackers, crumbled
1 clove garlic, minced
3 tablespoons olive oil
2 tablespoons fresh parsley, chopped
Sea salt and freshly ground black pepper, to taste
1 pound button mushrooms, stemmed

Directions

Toss your mushrooms with the remaining ingredients. Arrange them on a lightly greased Air Fryer basket.
Air fry the mushrooms at 375 degrees F for about 10 minutes, shaking the basket halfway through the cooking time.
Enjoy!

Spicy Crispy Tofu Cubes

(Ready in about 25 minutes | Servings 4)

Per serving: 173 Calories; 9.9g Fat; 12.3g Carbs; 11.6g Protein; 3.4g Sugars; 1.6g Fiber

Ingredients

14 ounces extra-firm tofu, pressed and cubed
2 tablespoons soy sauce
1 tablespoon Dijon mustard
1/4 cup red wine
2 teaspoons sesame oil
1 teaspoon garlic, minced
1 chili pepper, seeded and minced
4 tablespoons corn flour
Sea salt and ground black pepper, to taste

Directions

Toss the tofu with the soy sauce, mustard, red wine, sesame oil, garlic, and chili pepper. Let it marinate for 30 minutes.

Toss the tofu cubes with the corn flour, salt, and black pepper; place them in the Air Fryer cooking basket, discarding the marinade.
Cook the tofu cubes at 360 degrees F for 10 minutes; shake the basket and continue to cook for 12 minutes more. Bon appétit!

Traditional Lebanese Falafel

(Ready in about 20 minutes | Servings 4)
Per serving: 216 Calories; 9.4g Fat; 27.4g Carbs; 7.4g Protein; 5.5g Sugars; 6.7g Fiber
Ingredients
12 ounces canned chickpeas, rinsed and drained
1 bell pepper, seeded and minced
1 small onion, quartered
2 cloves garlic, roughly chopped
1/4 cup fresh parsley, roughly chopped
1/4 cup fresh scallions, chopped
1/2 teaspoon cumin, ground
Kosher salt and ground black pepper, to taste
1 teaspoon paprika
1 teaspoon coriander
2 tablespoons plain flour
2 tablespoons olive oil
Directions
Pulse all ingredients in your food processor until everything is well incorporated.
Shape the mixture into balls and place them in a lightly greased Air Fryer cooking basket.
Cook the falafel at 380 degrees F for about 15 minutes, shaking the basket occasionally to ensure even cooking.
Serve in pita bread with toppings of your choice. Enjoy!

Eggplant alla Milanese

(Ready in about 20 minutes | Servings 2)
Per serving: 407 Calories; 15g Fat; 56g Carbs; 15.5g Protein; 24.3g Sugars; 12g Fiber
Ingredients
2 small eggplants, halved lengthwise
2 tablespoons olive oil
Sea salt and ground black pepper, to taste
1 cup red lentils, canned, drained, and rinsed
1 tomato, crushed
1 tablespoon Italian seasoning mix
1/4 teaspoon grated nutmeg
Directions
Toss the eggplants with the oil; place them in the Air Fryer cooking basket.
Mix the remaining ingredients to make the filling.
Spoon the filling into the eggplant halves.
Cook the stuffed eggplants at 400 degrees F for about 15 minutes.
Bon appétit!

Roasted Sweet Potatoes

(Ready in about 40 minutes | Servings 3)
Per serving: 200 Calories; 9.2g Fat; 26.8g Carbs; 3.5g Protein; 1.3g Sugars; 3.5g Fiber
Ingredients
1 pound sweet potatoes, cubed
2 tablespoons coconut oil
Kosher salt and freshly ground black pepper, to taste
1 teaspoon garlic, minced
1/2 teaspoon ground cumin
2 tablespoons fresh coriander, chopped
2 tablespoons fresh parsley, chopped
2 tablespoons fresh scallions, chopped
Directions
Toss the sweet potatoes with the remaining ingredients.
Cook the sweet potatoes at 380 degrees F for 35 minutes, shaking the basket halfway through the cooking time.
Taste and adjust the seasonings. Bon appétit!

Roasted Chinese Cabbage

(Ready in about 10 minutes | Servings 3)
Per serving: 144 Calories; 11.2g Fat; 9.4g Carbs; 3g Protein; 4.9g Sugars; 2.3g Fiber
Ingredients
1 pound Chinese cabbage, cut into wedges
2 tablespoons olive oil
2 tablespoons soy sauce
1 tablespoon rice vinegar
1 teaspoon stoneground mustard
1 teaspoon granulated garlic
Sea salt and cayenne pepper, to taste
Directions
Toss the cabbage wedges with the remaining ingredients.
Cook the cabbage wedges at 350 degrees F for 7 minutes, shaking the basket halfway through the cooking time.
Taste and adjust the seasonings. Bon appétit!

Mediterranean-Style Parsnip Bites

(Ready in about 20 minutes | Servings 4)
Per serving: 94 Calories; 0.3g Fat; 21.4g Carbs; 1.6g Protein; 6g Sugars; 5.3g Fiber
Ingredients
1 pound parsnip timed and cut into sticks
1 tablespoon Mediterranean herb mix
1 teaspoon garlic, minced
Sea salt and ground black pepper, to taste
Directions
Toss the parsnip with the remaining ingredients; place them in the Air Fryer cooking basket.
Cook the parsnip slices at 400 degrees F for about 15 minutes, shaking the basket occasionally to ensure even cooking.
Serve warm and enjoy!

Balsamic-Glazed Red Beets

(Ready in about 35 minutes | Servings 4)
Per serving: 114 Calories; 2.4g Fat; 21.7g Carbs; 2.2g Protein; 17g Sugars; 3.3g Fiber
Ingredients
1 pound red beets, peeled and diced

2 teaspoons olive oil
Coarse sea salt and ground black pepper, to taste
2 tablespoons agave syrup
2 tablespoons balsamic vinegar

Directions

Toss the red beets with the remaining ingredients until well coated on all sides.
Air fry the red beets at 390 degrees F for about 30 minutes, tossing the basket every 10 minutes to ensure even cooking.
Bon appétit!

Vegan Cheese Stuffed Peppers

(Ready in about 20 minutes | Servings 3)

Per serving: 224 Calories; 16.6g Fat; 12.7g Carbs; 7.2g Protein; 6g Sugars; 2.1g Fiber

Ingredients

6 Italian peppers, seeded and stems removed
2 garlic cloves, minced
1 tablespoon taco seasoning mix
1/2 cup vegan cheddar cheese, grated
Sea salt and red pepper flakes, to taste
2 tablespoons olive oil

Directions

Arrange the peppers in the Air Fryer cooking basket.
Mix the remaining ingredients until well combined.
Dived the filling between the peppers.
Cook the peppers at 400 degrees F for about 15 minutes.
Bon appétit!

Smoked Breakfast Sausage

(Ready in about 20 minutes | Servings 3)

Per serving: 197 Calories; 9.6g Fat; 22.5g Carbs; 7g Protein; 1.9g Sugars; 4.9g Fiber

Ingredients

1 cup canned white beans, drained and rinsed
1 medium onion, chopped
2 cloves garlic, chopped
2 tablespoons olive oil
1 teaspoon liquid smoke
2 tablespoons buckwheat flour

Directions

Pulse all the ingredients in your food processor until everything is well incorporated.
Shape the mixture into three sausages and place them in a lightly greased Air Fryer basket.
Cook the sausage at 390 degrees F for about 15 minutes, shaking the basket halfway through the cooking time.
Bon appétit!

Classic Fried Mushrooms

(Ready in about 15 minutes | Servings 3)

Per serving: 217 Calories; 11.6g Fat; 24.3g Carbs; 6.7g Protein; 2.8g Sugars; 4.4g Fiber

Ingredients

10 ounces mushrooms
1/2 cup plain flour
1/2 tortilla chips, crushed
2 chia eggs (2 tablespoons ground chia seeds + 4 tablespoons water)
Sea salt and ground black pepper, to taste
1 teaspoon smoked paprika
1 teaspoon garlic powder
2 tablespoons olive oil

Directions

Toss your mushrooms with the remaining ingredients. Arrange them on a lightly greased Air Fryer basket.
Air fry the mushrooms at 375 degrees F for about 10 minutes, shaking the basket halfway through the cooking time.
Enjoy!

Fried Marinara Polenta

(Ready in about 15 minutes | Servings 2)

Per serving: 238 Calories; 14.1g Fat; 25.3g Carbs; 2.7g Protein; 1.8g Sugars; 2.1g Fiber

Ingredients

1/2 pound polenta
2 tablespoons olive oil, as needed
1 teaspoon dried basil
1 teaspoon dried oregano
1/4 cup marinara sauce

Directions

Cut the polenta into pieces. Toss each piece with the olive oil, basil, oregano, and marinara sauce.
Cook the polenta bites at 350 degrees F for about 15 minutes, turning them over halfway through the cooking time.
Enjoy!

Zucchini Boats with Mushrooms and Chickpeas

(Ready in about 15 minutes | Servings 2)

Per serving: 261 Calories; 14.6g Fat; 31.7g Carbs; 5.8g Protein; 3.6g Sugars; 5.9g Fiber

Ingredients

2 medium zucchinis, halved
2 tablespoons olive oil
1 teaspoon garlic, minced
1 shallot, minced
2 tablespoons marinara sauce
2 ounces canned chickpeas, drained and rinsed
2 ounces button mushrooms, chopped
Sea salt and ground black pepper, to taste

Directions

Arrange the zucchini halves in the Air Fryer cooking basket.
Mix the remaining ingredients until well combined.
Dived the filling between the zucchini halves.
Cook the zucchini halves at 390 degrees F for about 13 minutes.
Bon appétit!

Crispy Chickpea Meatballs

(Ready in about 20 minutes | Servings 4)

Per serving: 215 Calories; 7.4g Fat; 29g Carbs; 9.7g Protein; 4.8g Sugars; 8.3g Fiber

Ingredients
16 ounces canned chickpeas, rinsed and drained
1 shallot, chopped
4 cloves garlic, roughly chopped
1/4 cup fresh parsley, roughly chopped
1/4 cup fresh coriander, roughly chopped
1/2 teaspoon stone-ground mustard
1/2 teaspoon cumin, ground
2 tablespoons tahini
Kosher salt and ground black pepper, to taste
Directions
Pulse all ingredients in your food processor until everything is well incorporated.
Form the mixture into balls and place them in a lightly greased Air Fryer cooking basket.
Air fry the meatballs at 380 degrees F for about 15 minutes, shaking the basket occasionally to ensure even cooking.
Serve in pita bread with toppings of your choice.
Enjoy!

Classic Stuffed Eggplant

(Ready in about 20 minutes | Servings 2)
Per serving: 235 Calories; 8g Fat; 40g Carbs; 7.2g Protein; 23.8g Sugars; 18g Fiber
Ingredients
2 small eggplants, halved lengthwise
1 tablespoon olive oil
1 small shallot, chopped
2 garlic cloves, minced
1 bell pepper, chopped
1 medium tomato, chopped
2 tablespoons fresh parsley, minced
1 tablespoon fresh basil, minced
Sea salt and ground black pepper, to taste
Directions
Toss the eggplants with the oil; place them in the Air Fryer cooking basket.
Mix the remaining ingredients to make the filling. Spoon the filling into the eggplant halves.
Cook the stuffed eggplants at 400 degrees F for about 15 minutes.
Serve warm and enjoy!

Hot Spicy Potato Wedges

(Ready in about 25 minutes | Servings 4)
Per serving: 147 Calories; 6.8g Fat; 19.8g Carbs; 2.2g Protein; 0.8g Sugars; 2.5g Fiber
Ingredients
1 pound potatoes, peeled and cut into wedges
2 tablespoons olive oil
1 teaspoon red chili powder
1 teaspoon garlic powder
Kosher salt and ground black pepper, to taste
Directions
Toss the potatoes with the remaining ingredients until well coated on all sides. Arrange the potatoes in the Air Fryer basket.
Cook the potatoes at 400 degrees F for about 20 minutes, shaking the basket halfway through the cooking time.
Bon appétit!

Asian-Style Broccoli

(Ready in about 10 minutes | Servings 4)
Per serving: 88 Calories; 7g Fat; 5.7g Carbs; 2.6g Protein; 1.7g Sugars; 1.9g Fiber
Ingredients
1/2 pound broccoli florets
2 tablespoons sesame oil
2 scallions, chopped
1 teaspoon Five-spice powder
Sea salt and ground black pepper, to taste
Directions
Toss the broccoli florets with the remaining ingredients until well coated.
Arrange the broccoli florets in the Air Fryer basket.
Cook the broccoli florets at 395 degrees F for 6 minutes, shaking the basket halfway through the cooking time.
Bon appétit!

Moroccan-Style Cauliflower Bites

(Ready in about 20 minutes | Servings 4)
Per serving: 121 Calories; 7.4g Fat; 12.7g Carbs; 3g Protein; 2.7g Sugars; 3.1g Fiber
Ingredients
1 pound cauliflower florets
Sea salt and ground black pepper, to taste
1 teaspoon ground ginger
1/4 teaspoon ground cloves
1/2 teaspoon ground cumin
1/2 teaspoon coriander
1/2 cayenne pepper
2 tablespoons olive oil
4 tablespoons cornflour
Directions
Toss the cauliflower florets with the remaining ingredients.
Cook the cauliflower florets at 350 degrees F for about 15 minutes, turning them over halfway through the cooking time.
Bon appétit!

Lemon Garlicky Cabbage

(Ready in about 10 minutes | Servings 4)
Per serving: 99 Calories; 7g Fat; 7.4g Carbs; 1.6g Protein; 3.8g Sugars; 3g Fiber
Ingredients
1 pound cabbage, cut into wedges
2 tablespoons olive oil
1 teaspoon garlic, minced
Kosher salt and freshly ground black pepper, to taste
1/4 teaspoon cumin powder
1/2 teaspoon bay leaf, crushed
2 tablespoons fresh lemon juice
1 teaspoon red pepper flakes, crushed
Directions

Toss the cabbage wedges with the remaining ingredients.
Cook the cabbage wedges at 350 degrees F for 7 minutes, shaking the basket halfway through the cooking time.
Taste and adjust the seasonings. Bon appétit!

Panko Chickpea Patties

(Ready in about 20 minutes | Servings 4)
Per serving: 305 Calories; 10.2g Fat; 42.9g Carbs; 11.7g Protein; 7.8g Sugars; 9.3g Fiber
Ingredients
14 ounces chickpeas, canned and drained
1/2 large onion chopped
1 small onion, chopped
2 garlic cloves, minced
1 teaspoon ginger, grated
1/4 cup fresh scallions, chopped
1/4 cup fresh parsley, chopped
2 tablespoons olive oil
1 teaspoon ground cumin
Sea salt and ground black pepper, to taste
1/2 cup panko crumbs
1/2 teaspoon baking powder
Directions
Pulse all the ingredients in your food processor until everything is well incorporated.
Form the mixture into patties and place them in a lightly greased Air Fryer cooking basket.
Air fry the patties at 380 degrees F for about 15 minutes, shaking the basket occasionally to ensure even cooking.
Serve with toppings of choice. Enjoy!

Rosemary Orange Beets

(Ready in about 35 minutes | Servings 3)
Per serving: 185 Calories; 10.1g Fat; 20.9g Carbs; 3.4g Protein; 14g Sugars; 4.3g Fiber
Ingredients
1 pound beets, peeled and diced
2 tablespoons olive oil
Sea salt and ground black pepper, to taste
1 tablespoon stone-ground mustard
2 tablespoons balsamic vinegar
1/4 cup fresh orange juice
1 tablespoon fresh rosemary, chopped
Directions
Toss the red beets with the remaining ingredients until well coated on all sides.
Air fry the red beets at 390 degrees F for about 30 minutes, tossing the basket every 10 minutes to ensure even cooking.
Bon appétit!

Balsamic Peppers with Tofu

(Ready in about 20 minutes | Servings 3)
Per serving: 135 Calories; 10.5g Fat; 8g Carbs; 3.4g Protein; 4.9g Sugars; 1.3g Fiber
Ingredients
1 red bell pepper, seeded and halved
1 green bell pepper, seeded and halved
1 orange bell pepper, seeded and halved
2 tablespoons olive oil
2 tablespoons balsamic vinegar
Sea salt and red pepper flakes, to taste
3 ounces tofu cheese, crumbled
Directions
Toss the peppers with the olive oil, vinegar, salt, and red pepper; place them in the Air Fryer cooking basket.
Cook the peppers at 400 degrees F for about 15 minutes, shaking the basket halfway through the cooking time.
Serve the roasted peppers with tofu cheese. Bon appétit!

Greek-Style Stuffed Zucchini

(Ready in about 15 minutes | Servings 2)
Per serving: 148 Calories; 13.5g Fat; 6.4g Carbs; 1.5g Protein; 2.9g Sugars; 1.3g Fiber
Ingredients
2 medium zucchinis, halved
2 tablespoons olive oil
1 shallot, chopped
2 garlic cloves, minced
1 small tomato, chopped
1 teaspoon hot sauce
1 teaspoon tamari sauce
Sea salt and ground black pepper, to taste
Directions
Place the zucchini halves in a lightly oiled Air Fryer cooking basket.
Mix the remaining ingredients to make the filling; stuff the zucchini halves with the prepared filling.
Cook the zucchini at 390 degrees F for 10 minutes or until cooked through.
Bon appétit!

Old-Fashioned Smoked Sausage

(Ready in about 50 minutes | Servings 4)
Per serving: 211 Calories; 7.5g Fat; 12.5g Carbs; 25.5g Protein; 4.4g Sugars; 1.7g Fiber
Ingredients
1 onion, chopped
2 cloves garlic, minced
2 tablespoons olive oil
1/4 cup tomato paste
2 tablespoons sun-dried tomatoes, chopped
Kosher salt and ground black pepper, to taste
1/2 teaspoon liquid smoke
1 cup vital wheat gluten
Directions
Pulse all the ingredients in your food processor until everything is well incorporated.
Shape the mixture into three sausages and roll them in a piece of aluminum foil; twist the ends closed.
Then, steam the sausages for about 40 minutes.
Air fry the sausage at 390 degrees F for about 15 minutes, shaking the basket halfway through the cooking time.

Bon appétit!

Panko Garlic Baby Bellas

(Ready in about 15 minutes | Servings 4)

Per serving: 151 Calories; 7.9g Fat; 16g Carbs; 5.8g Protein; 3.7g Sugars; 2g Fiber

Ingredients

1 pound baby bella mushrooms, cleaned
4 garlic cloves, peeled and minced
1/2 panko crumbs
2 tablespoons sesame oil
Sea salt and ground black pepper, to taste
1/2 teaspoon onion powder
1/2 teaspoon smoked paprika

Directions

Toss your mushrooms with the remaining ingredients. Arrange them on a lightly greased Air Fryer basket.
Air fry the mushrooms at 375 degrees F for about 10 minutes, shaking the basket halfway through the cooking time.
Enjoy!

Traditional Masala Aloo

(Ready in about 25 minutes | Servings 4)

Per serving: 151 Calories; 6.9g Fat; 20.6g Carbs; 2.5g Protein; 1.4g Sugars; 2.7g Fiber

Ingredients

1 pound fingerling potatoes
2 tablespoons olive oil
1 teaspoon garam masala
Sea salt and ground black pepper, to taste

Directions

Toss the potatoes with the remaining ingredients until well coated on all sides.
Arrange the potatoes in the Air Fryer basket.
Cook the potatoes at 400 degrees F for about 20 minutes, shaking the basket halfway through the cooking time.
Bon appétit!

Classic Fried Tempeh

(Ready in about 25 minutes | Servings 3)

Per serving: 214 Calories; 12.2g Fat; 11.6g Carbs; 18g Protein; 2.2g Sugars; 0.7g Fiber

Ingredients

10 ounces tempeh
2 tablespoons soy sauce
1 tablespoon rice vinegar
1 teaspoon cayenne pepper
Sea salt and ground black pepper, to taste

Directions

Toss the tempeh with the remaining ingredients. Let it marinate for 30 minutes.
Place the tempeh in the Air Fryer cooking basket, discarding the marinade.
Cook the tempeh at 360 degrees F for 10 minutes; turning it over and continue to cook for 12 minutes more. Bon appétit!

Moroccan-Style Chickpea Meatballs

(Ready in about 20 minutes | Servings 4)

Per serving: 246 Calories; 10g Fat; 32.2g Carbs; 9g Protein; 7.2g Sugars; 8.8g Fiber

Ingredients

16 ounces canned chickpeas, rinsed and drained
1 medium onion, chopped
3 cloves garlic, roughly chopped
1 large carrot, peeled and roughly chopped
1/4 cup fresh parsley, roughly chopped
1/4 cup fresh coriander, roughly chopped
1/2 teaspoon ginger, peeled and grated
1/2 teaspoon cinnamon, ground
2 tablespoons olive oil
Sea salt and ground black pepper, to taste

Directions

Pulse all the ingredients in your food processor until everything is well incorporated.
Form the mixture into balls and place them in a lightly greased Air Fryer cooking basket.
Air fry the meatballs at 380 degrees F for about 15 minutes, shaking the basket occasionally to ensure even cooking.
Serve in pita bread with toppings of your choice.
Enjoy!

Fried Green Beans

(Ready in about 10 minutes | Servings 3)

Per serving: 174 Calories; 13.1g Fat; 12.2g Carbs; 4.9g Protein; 4.8g Sugars; 4g Fiber

Ingredients

3/4 pound green beans, trimmed and halved
1/2 cup vegan mayonnaise
1 teaspoon granulated garlic
1 teaspoon paprika
Kosher salt and ground black pepper, to taste

Directions

Toss the green beans with the remaining ingredients until well coated on all sides.
Air fry the green beans at 390 degrees F for about 6 minutes, tossing the basket halfway through the cooking time.
Enjoy!

Greek-Style Vegan Burgers

(Ready in about 20 minutes | Servings 4)

Per serving: 169 Calories; 4.1g Fat; 26.8g Carbs; 8.2g Protein; 4.9g Sugars; 8.2g Fiber

Ingredients

1 tablespoon ground chia seeds
14 ounces canned chickpeas, rinsed and drained
1/4 cup fresh coriander
1/4 cup fresh scallions
1 tablespoon rosemary
1 tablespoon thyme
1 tablespoon basil
2 garlic cloves, peeled
1/2 teaspoon ground cumin
Sea salt and ground black pepper, to taste
2 tablespoons fresh lemon juice

Directions

To make a flax egg, soak the ground flaxseeds in 2 tablespoons of water for 15 minutes.

In your blender or food processor, mix all the ingredients, including the flax egg, until everything is well incorporated.

Form the mixture into patties and place them in a lightly greased Air Fryer cooking basket.

Air fry the patties at 380 degrees F for about 15 minutes, turning them over halfway through the cooking time.

Bon appétit!

Golden Parsnip Sticks

(Ready in about 20 minutes | Servings 4)

Per serving: 169 Calories; 4.1g Fat; 26.8g Carbs; 8.2g Protein; 4.9g Sugars; 8.2g Fiber

Ingredients

1 pound parsnip, trimmed and cut into sticks
2 tablespoons olive oil
1 teaspoon garlic, minced
1 teaspoon turmeric powder
1 tablespoon Dijon mustard
Sea salt and ground black pepper, to taste

Directions

Toss the parsnip with the remaining ingredients; place them in the Air Fryer cooking basket.

Cook the parsnip sticks at 400 degrees F for about 15 minutes, shaking the basket occasionally to ensure even cooking.

Serve warm and enjoy!

Broccoli Vegan Tempura

(Ready in about 10 minutes | Servings 4)

Per serving: 232 Calories; 7.6g Fat; 33.8g Carbs; 6.9g Protein; 2.6g Sugars; 4.3g Fiber

Ingredients

1 cup all-purpose flour
1/2 cup beer
2 tablespoons sesame oil
1/2 teaspoon cayenne pepper
1 teaspoon chili powder
Sea salt and ground black pepper, to taste
1 pound broccoli florets

Directions

In a mixing bowl, thoroughly combine the flour, beer, oil, and spices.

Dip the broccoli florets in the tempura mixture and place them in a lightly oiled Air Fryer cooking basket.

Cook the broccoli florets at 395 degrees F for 6 minutes, shaking the basket halfway through the cooking time.

Bon appétit!

Classic Chickpea Burgers

(Ready in about 20 minutes | Servings 4)

Per serving: 281 Calories; 9.8g Fat; 38.2g Carbs; 11.1g Protein; 7.2g Sugars; 9g Fiber

Ingredients

16 ounces chickpeas, boiled and drained
2 tablespoons all-purpose flour
1/2 teaspoon baking soda
1/4 cup fresh parsley leaves, stems removed
1/4 cup fresh cilantro leaves, stems removed
1 teaspoon green chili paste
1 onion, quartered
4 garlic cloves, peeled
Sea salt and ground black pepper, to taste
2 tablespoons olive oil

Directions

Pulse all the ingredients in your food processor until everything is well incorporated.

Form the mixture into burgers and place them in a lightly greased Air Fryer cooking basket.

Cook the burgers at 380 degrees F for about 15 minutes, turning them occasionally to ensure even cooking.

Serve with burger buns and enjoy!

DESSERTS

Brownies with a Twist

(Ready in about 25 minutes | Servings 6)

Per serving: 325 Calories; 21.8g Fat; 30.8g Carbs; 4.2g Protein; 16.2g Sugars; 1.5g Fiber

Ingredients

1 stick butter, melted
1 cup brown sugar
2 eggs
3/4 cup all-purpose flour
1/2 teaspoon baking powder
1/4 cup cocoa powder
2 tablespoons coconut oil
1 teaspoon coconut extract
A pinch of sea salt

Directions

Start by preheating your Air Fryer to 340 degrees F. Now, spritz the sides and bottom of a baking pan with a nonstick cooking spray.
In a mixing bowl, beat the melted butter and sugar until fluffy. Next, fold in the eggs and beat again until well combined.
After that, add in the remaining ingredients. Mix until everything is well incorporated.
Bake in the preheated Air Fryer for 20 minutes. Enjoy!

Vanilla Pancake Cups

(Ready in about 25 minutes | Servings 4)

Per serving: 135 Calories; 6.3g Fat; 13.6g Carbs; 5.1g Protein; 1.2g Sugars; 0.7g Fiber

Ingredients

1/2 cup flour
2 eggs
1/3 cup coconut milk
1 tablespoon coconut oil, melted
1 teaspoon vanilla paste
1/4 teaspoon ground cinnamon
A pinch of ground cardamom

Directions

Mix all the ingredients until well combined.
Let the batter stand for 20 minutes. Spoon the batter into a greased muffin tin.
Cook at 330 degrees F for 4 to 5 minutes or until golden brown. Serve with toppings of choice.
Bon appétit!

Old-Fashioned Baked Apples

(Ready in about 20 minutes | Servings 2)

Per serving: 295 Calories; 22.2g Fat; 27.8g Carbs; 1.9g Protein; 19.2g Sugars; 6.1g Fiber

Ingredients

2 medium apples
4 tablespoons pecans, chopped
4 tablespoons Sultanas
2 tablespoons butter, at room temperature
1/2 teaspoon cinnamon
1/4 teaspoon grated nutmeg

Directions

Cut the apples in halves and spoon out some of the flesh.
In a mixing bowl, thoroughly combine the remaining ingredients. Stuff the apple halves and transfer them to the Air Fryer cooking basket.
Pour 1/4 cup of water into an Air Fryer safe dish. Place the apples in the dish.
Bake the apples at 340 degrees F for 17 minutes. Serve at room temperature. Bon appétit!

Favorite Raisin Scones

(Ready in about 20 minutes | Servings 5)

Per serving: 245 Calories; 1.2g Fat; 29.6g Carbs; 4.4g Protein; 10.2g Sugars; 0.7g Fiber

Ingredients

1 cup all-purpose flour
1/2 teaspoon baking powder
1/2 cup granulated sugar
2 tablespoons raisins
A pinch of coarse sea salt
A pinch of grated nutmeg
1 teaspoon lemon zest
1 teaspoon vanilla extract
1/4 cup butter, cold
2 eggs, whisked

Directions

Start by preheating your Air Fryer to 360 degrees F.
Mix all the ingredients until everything is well incorporated. Spoon the batter into baking cups; lower the cups into the Air Fryer basket.
Bake your scones for about 17 minutes or until a tester comes out dry and clean.
Bon appétit!

Traditional Danish Pastry

(Ready in about 25 minutes | Servings 5)

Per serving: 470 Calories; 26g Fat; 53.9g Carbs; 5.4g Protein; 20.2g Sugars; 2.4g Fiber

Ingredients

12 ounces refrigerated puff pastry
1 cup apple pie filling

Directions

Roll out the puff pastry sheet into a large rectangle; cut the pastry sheet into triangles.
Spoon the filling into each triangle; fold the pastry over and seal the edges with your fingers.
Bake the Danish pastry at 350 degrees F for 20 minutes or until the top is golden brown. Bon appétit!

Authentic Indian Gulgulas

(Ready in about 20 minutes | Servings 4)

Per serving: 194 Calories; 2.6g Fat; 37.7g Carbs; 4.6g Protein; 25.2g Sugars; 0.5g Fiber

Ingredients

1/2 cup all-purpose flour
1/2 teaspoon baking powder

1/2 cup sugar
1/4 teaspoon ground cardamom
1/4 teaspoon sea salt
1 tablespoon ghee
2 eggs, whisked
2 tablespoons Indian yogurt

Directions

In a mixing bowl, thoroughly combine all the ingredients.

Drop a spoonful of batter onto the greased Air Fryer pan. Cook in the preheated Air Fryer at 360 degrees F for 10 minutes, flipping them halfway through the cooking time.

Repeat with the remaining batter and serve warm. Enjoy!

Dessert Vanilla French Toast

(Ready in about 10 minutes | Servings 3)

Per serving: 164 Calories; 10.4g Fat; 11.7g Carbs; 4.6g Protein; 2.2g Sugars; 0.8g Fiber

Ingredients

1 egg, whisked
1/4 cup coconut milk
2 tablespoons butter, melted
1 teaspoon vanilla paste
1/2 teaspoon ground cinnamon
A pinch of grated nutmeg
3 slices bread

Directions

In a mixing bowl, thoroughly combine the eggs, milk, butter, vanilla, cinnamon, and nutmeg.

Then dip each piece of bread into the egg mixture; place the bread slices in a lightly greased baking pan.

Air Fryer the bread slices at 330 degrees F for about 4 minutes; turn them over and cook for a further 3 to 4 minutes. Enjoy!

Street-Style Spanish Churros

(Ready in about 20 minutes | Servings 4)

Per serving: 214 Calories; 12.4g Fat; 20.1g Carbs; 4.4g Protein; 2.1g Sugars; 0.6g Fiber

Ingredients

3/4 cup all-purpose flour
1/2 teaspoon baking powder
3/4 cup water
4 tablespoons butter
1 tablespoon granulated sugar
1/2 teaspoon vanilla extract
1/2 teaspoon sea salt
1 large egg

Directions

In a mixing bowl, thoroughly combine all ingredients.

Place the batter in a piping bag fitted with a large open star tip.

Pipe the churros into 6-inch long ropes and lower them onto the greased Air Fryer pan.

Cook your churros in the preheated Air Fryer at 360 degrees F for 10 minutes, flipping them halfway through the cooking time.

Repeat with the remaining batter and serve warm. Enjoy!

Vanilla-Cinnamon Pears in Wine

(Ready in about 20 minutes | Servings 3)

Per serving: 185 Calories; 0.2g Fat; 47.1g Carbs; 1g Protein; 42.2g Sugars; 4.4g Fiber

Ingredients

3 pears, peeled and cored
1 vanilla pod
1 cinnamon stick
2-3 cloves
1 cup caster sugar
1 cup red wine

Directions

Place the pears, vanilla, cinnamon, cloves, sugar, and wine in an Air Fryer safe dish.

Cook the pears at 340 degrees F for 17 minutes.

Serve at room temperature. Bon appétit!

Coconut Chocolate Cake

(Ready in about 25 minutes | Servings 6)

Per serving: 279 Calories; 20.8g Fat; 25.8g Carbs; 2.9g Protein; 16.9g Sugars; 2.5g Fiber

Ingredients

1/2 cup coconut oil, room temperature
1 cup brown sugar
2 chia eggs (2 tablespoons ground chia seeds + 4 tablespoons water)
1/4 cup all-purpose flour
1/4 cup coconut flour
1/2 cup cocoa powder
1/2 cup dark chocolate chips
A pinch of grated nutmeg
A pinch of sea salt
2 tablespoons coconut milk

Directions

Start by preheating your Air Fryer to 340 degrees F.

Now, spritz the sides and bottom of a baking pan with a nonstick cooking spray.

In a mixing bowl, beat the coconut oil and brown sugar until fluffy. Next, fold in the chia eggs and beat again until well combined.

After that, add in the remaining ingredients. Mix until everything is well incorporated.

Bake in the preheated Air Fryer for 20 minutes. Enjoy!

Easy Apple Pie

(Ready in about 40 minutes | Servings 4)

Per serving: 450 Calories; 21.8g Fat; 61.6g Carbs; 2.7g Protein; 14.9g Sugars; 3.7g Fiber

Ingredients

12 ounces refrigerated 2 pie crusts
3 cups apples, peeled and thinly sliced
1/4 cup brown sugar
1 tablespoon lemon juice
1 teaspoon pure vanilla extract
1/2 teaspoon cinnamon
A pinch of ground cardamom
A pinch of kosher salt

Directions
Place the first pie crust in a lightly greased pie plate.
In a mixing bowl, thoroughly combine the remaining ingredients to make the filling. Spoon the filling into the prepared pie crust.
Unroll the second pie crust and place it on top of the filling.
Bake the apple pie at 350 degrees F for 35 minutes or until the top is golden brown. Bon appétit!

Classic Homemade Beignets

(Ready in about 20 minutes | Servings 4)
Per serving: 250 Calories; 12.8g Fat; 25.6g Carbs; 7.7g Protein; 7g Sugars; 0.7g Fiber
Ingredients
3/4 cup all-purpose flour
1 teaspoon baking powder
1/4 teaspoon kosher salt
1/4 cup yogurt
2 eggs, beaten
1/4 cup granulated sugar
2 tablespoons coconut oil, melted
Directions
In a mixing bowl, thoroughly combine all the ingredients.
Drop a spoonful of batter onto the greased Air Fryer pan. Cook in the preheated Air Fryer at 360 degrees F for 10 minutes, flipping them halfway through the cooking time.
Repeat with the remaining batter and serve warm. Enjoy!

Classic Chocolate Cupcakes

(Ready in about 20 minutes | Servings 6)
Per serving: 337 Calories; 18g Fat; 40.6g Carbs; 5.5g Protein; 26.2g Sugars; 1.7g Fiber
Ingredients
3/4 cup all-purpose flour
1 teaspoon baking powder
1/4 teaspoon ground cinnamon
1/4 teaspoon ground cardamom
3/4 cup granulated sugar
1/4 cups unsweetened cocoa powder
A pinch of sea salt
1 stick butter, at room temperature
3/4 cup milk
2 eggs, beaten
Directions
Start by preheating your Air Fryer to 330 degrees F.
Mix all the ingredients in a bowl. Scrape the batter into silicone baking molds; place them in the Air Fryer basket.
Bake your cupcakes for about 15 minutes or until a tester comes out dry and clean.
Allow the cupcakes to cool before unmolding and serving. Bon appétit!

Southern-Style Peaches

(Ready in about 20 minutes | Servings 3)
Per serving: 280 Calories; 18.8g Fat; 31.8g Carbs; 1.4g Protein; 26.9g Sugars; 2.6g Fiber
Ingredients
3 peaches, halved
1 tablespoon fresh lime juice
1/2 teaspoon ground cinnamon
1/2 teaspoon grated nutmeg
1/2 cup brown sugar
4 tablespoons coconut oil
Directions
Toss the peaches with the remaining ingredients.
Pour 1/4 cup of water into an Air Fryer safe dish.
Place the peaches in the dish.
Bake the peaches at 340 degrees F for 15 minutes.
Serve at room temperature. Bon appétit!

Favorite Fudge Cake

(Ready in about 25 minutes | Servings 5)
Per serving: 431 Calories; 23.8g Fat; 49.5g Carbs; 6.6g Protein; 34.1g Sugars; 1.8g Fiber
Ingredients
1/2 cup butter, melted
1 cup turbinado sugar
3 eggs
1 teaspoon vanilla extract
1/4 teaspoon salt
1/4 teaspoon ground cloves
1/2 teaspoon ground cinnamon
1/2 cup all-purpose flour
1/4 cup almond flour
5 ounces chocolate chips
Directions
Start by preheating your Air Fryer to 340 degrees F.
Now, spritz the sides and bottom of a baking pan with a nonstick cooking spray.
In a mixing bowl, beat the butter and sugar until fluffy. Next, fold in the eggs and beat again until well combined.
After that, add in the remaining ingredients. Mix until everything is well combined.
Bake in the preheated Air Fryer for 20 minutes. Enjoy!

Cinnamon Apple Wedges

(Ready in about 20 minutes | Servings 2)
Per serving: 174 Calories; 4.8g Fat; 34.5g Carbs; 0.6g Protein; 27.1g Sugars; 5.1g Fiber
Ingredients
2 apples, peeled, cored, and cut into wedges
2 teaspoons coconut oil
2 tablespoons brown sugar
1 teaspoon pure vanilla extract
1 teaspoon ground cinnamon
1/4 cup water
Directions
Toss the apples with the coconut oil, sugar, vanilla, and cinnamon.
Pour 1/4 cup of water into an Air Fryer safe dish.
Place the apples in the dish.
Bake the apples at 340 degrees F for 17 minutes.
Serve at room temperature. Bon appétit!

Old-Fashioned Pumpkin Cake

(Ready in about 20 minutes | Servings 2)

Per serving: 269 Calories; 15.8g Fat; 20.5g Carbs; 10.6g Protein; 14.1g Sugars; 2.5g Fiber

Ingredients

1/3 cup pumpkin puree
1/2 cup peanut butter
2 eggs, beaten
1 teaspoon vanilla extract
1/2 teaspoon pumpkin pie spice
1/2 teaspoon baking powder

Directions

Mix all the ingredients to make the batter. Pour the batter into a lightly oiled baking pan.
Place the pan in the Air Fryer cooking basket.
Bake your cake at 350 degrees F for about 13 minutes or until it is golden brown around the edges.
Bon appétit!

Fluffy Scones with Cranberries

(Ready in about 20 minutes | Servings 4)

Per serving: 326 Calories; 14.8g Fat; 42.5g Carbs; 6g Protein; 16.1g Sugars; 1.7g Fiber

Ingredients

1 cup all-purpose flour
1 teaspoon baking powder
1/4 cup caster sugar
A pinch of sea salt
1/4 teaspoon ground cinnamon
4 tablespoons butter
1 egg, beaten
1/4 cup milk
2 ounces dried cranberries

Directions

Start by preheating your Air Fryer to 360 degrees F.
Mix all the ingredients until everything is well incorporated. Spoon the batter into baking cups; lower the cups into the Air Fryer basket.
Bake your scones for about 17 minutes or until a tester comes out dry and clean.
Bon appétit!

Grilled Plantain Boats

(Ready in about 10 minutes | Servings 2)

Per serving: 354 Calories; 7.6g Fat; 74.5g Carbs; 2.8g Protein; 44.1g Sugars; 5.3g Fiber

Ingredients

2 plantains, peeled
1/2 cup coconut, shredded
1 tablespoon coconut oil
4 tablespoons brown sugar
1/2 teaspoon cinnamon powder
1/2 teaspoon cardamom powder
4 tablespoons raisins

Directions

In the peel, slice your plantains lengthwise; make sure not to slice all the way through the plantains.
Divide the remaining ingredients between the plantain pockets.
Place the plantain boats in the Air Fryer grill pan.
Cook at 395 degrees F for 7 minutes.
Eat with a spoon and enjoy!

Almond Chocolate Cake

(Ready in about 25 minutes | Servings 6)

Per serving: 344 Calories; 22.8g Fat; 32.5g Carbs; 6g Protein; 21g Sugars; 3.1g Fiber

Ingredients

1 stick butter, melted
1/2 cups brown sugar
2 eggs, at room temperature
5 ounces chocolate chips
1/2 teaspoon pure vanilla extract
1/2 teaspoon pure almond extract
1/4 cup cocoa powder (Note 3)1/4 cup cocoa powder (Note 3)
1/4 cup all-purpose flour
1/2 cup almond flour
1/2 teaspoon baking powder
2 ounces almonds, slivered
4 tablespoons coconut milk

Directions

Start by preheating your Air Fryer to 340 degrees F. Then, brush the sides and bottom of a baking pan with a nonstick cooking spray.
In a mixing bowl, beat the butter and sugar until fluffy. Next, fold in the eggs and beat again until well combined.
After that, add in the remaining ingredients. Mix until everything is well combined.
Bake in the preheated Air Fryer for 20 minutes. Enjoy!

Classic Fried Plums

(Ready in about 20 minutes | Servings 4)

Per serving: 144 Calories; 7.2g Fat; 20.9g Carbs; 0.7g Protein; 19g Sugars; 1.6g Fiber

Ingredients

1 pound plums, halved and pitted
2 tablespoons coconut oil
4 tablespoons brown sugar
4 whole cloves
1 cinnamon stick
4 whole star anise

Directions

Toss the plums with the remaining ingredients.
Pour 1/4 cup of water into an Air Fryer safe dish.
Place the plums in the dish.
Bake the plums at 340 degrees F for 17 minutes.
Serve at room temperature. Bon appétit!

German Giant Pancake

(Ready in about 20 minutes | Servings 3)

Per serving: 174 Calories; 10.8g Fat; 16.1g Carbs; 3.5g Protein; 6g Sugars; 1.9g Fiber

Ingredients

1 small apple, peeled, cored, and sliced
1 tablespoon coconut oil, melted
1 egg, whisked
1/4 cup plain flour

1/4 teaspoon baking powder
1/4 cup full-fat coconut milk
A pinch of granulated sugar
A pinch of kosher salt
1/2 teaspoon vanilla paste

Directions

Drizzle the apple slices with the melted coconut oil; arrange the apple slices in a baking pan.
Mix the remaining ingredients to make the batter. Pour the batter over the apples. Transfer the baking pan to the Air Fryer cooking basket.
Bake your pancake at 350 degrees F for about 13 minutes or until it is golden brown around the edges.
Bon appétit!

Classic Cinnamon Donuts

(Ready in about 20 minutes | Servings 4)

Per serving: 374 Calories; 16.2g Fat; 52.1g Carbs; 5.5g Protein; 9g Sugars; 1.5g Fiber

Ingredients

12 ounces flaky large biscuits
1/4 cup granulated sugar
1 teaspoon ground cinnamon
1/4 teaspoon grated nutmeg
2 tablespoons coconut oil

Directions

Separate the dough into biscuits and place them in a lightly oiled Air Fryer cooking basket.
Mix the sugar, cinnamon, nutmeg, and coconut oil until well combined.
Drizzle your donuts with the cinnamon mixture.
Bake your donuts in the preheated Air Fryer at 340 degrees F for approximately 10 minutes or until golden. Repeat with the remaining donuts.
Bon appétit!

Classic Autumn Pie

(Ready in about 40 minutes | Servings 4)

Per serving: 534 Calories; 26.4g Fat; 72.3g Carbs; 3.9g Protein; 26g Sugars; 3g Fiber

Ingredients

12 ounces refrigerated pie crusts
1/2 cup pumpkin puree, canned
1 ounce walnuts, coarsely chopped
1/2 cup granulated sugar
1 teaspoon pumpkin pie spice mix
1 teaspoon fresh ginger, peeled and grated

Directions

Place the first pie crust in a lightly greased pie plate.
In a mixing bowl, thoroughly combine the remaining ingredients to make the filling. Spoon the filling into the prepared pie crust.
Unroll the second pie crust and place it on top of the filling.
Bake the pie at 350 degrees F for 35 minutes or until the top is golden brown. Bon appétit!

Traditional Thai Goreng Pisang

(Ready in about 20 minutes | Servings 2)

Per serving: 384 Calories; 12.2g Fat; 60.8g Carbs; 18.7g Protein; 19g Sugars; 5.2g Fiber

Ingredients

4 tablespoons rice flour
4 tablespoons all-purpose flour
1/4 teaspoon ground cinnamon
A pinch of sea salt
A pinch of grated nutmeg
4 tablespoons coconut flakes
2 teaspoons coconut oil
2 eggs, whisked
2 bananas, peeled and sliced

Directions

Start by preheating your Air Fryer to 390 degrees F.
In a mixing dish, thoroughly combine the flour, cinnamon, salt, nutmeg, and coconut flakes.
Now, add in the coconut oil and eggs. Roll each slice of banana over the egg/flour mixture.
Bake your bananas in the preheated Air Fryer approximately 13 minutes, turning them over halfway through the cooking time. Bon appétit!

Easy French Dessert

(Ready in about 10 minutes | Servings 2)

Per serving: 310 Calories; 20.4g Fat; 22.3g Carbs; 9g Protein; 4.1g Sugars; 1.3g Fiber

Ingredients

2 eggs
2 tablespoons coconut oil, melted
1/4 cup milk
1/2 teaspoon vanilla extract
1/4 teaspoon ground cinnamon
1/8 teaspoon ground nutmeg
4 thick slices baguette

Directions

In a mixing bowl, thoroughly combine the eggs, coconut oil, milk, vanilla, cinnamon, and nutmeg.
Then, dip each piece of bread into the egg mixture; place the bread slices in a lightly greased baking pan.
Air Fryer the bread slices at 330 degrees F for about 4 minutes; turn them over and cook for a further 3 to 4 minutes. Enjoy!

American-Style Crullers

(Ready in about 20 minutes | Servings 4)

Per serving: 250 Calories; 15.4g Fat; 19.3g Carbs; 7.9g Protein; 1.7g Sugars; 0.6g Fiber

Ingredients

3/4 cup all-purpose flour
1/4 cup butter
1/4 cup water
1/2 cup full-fat milk
1/4 teaspoon kosher salt
A pinch of grated nutmeg
3 eggs, beaten

Directions

In a mixing bowl, thoroughly combine all ingredients.
Place the batter in a piping bag fitted with a large open star tip.

Pipe your crullers into circles and lower them onto the greased Air Fryer pan.
Cook your crullers in the preheated Air Fryer at 360 degrees F for 10 minutes, flipping them halfway through the cooking time.
Repeat with the remaining batter and serve immediately. Enjoy!

Chocolate Cupcakes with Raisins

(Ready in about 20 minutes | Servings 4)

Per serving: 360 Calories; 18g Fat; 45.6g Carbs; 8.7g Protein; 22g Sugars; 4g Fiber

Ingredients

3/4 cup all-purpose flour
1/2 teaspoon baking powder
1/2 cup unsweetened cocoa powder
A pinch of kosher salt
1/4 teaspoon grated nutmeg
1/2 teaspoon ground cinnamon
4 tablespoons coconut oil
3/4 cup brown sugar
2 eggs, whisked
1/2 teaspoon vanilla extract
3/4 cup yogurt
2 tablespoons raisins

Directions

Start by preheating your Air Fryer to 330 degrees F.
Mix all the ingredients in a bowl. Scrape the batter into silicone baking molds; place them in the Air Fryer basket.
Bake your cupcakes for about 15 minutes or until a tester comes out dry and clean.
Allow the cupcakes to cool before unmolding and serving. Bon appétit!

Homemade Apple Fritters

(Ready in about 20 minutes | Servings 4)

Per serving: 287 Calories; 15.8g Fat; 32.6g Carbs; 4.9g Protein; 12.6g Sugars; 1.8g Fiber

Ingredients

1 apple, peeled and grated
1/4 cup coconut oil, melted
3/4 cup all-purpose flour
1 ¼ teaspoons baking powder
¼ teaspoon ground cinnamon
1 egg
1/2 cup milk
2 tablespoons granulated sugar

Directions

In a mixing bowl, thoroughly combine all the ingredients.
Drop a spoonful of batter onto the greased Air Fryer pan. Cook in the preheated Air Fryer at 360 degrees F for 10 minutes, flipping them halfway through the cooking time.
Repeat with the remaining batter and serve warm. Enjoy!

Old-Fashioned Chocolate Cake

(Ready in about 25 minutes | Servings 6)

Per serving: 306 Calories; 20.9g Fat; 29.5g Carbs; 4.6g Protein; 17.3g Sugars; 2.7g Fiber

Ingredients

1/2 cup coconut oil
1 cup white granulated sugar
2 eggs
1/2 cups all-purpose flour
1/4 cup coconut flour
1/2 teaspoon baking powder
1/2 cup cocoa powder, unsweetened
1/4 teaspoon salt
1/4 teaspoon grated nutmeg
1/2 teaspoon ground cinnamon
1/4 cup milk
1/2 teaspoon pure vanilla extract

Directions

Start by preheating your Air Fryer to 340 degrees F. Then, brush the sides and bottom of a baking pan with a nonstick cooking spray.
In a mixing bowl, beat the coconut oil and sugar until fluffy. Next, fold in the eggs and beat again until well combined.
After that, add in the remaining ingredients. Mix until everything is well combined.
Bake in the preheated Air Fryer for 20 minutes.
Bon appétit!

Greek-Style Stuffed Pears

(Ready in about 20 minutes | Servings 2)

Per serving: 182 Calories; 5.9g Fat; 32.4g Carbs; 5.5g Protein; 26.3g Sugars; 5.2g Fiber

Ingredients

2 pears
1/4 teaspoon cloves
1/8 teaspoon grated nutmeg
1/4 teaspoon ground cinnamon
2 tablespoons honey
2 tablespoons walnuts, chopped
2 ounces Greek-style yogurt

Directions

Cut the pears in half and spoon out some of the flesh.
In a mixing bowl, thoroughly combine the remaining ingredients. Stuff the pear halves and transfer them to the Air Fryer cooking basket.
Pour 1/4 cup of water into an Air Fryer safe dish. Place the pears in the dish.
Bake the apples at 340 degrees F for 17 minutes.
Serve at room temperature. Bon appétit!

Favorite Strawberry Fritters

(Ready in about 15 minutes | Servings 4)

Per serving: 199 Calories; 8.6g Fat; 24.4g Carbs; 5.8g Protein; 5.7g Sugars; 1.2g Fiber

Ingredients

3/4 cup all-purpose flour
1/2 teaspoon baking powder
2 tablespoons butter, melted
1/4 cup coconut milk
2 eggs, whisked
1 teaspoon lime juice

1/2 cup strawberries
2 tablespoons powdered sugar
Directions
In a mixing bowl, thoroughly combine all the ingredients.
Drop a spoonful of batter onto the greased Air Fryer pan. Cook in the preheated Air Fryer at 360 degrees F for 10 minutes, flipping them halfway through the cooking time.
Repeat with the remaining batter and serve warm. Enjoy!

Roasted Bourbon Cherries

(Ready in about 25 minutes | Servings 4)
Per serving: 70 Calories; 3.6g Fat; 10.4g Carbs; 0.8g Protein; 10.2g Sugars; 0.2g Fiber
Ingredients
2 cups cherries, pitted
4 tablespoons brown sugar
1 tablespoon coconut oil
2 tablespoons bourbon
1/4 teaspoon ground cinnamon
Directions
Toss the cherries with the remaining ingredients; place your cherries in a lightly greased baking dish.
Roast the cherries in the preheated Air Fryer at 370 degrees F for approximately 20 minutes.
Serve at room temperature. Bon appétit!

Easy Fudge Brownie

(Ready in about 25 minutes | Servings 6)
Per serving: 304 Calories; 20.9g Fat; 26.1g Carbs; 4.8g Protein; 10.4g Sugars; 2.4g Fiber
Ingredients
1/2 cup butter, melted
1/2 cup granulated sugar
2 eggs, whisked
3/4 cup self-raising flour
1/4 cup cocoa powder
1 teaspoon vanilla extract
1/2 cup chocolate chips
Directions
Start by preheating your Air Fryer to 340 degrees F. Now, spritz the sides and bottom of a baking pan with a nonstick cooking spray.
In a mixing bowl, beat the melted butter and sugar until fluffy. Next, fold in the eggs and beat again until well combined.
After that, add in the remaining ingredients. Mix until everything is well incorporated.
Bake your brownie in the preheated Air Fryer for approximately 20 minutes. Enjoy!

Purple Plum Mini Pies

(Ready in about 25 minutes | Servings 6)
Per serving: 257 Calories; 9g Fat; 40.4g Carbs; 3.7g Protein; 28.7g Sugars; 2g Fiber
Ingredients
1 cup purple plums, pitted and coarsely chopped
1/2 cup brown sugar
1/2 teaspoon ground cinnamon
12 ounces refrigerated flaky cinnamon rolls
Directions
Toss the plums with the sugar and cinnamon.
Spray the muffin cups with a nonstick cooking spray.
Separate dough into 6 rolls and press them into the prepared muffin cups.
Spoon the filling into each dough-lined cup.
Bake the plum pie cups at 350 degrees F for 20 minutes or until the top is golden brown. Bon appétit!

Grandma's Apple Cakes

(Ready in about 20 minutes | Servings 4)
Per serving: 247 Calories; 9g Fat; 34g Carbs; 7.7g Protein; 8.2g Sugars; 3.8g Fiber
Ingredients
1/2 cup all-purpose flour
1/2 cup oats, ground
1/2 teaspoon baking powder
1 apple, peeled and grated
1/4 cup dried cranberries
2 tablespoons butter
1/2 teaspoon ground cinnamon
1/2 cup full-fat milk
1 egg, whisked
Directions
In a mixing bowl, thoroughly combine all the ingredients.
Drop a spoonful of batter onto the greased Air Fryer pan. Cook in the preheated Air Fryer at 360 degrees F for 10 minutes, flipping them halfway through the cooking time.
Repeat with the remaining batter and serve warm. Enjoy!

Chocolate Chip Cupcakes

(Ready in about 20 minutes | Servings 6)
Per serving: 247 Calories; 10g Fat; 36.6g Carbs; 4.7g Protein; 21g Sugars; 1.8g Fiber
Ingredients
3/4 cup plain flour
1/2 teaspoon baking powder
1/4 cup cocoa powder
3/4 cup caster sugar
1 egg, whisked
2 ounces butter, at room temperature
3/4 cup whole milk
2 ounces chocolate chips
1/2 teaspoon vanilla extract
Directions
Start by preheating your Air Fryer to 330 degrees F.
Mix all the ingredients in a bowl. Scrape the batter into silicone baking molds; place them in the Air Fryer basket.
Bake your cupcakes for about 15 minutes or until a tester comes out dry and clean.
Allow the cupcakes to cool before unmolding and serving. Bon appétit!

Favorite Banana Fritters

(Ready in about 15 minutes | Servings 1)
Per serving: 317 Calories; 18g Fat; 35g Carbs; 6.7g Protein; 22.2g Sugars; 3.4g Fiber
Ingredients
1 banana, mashed
1 egg, beaten
1 tablespoon coconut oil
1/4 teaspoons ground cinnamon
1 tablespoon brown sugar
Directions
In a mixing bowl, thoroughly combine all the ingredients.
Ladle the batter into a lightly greased Air Fryer pan.
Cook the fritter in the preheated Air Fryer at 360 degrees F for 10 minutes, flipping it halfway through the cooking time.
Enjoy!

Vanilla Apricots in Rosé Wine

(Ready in about 20 minutes | Servings 3)
Per serving: 132 Calories; 4g Fat; 22.4g Carbs; 1.1g Protein; 22.3g Sugars; 1.3g Fiber
Ingredients
5 ripe apricots, halved and pitted
1/2 cup caster sugar
1/2 cup rosé wine
1/2 vanilla bean, split
1/2 cinnamon stick
3-4 whole star anise
1 tablespoon butter
1 teaspoon lemon peel
Directions
Toss the apricots with the caster sugar.
Pour the wine into an Air Fryer safe dish. Place the apricots along with the spices and butter in the dish.
Cook the apricots at 340 degrees F for 16 minutes.
Serve at room temperature. Bon appétit!

Easy Mug Cake

(Ready in about 25 minutes | Servings 2)
Per serving: 386 Calories; 26.9g Fat; 36.5g Carbs; 7.6g Protein; 17g Sugars; 7g Fiber
Ingredients
2 tablespoons coconut flour
2 tablespoons almond flour
2 tablespoons all-purpose flour
1/2 teaspoon baking powder
4 tablespoons unsweetened cocoa powder
2 ounces chocolate chips
A pinch of salt
A pinch of grated nutmeg
2 tablespoons coconut oil
4 tablespoons coconut milk
1/2 teaspoon pure almond extract
Directions
Start by preheating your Air Fryer to 350 degrees F.
Thoroughly combine all the ingredients; mix until well combined.
Divide the mixture between two mugs and place them in the Air Fryer cooking basket.
Air fry the mug cakes for approximately 20 minutes.
Bon appétit!

Butter Fried Pears

(Ready in about 20 minutes | Servings 2)
Per serving: 156 Calories; 11.9g Fat; 13.7g Carbs; 0.7g Protein; 8.7g Sugars; 4.8g Fiber
Ingredients
2 pears, peeled, cored, and cut into sticks
2 tablespoons butter
A pinch of grated nutmeg
A pinch of sea salt
1/2 teaspoon ground cinnamon
1 teaspoon fresh ginger, grated
Directions
Toss the pears with the remaining ingredients.
Pour 1/4 cup of water into an Air Fryer safe dish.
Place the pears in the dish.
Bake the pears at 340 degrees F for 17 minutes.
Serve at room temperature. Bon appétit!

Autumn Pumpkin Cake

(Ready in about 20 minutes | Servings 3)
Per serving: 265 Calories; 10.7g Fat; 37g Carbs; 7.7g Protein; 25.5g Sugars; 2.8g Fiber
Ingredients
4 tablespoons all-purpose flour
4 tablespoons almond flour
1 teaspoon baking powder
4 tablespoons honey
1 teaspoon pumpkin pie spice blend
A pinch of Himalayan salt
1/4 cup milk
1/4 cup canned pumpkin
1 egg, beaten
Directions
Mix all the ingredients to make the batter. Pour the batter into a lightly oiled baking pan.
Place the pan in the Air Fryer cooking basket.
Bake your cake at 350 degrees F for about 13 minutes or until it is golden brown around the edges.
Bon appétit!

Old-Fashioned Donuts

(Ready in about 20 minutes | Servings 4)
Per serving: 262 Calories; 10g Fat; 37.6g Carbs; 5.7g Protein; 13.1g Sugars; 1.2g Fiber
Ingredients
1 cup all-purpose flour
1/2 teaspoon baking powder
1/4 teaspoon sea salt
1/2 cup white sugar
2 large eggs, whisked
2 tablespoons canola oil
1/4 cup milk
1/2 teaspoon cinnamon powder
Directions
In a mixing bowl, thoroughly combine all-purpose flour with baking powder, salt, and sugar.

In a separate bowl, beat the eggs until frothy using a hand mixer; add in the oil and milk and beat again; lastly, stir in cinnamon powder and mix again until everything is well combined.
Then, stir the egg mixture into the flour mixture and continue mixing until a dough ball forms. Try not to over-mix your dough. Transfer to a lightly floured surface.
Roll out your dough to a 1/4-inch thickness using a rolling pin. Cut out doughnuts using a 3-inch round cutter; now, use a 1-inch round cutter to remove the center.
Bake in the preheated Air Fryer at 340 degrees F for approximately 10 minutes or until golden. Repeat with the remaining doughnuts.
Bon appétit!

Homemade Chocolate Eclairs

(Ready in about 30 minutes | Servings 4)
Per serving: 403 Calories; 29.6g Fat; 28.6g Carbs; 7.7g Protein; 9.1g Sugars; 1.4g Fiber
Ingredients
Choux Pastry:
3/4 cup all-purpose flour
1/4 cup almond milk
1/2 cup water
6 tablespoons butter, room temperature
1 teaspoon brown sugar
1/4 teaspoon kosher salt
1/4 teaspoon grated nutmeg
3 eggs
Chocolate Glaze:
1/3 cup heavy whipping cream
2 ounces semi-sweet chocolate chips
Directions
In a mixing bowl, thoroughly combine all the ingredients for the pastry. Place the batter in a piping bag fitted with a large open star tip.
Pipe your eclairs into strips and lower them onto the greased Air Fryer pan.
Cook your eclairs in the preheated Air Fryer at 360 degrees F for 10 minutes, flipping them halfway through the cooking time.
Repeat with the remaining batter. Place the eclairs in your refrigerator while making the chocolate glaze.
Heat the whipping cream in a microwave; add in the chocolate and whisk until smooth sauce forms.
Top the chilled eclairs with the chocolate glaze and let it sit for about 30 minutes before serving. Bon appétit!

Autumn Pear Pancake

(Ready in about 15 minutes | Servings 4)
Per serving: 183 Calories; 6.6g Fat; 24.6g Carbs; 5.7g Protein; 10.1g Sugars; 2.1g Fiber
Ingredients
1 pear, peeled, cored and sliced
1 tablespoon lemon juice
1 tablespoon coconut oil
1/2 cup all-purpose flour
1/2 teaspoon baking powder
2 tablespoons brown sugar
1/2 teaspoon cinnamon
2 eggs, whisked
1/2 cup milk
1/2 teaspoon vanilla extract
Directions
Drizzle the pear slices with the lemon juice and melted coconut oil; arrange the pear slices in a baking pan.
Mix the remaining ingredients to make the batter. Pour the batter over the pears. Transfer the baking pan to the Air Fryer cooking basket.
Bake your pancake at 350 degrees F for about 13 minutes or until it is golden brown around the edges.
Bon appétit!

Colorful Fruit Kabobs

(Ready in about 15 minutes | Servings 4)
Per serving: 167 Calories; 7g Fat; 27.6g Carbs; 1.3g Protein; 22.1g Sugars; 2.3g Fiber
Ingredients
1 cup melon, cut into 1-inch chunks
1 cup pineapple, cut into 1-inch chunks
1 banana, cut into 1-inch chunks
1 peach, cut into 1-inch chunks
2 tablespoons coconut oil, melted
2 tablespoons honey
Directions
Toss your fruits with the coconut oil and honey.
Thread the fruits onto skewers and place them in the Air Fryer cooking basket.
Then, cook the skewers at 400 degrees F for approximately 10 minutes, turning them over halfway through the cooking time.
Bon appétit!

Favorite Almond Cupcakes

(Ready in about 20 minutes | Servings 6)
Per serving: 373 Calories; 24.6g Fat; 33.6g Carbs; 7.7g Protein; 18.1g Sugars; 2.7g Fiber
Ingredients
3/4 cup self-raising flour
1/4 cup cocoa powder
2 eggs, beaten
1 stick butter, at room temperature
1 cup granulated sugar
1/2 cup almond milk
2 ounces almonds, slivered
Directions
Start by preheating your Air Fryer to 330 degrees F.
Mix all the ingredients in a bowl. Scrape the batter into silicone baking molds; place them in the Air Fryer basket.
Bake your cupcakes for about 15 minutes or until a tester comes out dry and clean.
Allow the cupcakes to cool before unmolding and serving. Bon appétit!

Mini Monkey Rolls

(Ready in about 25 minutes | Servings 4)
Per serving: 383 Calories; 16.6g Fat; 52g Carbs; 7.4g Protein; 13.6g Sugars; 3.7g Fiber
Ingredients
12 ounces refrigerated dinner roll dough
1/2 cup brown sugar
1 teaspoon ground cinnamon
1/4 cup almonds, chopped
1/4 cup butter, melted
Directions
Spritz muffin cups with a nonstick cooking spray. Separate the dough into biscuits. In a shallow bowl, thoroughly combine the sugar, cinnamon, almonds, and butter.
Roll the biscuits over the sugar/cinnamon mixture. Divide them between muffin cups.
Bake the mini monkey rolls at 340 degrees F for about 20 minutes or until golden brown. Turn them upside down and serve.

Indian Vettu Cake

(Ready in about 15 minutes | Servings 4)
Per serving: 225 Calories; 9g Fat; 30.7g Carbs; 5.2g Protein; 12.3g Sugars; 0.8g Fiber
Ingredients
3/4 cup all-purpose flour
1/2 teaspoon baking powder
1/4 teaspoon cardamom powder
1/4 teaspoon cinnamon powder
2 eggs, whisked
1/2 cup caster sugar
2 tablespoons coconut oil
Directions
Mix all the ingredients to make the batter. Pour the batter into a lightly oiled baking pan.
Place the pan in the Air Fryer cooking basket.
Air fry your fritters at 350 degrees F for about 13 minutes or until they are golden brown around the edges.
Bon appétit!

Harvest Apple Cake

(Ready in about 20 minutes | Servings 3)
Per serving: 215 Calories; 5.7g Fat; 34.7g Carbs; 6.2g Protein; 19.8g Sugars; 3.6g Fiber
Ingredients
1/3 cup all-purpose flour
1/4 cup coconut flour
1/2 teaspoon baking powder
1/2 teaspoon ground cinnamon
3 tablespoons brown sugar
A pinch of kosher salt
2 eggs, beaten
1/2 teaspoon pure vanilla extract
1/4 cup full-fat milk
2 small apples, peeled, cored, and grated
Directions
Mix all the ingredients to make the batter. Pour the batter into a lightly oiled baking pan.
Place the pan in the Air Fryer cooking basket.
Bake your cake at 350 degrees F for about 13 minutes or until it is golden brown around the edges.
Bon appétit!

Mini Maraschino Cherry Pies

(Ready in about 25 minutes | Servings 6)
Per serving: 265 Calories; 9.7g Fat; 41.7g Carbs; 3.3g Protein; 22.2g Sugars; 1.6g Fiber
Ingredients
1/2 cup Maraschino cherries, pitted
1/2 cup granulated sugar
1/2 teaspoon ground cardamom
1 teaspoon pure vanilla extract
2 tablespoons hazelnuts, chopped
12 ounces refrigerated flaky cinnamon rolls
Directions
Toss the cherries with the sugar, cardamom, vanilla, and hazelnuts.
Spray muffin cups with a nonstick cooking spray.
Separate the dough into 6 rolls and press them into the prepared muffin cups.
Spoon the filling into each dough-lined cup.
Bake the mini pies at 350 degrees F for 20 minutes or until the top is golden brown. Bon appétit!

Fluffy Blueberry Fritters

(Ready in about 15 minutes | Servings 4)
Per serving: 195 Calories; 8g Fat; 25.4g Carbs; 4.9g Protein; 6.9g Sugars; 1g Fiber
Ingredients
3/4 cup all-purpose flour
1 teaspoon baking powder
1/2 cup coconut milk
2 tablespoons coconut sugar
A pinch of sea salt
1 egg
2 tablespoons melted butter
2 ounces fresh blueberries
Directions
In a mixing bowl, thoroughly combine all the ingredients.
Drop a spoonful of batter onto the greased Air Fryer pan. Cook in the preheated Air Fryer at 360 degrees F for 10 minutes, flipping them halfway through the cooking time.
Repeat with the remaining batter and serve warm. Enjoy!

Cranberry Chocolate Cupcakes

(Ready in about 20 minutes | Servings 6)
Per serving: 545 Calories; 35.1g Fat; 54.4g Carbs; 6.2g Protein; 36g Sugars; 3.1g Fiber
Ingredients
Cupcakes:
3/4 cup self-raising flour
3/4 cup caster sugar
1/4 cup cocoa powder
A pinch of sea salt
A pinch of grated nutmeg
2 eggs, whisked

1/2 cup buttermilk
1/2 stick butter, melted
2 ounces dried cranberries
Frosting:
1/2 cup butter, room temperature
1 teaspoon vanilla extract
3 ounces chocolate chips, melted
4 tablespoons heavy whipping cream

Directions

Start by preheating your Air Fryer to 330 degrees F.
Mix all the ingredients for the cupcakes. Scrape the batter into silicone baking molds; place them in the Air Fryer basket.
Bake your cupcakes for about 15 minutes or until a tester comes out dry and clean.
Beat all the ingredients for the frosting using an electric mixer. Pipe the frosting onto the cupcakes.
Bon appétit!

Indian-Style Unnakai Malabar

(Ready in about 15 minutes | Servings 1)

Per serving: 545 Calories; 35.1g Fat; 54.4g Carbs; 6.2g Protein; 36g Sugars; 3.1g Fiber

Ingredients

1 plantain, peeled
1/4 cup coconut flakes
1/4 teaspoon cinnamon powder
1/4 teaspoon cardamom powder
1 tablespoon ghee
2 tablespoons brown sugar

Directions

Preheat your Air Fryer to 390 degrees F.
Toss the plantain with the remaining ingredients.
Bake the prepared plantain in the preheated Air Fryer approximately 13 minutes, flipping it halfway through the cooking time.
Bon appétit!

Squash Fried Cake

(Ready in about 15 minutes | Servings 4)

Per serving: 155 Calories; 5.7g Fat; 20.4g Carbs; 5.2g Protein; 1.6g Sugars; 1.9g Fiber

Ingredients

2 cups butternut squash, shredded
1/2 cup all-purpose flour
2 eggs, beaten
1 tablespoon coconut oil
1 teaspoon pumpkin pie spice mix

Directions

In a mixing bowl, thoroughly combine all the ingredients.
Drop a spoonful of batter onto the greased Air Fryer pan. Cook in the preheated Air Fryer at 360 degrees F for 10 minutes, flipping them halfway through the cooking time.
Repeat with the remaining batter and serve warm.
Enjoy!

Honey and Coconut Apricots

(Ready in about 20 minutes | Servings 4)

Per serving: 176 Calories; 6.8g Fat; 28.4g Carbs; 2.8g Protein; 26g Sugars; 1.8g Fiber

Ingredients

8 apricots, halved and pitted
1 tablespoon coconut oil, melted
2 tablespoons honey
1 teaspoon ground cinnamon
2 ounces mascarpone cheese
1 tablespoon coconut flakes

Directions

Toss the apricots with the coconut oil, honey, and cinnamon.
Place the apricots in a lightly oiled Air Fryer cooking basket.
Cook the apricots at 340 degrees F for 16 minutes.
Top the fried apricots with mascarpone cheese and coconut flakes.
Bon appétit!

Danish Cinnamon Rolls

(Ready in about 15 minutes | Servings 4)

Per serving: 356 Calories; 20.3g Fat; 39.4g Carbs; 2.8g Protein; 24.2g Sugars; 1.1g Fiber

Ingredients

9 ounces refrigerated crescent rolls
1 tablespoon coconut oil
4 tablespoons caster sugar
1 teaspoon ground cinnamon

Directions

Separate the dough into rectangles. Mix the remaining ingredients until well combined.
Spread each rectangle with the cinnamon mixture; roll them up tightly.
Place the rolls in the Air Fryer cooking basket.
Bake the rolls at 300 degrees F for about 5 minutes; turn them over and bake for a further 5 minutes.
Bon appétit!

Festive Rum Fritters

(Ready in about 25 minutes | Servings 4)

Per serving: 235 Calories; 11.7g Fat; 26.7g Carbs; 3g Protein; 5.6g Sugars; 1.4g Fiber

Ingredients

3/4 cup all-purpose flour
3/4 cup water
1 tablespoon rum
4 tablespoons butter
1 banana, mashed
1 tablespoon caster sugar
1/4 teaspoon salt
1/4 teaspoon grated nutmeg

Directions

In a mixing bowl, thoroughly combine all the ingredients.
Drop a spoonful of batter onto the greased Air Fryer pan. Cook in the preheated Air Fryer at 360 degrees F for 10 minutes, flipping them halfway through the cooking time.
Repeat with the remaining batter and serve warm.
Enjoy!

Vanilla Mug Cake

(Ready in about 25 minutes | Servings 1)

Per serving: 476 Calories; 39g Fat; 28.5g Carbs; 8.8g Protein; 7g Sugars; 6.2g Fiber

Ingredients

2 tablespoons all-purpose flour
2 tablespoons almond flour
2 tablespoons cocoa powder, unsweetened
2 tablespoons agave nectar
1/4 teaspoon baking powder
1 teaspoon pure vanilla extract
A pinch of kosher salt
A pinch of grated nutmeg
2 tablespoons coconut oil, at room temperature
2 tablespoons full-fat milk

Directions

Start by preheating your Air Fryer to 350 degrees F.
Thoroughly combine all the ingredients; mix until well combined.
Spoon the mixture into a mug and place it in the Air Fryer cooking basket.
Air fry the mug cake for approximately 20 minutes.
Bon appétit!

Grandma's Fried Banana

(Ready in about 20 minutes | Servings 1)

Per serving: 286 Calories; 14.9g Fat; 43.5g Carbs; 1.3g Protein; 30.7g Sugars; 3.8g Fiber

Ingredients

1 banana, peeled and sliced
1 tablespoon coconut oil
2 tablespoons granulated sugar
1/2 teaspoon ground cloves
1/2 teaspoon ground cinnamon

Directions

Preheat your Air Fryer to 390 degrees F.
Toss banana slices with the remaining ingredients.
Bake the prepared banana slices in the preheated Air Fryer approximately 13 minutes, flipping them halfway through the cooking time.
Bon appétit!

OTHER AIR FRYER FAVORITES

Tomato and Cheese Frittata

(Ready in about 20 minutes | Servings 3)

Per serving: 236 Calories; 17.9g Fat; 5.5g Carbs; 13g Protein; 2.3g Sugars; 1.2g Fiber

Ingredients

4 tablespoons sour cream
5 eggs
1/4 cup mozzarella cheese, crumbled
2 tablespoons olive oil
1 medium tomato, chopped
1/4 cup fresh parsley, chopped
1/4 cup fresh chives, chopped
1/2 teaspoon dried oregano
Sea salt and ground black pepper, to taste

Directions

Start by preheating your Air Fryer to 350 degrees F. Then, spritz the sides and bottom of a baking pan with a nonstick cooking oil.
In a mixing bowl, thoroughly combine all the ingredients.
Pour the mixture into the prepared baking pan and lower the pan into the Air Fryer basket.
Cook your frittata in the preheated Air Fryer for approximately 15 minutes, or until a toothpick comes out dry and clean.
Bon appétit!

Creamed Corn Fried Cakes

(Ready in about 20 minutes | Servings 4)

Per serving: 296 Calories; 12.7g Fat; 32.5g Carbs; 13g Protein; 2.3g Sugars; 1.8g Fiber

Ingredients

1 cup all-purpose flour
1/2 teaspoon baking powder
1 cup sweet corn kernels, canned and drained
2 eggs
1/4 cup buttermilk
1/2 teaspoon sea salt
1/4 teaspoon freshly ground black pepper, or more to taste
1 garlic clove, minced
1 tablespoon butter, melted
2 ounces Swiss cheese, shredded

Directions

Start by preheating your Air Fryer to 380 degrees F.
Mix all the ingredients until everything is well combined. Form the mixture into patties.
Cook your fritters for about 15 minutes or until cooked through. Turn them over halfway through the cooking time.
Bon appétit!

Classic Potato Croquettes

(Ready in about 15 minutes | Servings 4)

Per serving: 363 Calories; 19g Fat; 36.2g Carbs; 11.5g Protein; 1.6g Sugars; 2.9g Fiber

Ingredients

1/2 cup all-purpose flour
3/4 pound potatoes, peeled and grated
2 eggs, whisked
2 tablespoons butter
2 ounces Parmesan cheese, grated
2 ounces breadcrumbs
2 tablespoons olive oil
1 teaspoon paprika
Kosher salt and freshly ground black pepper, to taste

Directions

Mix all the ingredients in a bowl. Shape the mixture into bite-sized balls and place them in a lightly oiled Air Fryer cooking basket.
Cook your croquettes at 400 degrees F for about 14 minutes, shaking the basket halfway through the cooking time.
Bon appétit!

The Best Griddlecake Ever

(Ready in about 15 minutes | Servings 4)

Per serving: 163 Calories; 3.3g Fat; 23.2g Carbs; 6.5g Protein; 5.5g Sugars; 0.9g Fiber

Ingredients

3/4 cup all-purpose flour
1/2 teaspoon baking powder
2 tablespoons brown sugar
1/2 cup yogurt
2 eggs, whisked
1/2 teaspoon ground cinnamon
1/2 teaspoon vanilla extract

Directions

In a mixing bowl, thoroughly combine all the ingredients.
Drop a spoonful of batter onto the greased Air Fryer pan. Cook in the preheated Air Fryer at 360 degrees F for 10 minutes, flipping them halfway through the cooking time.
Repeat with the remaining batter and serve warm.
Enjoy!

Classic Spinach Egg Cups

(Ready in about 20 minutes | Servings 4)

Per serving: 146 Calories; 11.9g Fat; 3.6g Carbs; 7.3g Protein; 1.9g Sugars; 1g Fiber

Ingredients

4 eggs
4 tablespoons cream cheese
1 tablespoon butter, melted
Sea salt and ground black pepper, to taste
1/2 teaspoon cayenne pepper
1 cup baby spinach, chopped
1 small tomato, chopped
2 garlic cloves, minced

Directions

Start by preheating your Air Fryer to 350 degrees F. Then, spritz silicone molds with a nonstick cooking oil.
In a mixing bowl, thoroughly combine all the ingredients.
Pour the mixture into the prepared silicone molds and lower them into the Air Fryer basket.
Cook the egg cups in the preheated Air Fryer for approximately 15 minutes, or until a toothpick comes out dry and clean.
Bon appétit!

Indian Roti Canai

(Ready in about 20 minutes | Servings 4)
Per serving: 176 Calories; 6.1g Fat; 24.1g Carbs; 5.3g Protein; 6.3g Sugars; 0.6g Fiber
Ingredients
3/4 cup flour
1/2 teaspoons baking soda
A pinch of kosher salt
A pinch of grated nutmeg
3/4 cup milk
1 egg
2 tablespoons brown sugar
1 tablespoon coconut oil, melted
Directions
Thoroughly combine all the ingredients in a mixing bowl.
Drop a spoonful of batter onto the greased Air Fryer pan.
Cook in the preheated Air Fryer at 360 degrees F for 10 minutes, flipping them halfway through the cooking time.
Repeat with the remaining batter and serve warm.
Bon appétit!

Smoked Sausage Cheese Rolls

(Ready in about 15 minutes | Servings 4)
Per serving: 412 Calories; 26.1g Fat; 24g Carbs; 18.3g Protein; 2g Sugars; 2g Fiber
Ingredients
6 ounces refrigerated crescent dinner rolls
1/2 pound smoked sausage, chopped
4 ounces Swiss cheese, shredded
1/2 teaspoon dried oregano
2 tablespoons tomato paste
Directions
Separate the dough into rectangles. In a bowl, combine the remaining ingredients.
Spread each rectangle with the sausage mixture; roll them up tightly.
Place the rolls in the Air Fryer cooking basket.
Bake the rolls at 300 degrees F for about 5 minutes; turn them over and bake for a further 5 minutes.
Bon appétit!

Old-Fashioned Rissoles

(Ready in about 20 minutes | Servings 4)
Per serving: 342 Calories; 26.2g Fat; 5g Carbs; 21.3g Protein; 1.1g Sugars; 0.5g Fiber
Ingredients
1 slice bread, crusts removed and soaked
1 shallot, chopped
2 cloves garlic, minced
1/2 pound ground beef
1/2 pound pork sausage, crumbled
1 egg, beaten
Sea salt and ground black pepper, to taste
Directions
Mix all the ingredients until everything is well combined. Form the mixture into balls.
Cook the meatballs at 380 degrees F for about 15 minutes or until cooked through, shaking the basket halfway through the cooking time.
Bon appétit!

Breakfast French Toast

(Ready in about 10 minutes | Servings 2)
Per serving: 192 Calories; 9.1g Fat; 21.5g Carbs; 5.5g Protein; 10.1g Sugars; 0.8g Fiber
Ingredients
2 tablespoons butter, melted
2 eggs, whisked
4 tablespoons coconut milk
1/2 teaspoon ground cinnamon
1/2 teaspoon vanilla extract
4 tablespoons brown sugar
4 slices stale French bread
Directions
In a mixing bowl, thoroughly combine the butter, eggs, coconut milk, cinnamon, vanilla, and brown sugar.
Then dip each piece of bread into the egg mixture; place the bread slices in a lightly greased baking pan.
Air Fryer the bread slices at 330 degrees F for about 4 minutes; turn them over and cook for a further 3 to 4 minutes. Enjoy!

Mini Crescent Dogs

(Ready in about 10 minutes | Servings 4)
Per serving: 342 Calories; 25g Fat; 14.9g Carbs; 13.3g Protein; 1.8g Sugars; 0.8g Fiber
Ingredients
4 ounces refrigerated crescent rolls
1 tablespoon Dijon mustard
8 cocktail sausages
Directions
Separate the dough into triangles. Cut them lengthwise into triangles. Spread each triangle with the mustard.
Place a cocktail sausage on the shortest side of each triangle and roll it up.
Place the rolls in the Air Fryer cooking basket.
Bake the rolls at 320 degrees F for about 8 minutes, turning them over halfway through the cooking time.
Bon appétit!

Herb and Ricotta Cheese Frittata

(Ready in about 20 minutes | Servings 3)

Per serving: 277 Calories; 21.5g Fat; 5g Carbs; 15.6g Protein; 1.9g Sugars; 0.5g Fiber

Ingredients

6 eggs
6 tablespoons half-and-half
1/4 teaspoon salt
1/4 teaspoon ground black pepper
3 ounces Ricotta cheese crumbled
2 cups baby spinach
1 tablespoon fresh cilantro, chopped
2 tablespoons olive oil

Directions

Start by preheating your Air Fryer to 350 degrees F. Then, spritz the sides and bottom of a baking pan with a nonstick cooking oil.
In a mixing bowl, thoroughly combine all the ingredients.
Pour the mixture into the prepared baking pan and lower the pan into the Air Fryer basket.
Cook your frittata in the preheated Air Fryer for approximately 15 minutes, or until a toothpick comes out dry and clean.
Bon appétit!

Colorful Vegetable Croquettes

(Ready in about 15 minutes | Servings 4)

Per serving: 227 Calories; 15.5g Fat; 9.5g Carbs; 12.6g Protein; 2.7g Sugars; 1.6g Fiber

Ingredients

2 eggs, whisked
1/2 cup chickpea flour
2 ounces feta cheese, crumbled
2 ounces Swiss cheese, shredded
1 bell pepper, chopped
1 small zucchini, chopped
1 clove garlic, minced
1/2 teaspoon smoked paprika
Kosher salt and freshly ground black pepper, to taste
2 tablespoons butter, melted

Directions

Mix all the ingredients in a bowl. Shape the mixture into bite-sized balls and place them in a lightly oiled Air Fryer cooking basket.
Cook your croquettes at 400 degrees F for about 14 minutes, shaking the basket halfway through the cooking time.
Bon appétit!

Mom's Rosemary Popovers

(Ready in about 20 minutes | Servings 4)

Per serving: 299 Calories; 20.6g Fat; 14.3g Carbs; 13.3g Protein; 2.2g Sugars; 0.4g Fiber

Ingredients

6 large-sized eggs
1/2 cup all-purpose flour
1/2 teaspoon baking powder
4 tablespoons butter, melted
1/2 cup milk
1/2 teaspoon granulated sugar
1/4 teaspoon kosher salt
1 teaspoon dried rosemary

Directions

Start by preheating your Air Fryer to 350 degrees F. Then, spritz mini muffin cups with a nonstick cooking oil.
In a mixing bowl, thoroughly combine all the ingredients.
Pour the mixture into the prepared mini muffin cups and lower them into the Air Fryer basket.
Cook your tartlets in the preheated Air Fryer for approximately 15 minutes, or until a toothpick comes out dry and clean.
Bon appétit!

Hard-Boiled Eggs

(Ready in about 20 minutes | Servings 2)

Per serving: 144 Calories; 9.6g Fat; 0.7g Carbs; 12.3g Protein; 0.2g Sugars; 0g Fiber

Ingredients

4 eggs
Sea salt, to taste

Directions

Place the eggs in the Air Fryer cooking basket.
Air fry your eggs at 270 degrees F for about 15 minutes.
Peel the eggs and season them with the salt. Bon appétit!

The Best Broccoli Salad Ever

(Ready in about 10 minutes | Servings 4)

Per serving: 214 Calories; 18.2g Fat; 10.7g Carbs; 5.6g Protein; 2.9g Sugars; 4g Fiber

Ingredients

1 pound broccoli florets
2 tablespoons sunflower seeds
2 tablespoons pepitas
2 tablespoons Sultanas
1 small shallot, chopped
1 teaspoon garlic, minced
1/4 cup extra-virgin olive oil
1 tablespoon yellow mustard
Sea salt and ground black pepper, to taste

Directions

Place the broccoli florets in a lightly greased Air Fryer basket.
Cook the broccoli florets at 395 degrees F for 9 minutes, shaking the basket halfway through the cooking time.
Toss the broccoli florets with the remaining ingredients. Serve at room temperature and enjoy!

Chickpea Buddha Bowl

(Ready in about 30 minutes | Servings 3)

Per serving: 240 Calories; 11.2g Fat; 29.7g Carbs; 8.6g Protein; 7.1g Sugars; 7.4g Fiber

Ingredients

8 ounces chickpeas, drained and rinsed
2 tablespoons olive oil
Sea salt and ground black pepper, to taste
1 teaspoon paprika

2 bell peppers, seeded and halved
1 small onion, thinly sliced
2 cups baby spinach
2 lemon wedges
Directions
Toss the chickpeas with the olive oil, salt, black pepper, and paprika in the Air Fryer cooking basket.
Air fry the chickpeas at 390 degrees F for about 13 minutes, tossing the basket a couple of times; reserve.
Then, air fry the peppers at 400 degrees F for about 15 minutes, shaking the basket halfway through the cooking time.
Arrange the bowl with the roasted chickpeas, peppers, and the other ingredients. Bon appétit!

Red Kidney Bean Sausage

(Ready in about 20 minutes | Servings 4)
Per serving: 228 Calories; 8.2g Fat; 30.7g Carbs; 9.6g Protein; 5.1g Sugars; 6.7g Fiber
Ingredients
1 cup cooked quinoa
10 ounces canned red kidney beans, rinsed and dried
1/2 cup walnuts, ground
1 red onion, chopped
2 cloves garlic, minced
1 teaspoon smoked paprika
Sea salt and ground black pepper, to taste
Directions
Mix all the ingredients in your blender or food processor. Form the mixture into logs and arrange them in a lightly greased Air Fryer basket.
Cook the sausages at 380 degrees F for about 15 minutes or until cooked through. Tun them over halfway through the cooking time.
Bon appétit!

Keto Cauliflower Fat Bombs

(Ready in about 20 minutes | Servings 4)
Per serving: 180 Calories; 15.2g Fat; 5g Carbs; 4.6g Protein; 2.3g Sugars; 1.3g Fiber
Ingredients
2 cups cauliflower florets
4 tablespoons butter
1 teaspoon dried parsley flakes
1 teaspoon dried rosemary
2 garlic cloves, minced
Sea salt and ground black pepper, to taste
1/2 cup feta cheese
Directions
Arrange the cauliflower florets in a lightly greased Air Fryer basket.
Cook the cauliflower florets at 400 degrees F for about 15 minutes, shaking the basket halfway through the cooking time.
Chop the roasted cauliflower and combine it with the remaining ingredients. Shape the mixture into balls.
Bon appétit!

Bulgarian Cheese Toast

(Ready in about 10 minutes | Servings 3)
Per serving: 255 Calories; 17.6g Fat; 10.8g Carbs; 12.3g Protein; 2g Sugars; 0.5g Fiber
Ingredients
2 ounces goat cheese, crumbled
1 ounce butter, melted
1 ounce yogurt
2 eggs
1/4 teaspoon sea salt
3 stale Brioche bread slices
Directions
In a mixing bowl, thoroughly combine the cheese, butter, yogurt, eggs, and sea salt.
Then dip each piece of bread into the egg mixture; place the bread slices in a lightly greased baking pan.
Air Fryer the bread slices at 330 degrees F for about 4 minutes; turn them over and cook for a further 3 to 4 minutes. Enjoy!

Authentic Tater Tots

(Ready in about 20 minutes | Servings 4)
Per serving: 232 Calories; 9.3g Fat; 30.3g Carbs; 6.6g Protein; 1.4g Sugars; 1.8g Fiber
Ingredients
3/4 cup all-purpose flour
1 cup boiled potatoes, mashed
2 eggs, whisked
1 tablespoon fresh parsley, chopped
1 tablespoon fresh cilantro, chopped
2 tablespoons fresh scallions, chopped
Sea salt and ground black pepper, to taste
1/2 cup fresh breadcrumbs
2 tablespoons olive oil
Directions
Mix all the ingredients in a bowl. Shape the mixture into bite-sized balls and place them in a lightly oiled Air Fryer cooking basket.
Cook your tater tots at 400 degrees F for about 14 minutes, shaking the basket halfway through the cooking time.
Bon appétit!

Spring Mushroom Frittata

(Ready in about 20 minutes | Servings 3)
Per serving: 340 Calories; 25.5g Fat; 8.5g Carbs; 19.6g Protein; 2.5g Sugars; 1.5g Fiber
Ingredients
6 eggs
1/4 cup sour cream
1/2 cup Swiss cheese, shredded
Kosher salt and ground black pepper, to taste
1 teaspoon hot paprika
2 tablespoons olive oil
2 cloves garlic, crushed
6 ounces brown mushrooms, sliced
2 tablespoons fresh parsley, roughly chopped
Directions
Start by preheating your Air Fryer to 350 degrees F.
Then, spritz the sides and bottom of a baking pan with a nonstick cooking oil.

In a mixing bowl, thoroughly combine all the ingredients.
Pour the mixture into the prepared baking pan and lower the pan into the Air Fryer basket.
Cook your frittata in the preheated Air Fryer for approximately 15 minutes, or until a toothpick comes out dry and clean.
Bon appétit!

Asian-Style Sticks

(Ready in about 20 minutes | Servings 4)

Per serving: 364 Calories; 15.5g Fat; 40.5g Carbs; 16g Protein; 2g Sugars; 2.5g Fiber

Ingredients

1 cup boiled potato, mashed
1 cup cheddar, grated
1 tablespoon miso paste
1 cup all-purpose flour
1/2 teaspoon coriander seeds
Sea salt and ground black pepper, to taste
1 egg, beaten
1 cup breadcrumbs
2 tablespoons Kewpie Japanese mayonnaise

Directions

Mix all the ingredients, except for the breadcrumbs, in a bowl. Press the mixture into a parchment-lined baking sheet and allow it to freeze until firm.
Cut the mixture into sticks and roll them into the breadcrumbs; place the sticks in a lightly oiled Air Fryer cooking basket.
Cook the sticks at 400 degrees F for about 14 minutes, shaking the basket halfway through the cooking time.
Bon appétit!

Italian Nona's Meatballs

(Ready in about 20 minutes | Servings 4)

Per serving: 296 Calories; 19.5g Fat; 5g Carbs; 24.6g Protein; 1.2g Sugars; 0.6g Fiber

Ingredients

1/2 pound ground pork
1/2 pound ground turkey
1 onion, minced
2 garlic cloves, minced
1/4 cup Italian-style bread crumbs
1/4 cup parmesan cheese, grated
1 large-sized egg, whisked
Sea salt and ground black pepper, to taste

Directions

Mix all the ingredients until everything is well combined. Form the mixture into balls.
Cook the meatballs at 380 degrees F for about 15 minutes or until cooked through, shaking the basket halfway through the cooking time.
Bon appétit!

Classic Egg Salad

(Ready in about 20 minutes | Servings 4)

Per serving: 206 Calories; 16.5g Fat; 2.7g Carbs; 10.1g Protein; 1.5g Sugars; 0.5g Fiber

Ingredients

6 eggs
4 tablespoons Greek-style yogurt
4 tablespoons mayonnaise
3 tablespoons scallions, chopped
1 tablespoon Dijon mustard
Sea salt and ground black pepper, to taste

Directions

Place the eggs in the Air Fryer cooking basket.
Air fry your eggs at 270 degrees F for about 15 minutes.
Peel and chop the eggs; place them in a salad bowl and add in the remaining ingredients. Gently toss to combine.
Place the salad in your refrigerator until ready to serve. Bon appétit!

Rustic Egg Muffins

(Ready in about 20 minutes | Servings 4)

Per serving: 205 Calories; 14.5g Fat; 3.3g Carbs; 14.6g Protein; 1.6g Sugars; 0.6g Fiber

Ingredients

6 eggs
6 tablespoons Cottage cheese, crumbled
2 tablespoons scallions, chopped
1 teaspoon garlic, minced
3 ounces bacon, chopped
1 teaspoon paprika
Sea salt and ground black pepper, to taste

Directions

Start by preheating your Air Fryer to 350 degrees F. Then, spritz silicone molds with a nonstick cooking oil.
In a mixing bowl, thoroughly combine all the ingredients.
Pour the mixture into the prepared silicone molds and lower them into the Air Fryer basket.
Cook the egg muffins in the preheated Air Fryer for approximately 15 minutes, or until a toothpick comes out dry and clean.
Bon appétit!

Hot and Spicy Roasted Chickpeas

(Ready in about 15 minutes | Servings 4)

Per serving: 155 Calories; 5.5g Fat; 21.3g Carbs; 6.6g Protein; 4.1g Sugars; 5.8g Fiber

Ingredients

10 ounces chickpeas, drained and rinsed
1 tablespoon olive oil
Coarse sea salt and ground black pepper, to taste
1/2 teaspoon garlic powder
1 teaspoon cayenne pepper
1/2 teaspoon red chili powder

Directions

Toss the chickpeas with the other ingredients in the Air Fryer cooking basket.
Air fry the chickpeas at 390 degrees F for about 13 minutes, tossing the basket a couple of times.
Bon appétit!

Roasted Tofu and Pepper Bowl

(Ready in about 22 minutes | Servings 4)

Per serving: 215 Calories; 14.5g Fat; 11.3g Carbs; 14.6g Protein; 1g Sugars; 3.2g Fiber

Ingredients

2 bell peppers, sliced
12 ounces firm tofu, pressed and cut into bite-sized cubes
2 tablespoons tamari sauce
2 tablespoons rice wine
2 tablespoons sesame oil
1 chili pepper, minced
1 garlic clove, minced

Directions

Start by preheating your Air Fryer to 390 degrees F.
Toss the peppers and tofu with the remaining ingredients in the Air Fryer cooking basket.
Cook the peppers for about 10 minutes, shaking the basket halfway through the cooking time.
Add in the tofu cubes, reduce temperature to 360 degrees F, and continue to cook for approximately 10 minutes.
Bon appétit!

Spicy Lentil Burgers

(Ready in about 20 minutes | Servings 4)

Per serving: 185 Calories; 7.5g Fat; 22.3g Carbs; 8.6g Protein; 4.1g Sugars; 8.1g Fiber

Ingredients

12 ounces canned lentils, drained and rinsed
1 medium carrot, grated
1 medium onion, grated
1 garlic clove, minced
1 teaspoon smoked paprika
Sea salt and ground black pepper, to taste
2 tablespoons olive oil

Directions

Mix all the ingredients until everything is well combined. Form the mixture into four patties and arrange them in a lightly greased Air Fryer basket.
Cook the burgers at 380 degrees F for about 15 minutes or until cooked through. Tun them over halfway through the cooking time.
Bon appétit!

Favorite Reuben Sandwich

(Ready in about 15 minutes | Servings 2)

Per serving: 580 Calories; 36.5g Fat; 20.7g Carbs; 41.6g Protein; 2.4g Sugars; 1.1g Fiber

Ingredients

4 slices sourdough bread
2 tablespoons butter, room temperature
4 slices Cheddar cheese
1/2 pound corned beef

Directions

Butter one side of each slice of bread.
Assemble your sandwiches with cheese and corned beef.
Air fry the sandwiches at 380 degrees F for about 10 minutes.
Bon appétit!

Roasted Cauliflower Salad

(Ready in about 15 minutes | Servings 4)

Per serving: 158 Calories; 13.8g Fat; 8.3g Carbs; 2.6g Protein; 3.2g Sugars; 2.6g Fiber

Ingredients

1 pound cauliflower florets
Sea salt and ground black pepper, to taste
4 tablespoons freshly squeezed lemon juice
1/4 cup extra-virgin olive oil
1 teaspoon fresh garlic, minced
1 tablespoon fresh parsley, chopped
2 tablespoons fresh scallions, chopped

Directions

Arrange the cauliflower florets in a lightly greased Air Fryer basket.
Cook the cauliflower florets at 400 degrees F for about 13 minutes, shaking the basket halfway through the cooking time.
Toss the cauliflower florets with the remaining ingredients.
Bon appétit!

Bacon and Pepper Frittata

(Ready in about 20 minutes | Servings 4)

Per serving: 258 Calories; 21.5g Fat; 4.5g Carbs; 12.4g Protein; 1.6g Sugars; 0.6g Fiber

Ingredients

7 eggs
4 tablespoons sour cream
1 teaspoon paprika
Kosher salt and ground black pepper, to taste
2 tablespoons olive oil
2 ounces bacon, diced
1 bell pepper, seeded and diced
2 garlic cloves, minced

Directions

Start by preheating your Air Fryer to 350 degrees F. Then, spritz the sides and bottom of a baking pan with a nonstick cooking oil.
In a mixing bowl, thoroughly combine all the ingredients.
Pour the mixture into the prepared baking pan and lower the pan into the Air Fryer basket.
Cook your frittata in the preheated Air Fryer for approximately 15 minutes, or until a toothpick comes out dry and clean.
Bon appétit!

Traditional Portuguese Rabanadas

(Ready in about 10 minutes | Servings 2)

Per serving: 318 Calories; 19.5g Fat; 28g Carbs; 9g Protein; 19.6g Sugars; 0.7g Fiber

Ingredients

4 slices baguette
1/2 cup full-fat milk
4 tablespoons granulated sugar
2 eggs, beaten
1/2 teaspoon ground cinnamon

2 tablespoons coconut oil

Directions

Toss the bread slices with the remaining ingredients.

Air Fryer the bread slices at 330 degrees F for about 4 minutes; turn them over and cook for a further 3 to 4 minutes.

Bon appétit!

Roasted Brussels Sprout Salad

(Ready in about 12 minutes | Servings 4)

Per serving: 241 Calories; 11.5g Fat; 29g Carbs; 8.9g Protein; 18.6g Sugars; 6.3g Fiber

Ingredients

1 pound fresh Brussels sprouts, trimmed
1 Vidalia onion, peeled and thinly sliced
1 garlic clove, minced
1 apple, cored and sliced
1/4 cup pomegranate arils
2 ounces goat cheese, crumbled
1 tablespoon fresh lemon juice
1/4 cup extra-virgin olive oil
2 tablespoons honey
1 tablespoon Dijon mustard

Directions

Arrange the Brussels sprouts in the Air Fryer cooking basket.

Cook the Brussels sprouts at 380 degrees F for 10 minutes, shaking the basket halfway through the cooking time.

Toss the Brussels sprouts with the remaining ingredients and serve at room temperature. Enjoy!

Fried Buckwheat Balls

(Ready in about 20 minutes | Servings 4)

Per serving: 335 Calories; 10.3g Fat; 49g Carbs; 11.4g Protein; 1.6g Sugars; 2.8g Fiber

Ingredients

1 ½ cups cooked buckwheat
1 cup rice flour
1/2 teaspoon baking powder
1/2 cup Parmesan, grated
2 eggs, beaten
2 tablespoons olive oil
Sea salt and ground black pepper, to taste

Directions

Start by preheating your Air Fryer to 380 degrees F.

Mix all the ingredients until everything is well combined. Form the mixture into balls.

Air fry the balls for about 15 minutes or until cooked through, shaking the basket halfway through the cooking time.

Bon appétit!

Authentic Potato Sinkers

(Ready in about 20 minutes | Servings 4)

Per serving: 184 Calories; 2.5g Fat; 32.2g Carbs; 6.7g Protein; 0.6g Sugars; 1.7g Fiber

Ingredients

1 cup boiled potatoes, mashed
1 cup all-purpose flour
1/2 teaspoon baking powder
2 eggs, beaten
1/2 teaspoon cayenne pepper
1/4 teaspoon dried dill weed
1/2 teaspoon salt
1/4 teaspoon ground black pepper

Directions

Mix all the ingredients in a bowl. Shape the mixture into bite-sized balls and place them in a lightly oiled Air Fryer cooking basket.

Cook your sinkers at 400 degrees F for about 14 minutes, shaking the basket halfway through the cooking time.

Bon appétit!

Creamy Basil Egg Salad

(Ready in about 20 minutes | Servings 4)

Per serving: 146 Calories; 11.4g Fat; 2g Carbs; 8.4g Protein; 0.4g Sugars; 0.7g Fiber

Ingredients

5 eggs
4 tablespoons sour cream
1/4 cup mayonnaise
1 tablespoon Dijon mustard
2 tablespoons fresh basil, snipped
Sea salt and ground black pepper, to taste

Directions

Place the eggs in the Air Fryer cooking basket.

Air fry your eggs at 270 degrees F for about 15 minutes.

Peel and chop the eggs; place them in a salad bowl and add in the remaining ingredients. Gently toss to combine.

Place the salad in your refrigerator until ready to serve. Bon appétit!

Hot and Spicy Barley Croquettes

(Ready in about 20 minutes | Servings 4)

Per serving: 296 Calories; 19g Fat; 24g Carbs; 7.7g Protein; 1.7g Sugars; 3.8g Fiber

Ingredients

1 ½ cups cooked barley
2 large eggs, beaten
1 cup bread crumbs
Kosher salt and cayenne pepper, to taste
1 teaspoon red chili powder
2 ounces ground walnuts
2 tablespoons olive oil

Directions

Start by preheating your Air Fryer to 380 degrees F.

Mix all the ingredients until everything is well combined. Form the mixture into balls.

Air fry the balls for about 15 minutes or until cooked through, shaking the basket halfway through the cooking time.

Bon appétit!

Sweet Potatoes and Lentil Patties

(Ready in about 20 minutes | Servings 4)

Per serving: 199 Calories; 7.2g Fat; 28.4g Carbs; 6.5g Protein; 6.6g Sugars; 5.8g Fiber

Ingredients

1 cup red lentils
2 tablespoons tomato paste
1 sweet potato, peeled and grated
Sea salt and ground black pepper, to taste
1 small onion, chopped
1 tablespoon fresh parsley, chopped
1 tablespoon fresh coriander, chopped
2 tablespoons olive oil

Directions

Mix all the ingredients until everything is well combined. Form the mixture into four patties and arrange them in a lightly greased Air Fryer basket.
Cook the burgers at 380 degrees F for about 15 minutes or until cooked through. Tun them over halfway through the cooking time.
Bon appétit!

Holiday Cauliflower Steaks

(Ready in about 20 minutes | Servings 4)

Per serving: 129 Calories; 10.6g Fat; 7.4g Carbs; 2.5g Protein; 2.6g Sugars; 2.6g Fiber

Ingredients

1 pound cauliflower, cut into 4 steaks
4 tablespoons olive oil
1 teaspoon garlic, minced
1 teaspoon cayenne pepper
1/2 teaspoon cumin seeds
Coarse sea salt and ground black pepper, to taste

Directions

Toss the cauliflower steaks with the remaining ingredients.
Place the cauliflower steaks in a lightly greased Air Fryer basket.
Cook the cauliflower steaks at 390 degrees F for about 20 minutes, turning them over halfway through the cooking time.
Bon appétit!

Bulgur and Mushroom Fritters

(Ready in about 20 minutes | Servings 4)

Per serving: 196 Calories; 9g Fat; 24g Carbs; 4.7g Protein; 2.7g Sugars; 4.1g Fiber

Ingredients

1 ½ cups cooked bulgur
1 cup brown mushrooms, chopped
1 medium onion, chopped
2 cloves garlic, finely chopped
1 cup crackers, crushed
2 tablespoons butter
2 tablespoons fresh parsley, chopped
Sea salt and ground black pepper, to season

Directions

Start by preheating your Air Fryer to 380 degrees F.
Mix all the ingredients until everything is well combined. Form the mixture into balls.
Air fry the balls for about 15 minutes or until cooked through, shaking the basket halfway through the cooking time.
Bon appétit!

Spinach Quiche with Canadian Bacon

(Ready in about 20 minutes | Servings 4)

Per serving: 220 Calories; 11.3g Fat; 12.5g Carbs; 16.4g Protein; 2.6g Sugars; 1.6g Fiber

Ingredients

6 eggs, whisked
6 tablespoons all-purpose flour
1/2 teaspoon baking soda
6 tablespoons full-fat milk
4 ounces Canadian bacon, diced
1 tablespoon olive oil
2 cups baby spinach
1 tomato, chopped
1 Serrano peppers, chopped
Kosher salt and freshly ground black pepper, to taste

Directions

Start by preheating your Air Fryer to 350 degrees F. Then, spritz the sides and bottom of a baking pan with a nonstick cooking oil.
In a mixing bowl, thoroughly combine all the ingredients.
Pour the mixture into the prepared baking pan and lower the pan into the Air Fryer basket.
Cook your frittata in the preheated Air Fryer for approximately 15 minutes, or until a toothpick comes out dry and clean.
Bon appétit!

Indian-Style Dosas

(Ready in about 20 minutes | Servings 4)

Per serving: 176 Calories; 6.1g Fat; 24.1g Carbs; 5.3g Protein; 6.3g Sugars; 0.6g Fiber

Ingredients

1/2 cup all-purpose flour
1/2 cup rice flour
1/2 teaspoon baking powder
1/2 cup water
1 clove garlic, minced
1/2 teaspoon ground turmeric
1/2 teaspoon ground cumin
1/2 teaspoon mustard seeds

Directions

Thoroughly combine all the ingredients in a mixing bowl.
Drop a spoonful of batter onto the greased Air Fryer pan.
Cook the cakes in the preheated Air Fryer at 360 degrees F for 10 minutes, flipping them halfway through the cooking time.
Repeat with the remaining batter and serve warm.
Bon appétit!

German Königsberger Klopse

(Ready in about 20 minutes | Servings 4)

Per serving: 256 Calories; 14.6g Fat; 8.7g Carbs; 22.3g Protein; 1g Sugars; 0.8g Fiber

Ingredients

1/3 pound ground beef
1/2 pound ground turkey
1 egg, slightly beaten
1/4 cup tortilla chips, crushed
1/2 cup cheddar cheese, grated
1 small onion, chopped
1 teaspoon garlic, minced
Sea salt and fresh ground black pepper, to taste
1 teaspoon dried parsley flakes
1 teaspoon dried oregano
1 teaspoon dried basil

Directions

Mix all the ingredients until everything is well combined. Form the mixture into balls.
Cook the meatballs at 380 degrees F for about 15 minutes or until cooked through, shaking the basket halfway through the cooking time.
Bon appétit!

Easy Cinnamon Toast

(Ready in about 10 minutes | Servings 2)

Per serving: 168 Calories; 12.2g Fat; 11g Carbs; 1.9g Protein; 1.7g Sugars; 1.2g Fiber

Ingredients

2 bread slices
1 teaspoon ground cinnamon
2 tablespoons butter, softened

Directions

Toss the bread slices with cinnamon and butter.
Air Fryer the bread slices at 330 degrees F for about 4 minutes; turn them over and cook for a further 3 to 4 minutes.
Bon appétit!

Easy Birthday Tartlets

(Ready in about 20 minutes | Servings 4)

Per serving: 220 Calories; 17g Fat; 4.4g Carbs; 12.6g Protein; 2.5g Sugars; 0.7g Fiber

Ingredients

5 eggs
2 tablespoons butter, room temperature
1 cup baby spinach
1 bell pepper, chopped
1 shallot, chopped
Kosher salt ground black pepper, to taste
1/2 teaspoon dried basil
1/2 teaspoon dried oregano
3 ounces feta cheese, crumbled

Directions

Start by preheating your Air Fryer to 350 degrees F. Then, spritz mini muffin cups with a nonstick cooking oil.
In a mixing bowl, thoroughly combine all the ingredients.
Pour the mixture into the prepared mini muffin cups and lower them into the Air Fryer basket.
Cook your tartlets in the preheated Air Fryer for approximately 15 minutes, or until a toothpick comes out dry and clean.
Bon appétit!

Breakfast Waffle with Blueberries

(Ready in about 10 minutes | Servings 1)

Per serving: 134 Calories; 7g Fat; 16.4g Carbs; 2.7g Protein; 3.1g Sugars; 1g Fiber

Ingredients

1 frozen waffle
1 tablespoon blueberries
1 tablespoon whipped cream

Directions

Place the frozen waffle in a lightly greased Air Fryer cooking basket.
Air fry your waffle at 360 degrees F for 7 minutes, turning it over halfway through the cooking time.
Serve your waffle with blueberries and whipped cream. Bon appétit!

Roasted Green Bean Salad

(Ready in about 10 minutes | Servings 4)

Per serving: 204 Calories; 16.7g Fat; 10.4g Carbs; 4.5g Protein; 5.1g Sugars; 3.4g Fiber

Ingredients

1 pound green beans, trimmed
Sea salt and ground black pepper, to taste
1 shallot, finely chopped
1 teaspoon garlic, minced
1/4 cup extra-virgin olive oil
2 tablespoons white wine vinegar
1/4 cup fresh parsley, chopped
2 ounces feta cheese, crumbled

Directions

Arrange the green beans in a lightly greased Air Fryer basket.
Cook the green beans at 375 degrees F for 7 minutes; make sure to check the green beans halfway through the cooking time.
Add the green beans to a salad bowl; add in the remaining ingredients and stir to combine well.
Enjoy!

Classic Corn Salad

(Ready in about 15 minutes | Servings 2)

Per serving: 259 Calories; 19g Fat; 23.4g Carbs; 3.9g Protein; 5.6g Sugars; 3.4g Fiber

Ingredients

2 corn on the cob, husked and halved
2 teaspoons ghee
Sea salt and ground black pepper, to taste
1 Vidalia onion, thinly sliced
1 bell pepper, thinly sliced
2 tablespoons lime juice
2 tablespoons extra-virgin olive oil

Directions

Toss the ears of corn with the ghee, salt, and pepper.
Arrange the ears of corn in the Air Fryer cooking basket.

Cook the ears of corn at 390 degrees F for about 10 minutes, tossing them halfway through the cooking time.
Next, cut the kernels off the cob. Toss the corn kernels with the remaining ingredients. Bon appétit!

Roasted Ranch Garbanzo Beans

(Ready in about 15 minutes | Servings 4)
Per serving: 159 Calories; 5.9g Fat; 20.4g Carbs; 6g Protein; 3.6g Sugars; 5.7g Fiber
Ingredients
12 ounces canned garbanzo beans, drained and rinsed
1 tablespoon olive oil
1 tablespoon Ranch seasoning mix
Directions
Toss the garbanzo beans with the other ingredients in the Air Fryer cooking basket.
Air fry your garbanzo beans at 390 degrees F for about 13 minutes, tossing the basket a couple of times.
Bon appétit!

Authentic Italian Arancini

(Ready in about 20 minutes | Servings 4)
Per serving: 248 Calories; 12.5g Fat; 23.7g Carbs; 9.4g Protein; 0.8g Sugars; 2g Fiber
Ingredients
1 ½ cups cooked Arborio rice
1/2 cup Parmesan cheese, grated
1 cup panko crumbs
2 large eggs, whisked
1 teaspoon dried parsley flakes
Kosher salt and freshly ground black pepper, to taste
2 tablespoons butter
Directions
Start by preheating your Air Fryer to 380 degrees F.
Mix all the ingredients until everything is well combined. Form the mixture into balls.
Air fry the balls for about 15 minutes or until cooked through, shaking the basket halfway through the cooking time.
Bon appétit!

Classic Vegetarian Frittata

(Ready in about 20 minutes | Servings 4)
Per serving: 320 Calories; 24.3g Fat; 4.5g Carbs; 19.4g Protein; 1.8g Sugars; 0.6g Fiber
Ingredients
8 eggs
6 tablespoons sour cream
Coarse sea salt and ground black pepper, to taste
1 teaspoon cayenne pepper
1/2 teaspoon dried oregano
1 teaspoon dried basil
4 ounces gouda cheese, shredded
2 tablespoons olive oil
1 small zucchini, shredded
1 small shallot, chopped
Directions
Start by preheating your Air Fryer to 350 degrees F.
Then, spritz the sides and bottom of a baking pan with a nonstick cooking oil.
In a mixing bowl, thoroughly combine all the ingredients.
Pour the mixture into the prepared baking pan and lower the pan into the Air Fryer basket.
Cook your frittata in the preheated Air Fryer for approximately 15 minutes, or until a toothpick comes out dry and clean.
Bon appétit!

Parmesan Potato Croquettes

(Ready in about 20 minutes | Servings 4)
Per serving: 273 Calories; 12.9g Fat; 30.2g Carbs; 10g Protein; 1.4g Sugars; 2.7g Fiber
Ingredients
1/2 cup flour
1 teaspoon baking powder
3/4 pounds potatoes, grated
2 eggs, whisked
1/2 cup parmesan cheese, grated
1 tablespoon parsley, chopped
1 tablespoon cilantro, chopped
1 tablespoon chives, chopped
1 teaspoon smoked paprika
Kosher salt and ground black pepper, to taste
2 tablespoons olive oil
Directions
Mix all the ingredients in a bowl. Shape the mixture into bite-sized balls and place them in a lightly oiled Air Fryer cooking basket.
Cook your croquettes at 400 degrees F for about 14 minutes, shaking the basket halfway through the cooking time.
Bon appétit!

Egg Salad Sandwich

(Ready in about 25 minutes | Servings 3)
Per serving: 503 Calories; 27.7g Fat; 40.2g Carbs; 23.4g Protein; 6.6g Sugars; 6.5g Fiber
Ingredients
6 eggs
2 tablespoons scallions, chopped
2 garlic cloves, minced
1/4 cup sour cream
1/4 cup mayonnaise
1 teaspoon yellow mustard
Sea salt and ground black pepper, to taste
1 garlic clove, minced
6 slices whole-grain bread
Directions
Place the eggs in the Air Fryer cooking basket.
Air fry your eggs at 270 degrees F for about 15 minutes.
Peel and chop the eggs; place them in a salad bowl and add in the remaining ingredients. Gently toss to combine.

Next, air fry the bread slices at 330 degrees F for about 4 minutes; turn them over and cook for a further 3 to 4 minutes.
Lastly, assemble your sandwiches with the egg salad and toasted bread.
Bon appétit!

French-Style Carrot Salad

(Ready in about 20 minutes | Servings 4)
Per serving: 153 Calories; 0.7g Fat; 38.2g Carbs; 2.4g Protein; 25.1g Sugars; 5.5g Fiber
Ingredients
1 pound carrots, sliced
1/2 golden raisins
1 sweet onion, chopped
1 apple, peeled cored and diced
1 tablespoon fresh lemon juice
1 tablespoon white vinegar
Directions
Place the carrots in a lightly oiled Air Fryer cooking basket.
Air fry the carrots at 380 degrees F for 15 minutes; make sure to check the carrots halfway through the cooking time.
Toss the carrots with the remaining ingredients. Bon appétit!

Corn with Butter and Scallions

(Ready in about 12 minutes | Servings 2)
Per serving: 213 Calories; 14.8g Fat; 19.2g Carbs; 3.5g Protein; 4.1g Sugars; 2.9g Fiber
Ingredients
2 ears corn, husked and halved
1 teaspoon olive oil
Coarse sea salt and cayenne pepper, to taste
2 tablespoons butter, cold
1/2 teaspoon garlic, crushed
1 tablespoon fresh scallions, chopped
Directions
Toss the ears of corn with the oil, salt, and cayenne pepper. Arrange the ears of corn in the Air Fryer cooking basket.
Cook the ears of corn at 390 degrees F for about 10 minutes, tossing them halfway through the cooking time.
Garnish the ears of corn with the butter, garlic, and fresh scallions. Bon appétit!

Sweet Potato Salad Bowl

(Ready in about 20 minutes | Servings 2)
Per serving: 208 Calories; 14.3g Fat; 18.7g Carbs; 2.8g Protein; 5.6g Sugars; 3.7g Fiber
Ingredients
1 (5-inch) long sweet potato, peeled and cut into slices
2 tablespoons extra-virgin olive oil
Sea salt and ground black pepper, to taste
2 cups baby spinach
1 tomato, diced
1 bell pepper, seeded and sliced
1 tablespoon white wine vinegar
Directions
Start by preheating your Air Fryer to 360 degrees F.
Toss the sweet potato with 1 tablespoon of olive oil and place them in the Air Fryer cooking basket.
Air fry the sweet potato for 15 minutes, tossing halfway through the cooking time, working in batches.
Toss the roasted potatoes with the remaining ingredients and serve immediately.
Enjoy!

Classic Rice Patties

(Ready in about 20 minutes | Servings 4)
Per serving: 168 Calories; 9.3g Fat; 16.7g Carbs; 4.8g Protein; 2.8g Sugars; 2.2g Fiber
Ingredients
1 cup cooked brown rice
2 eggs, beaten
1 cup eggplant, peeled and chopped
1 cup breadcrumbs
1 bell pepper, chopped
1 small onion, chopped
2 cloves garlic, minced
Sea salt and ground black pepper, to taste
2 tablespoons olive oil
Directions
Start by preheating your Air Fryer to 380 degrees F.
Mix all the ingredients until everything is well combined. Form the mixture into patties.
Air fry the patties for about 15 minutes or until cooked through. Turn them over halfway through the cooking time.
Bon appétit!

Vegan Black Bean Hoagie

(Ready in about 20 minutes | Servings 4)
Per serving: 368 Calories; 10.3g Fat; 50.1g Carbs; 12.8g Protein; 8.8g Sugars; 7.2g Fiber
Ingredients
For Burgers:
14 ounces canned black beans, drained and rinsed
1 chia egg (1 tablespoon ground chia seeds + 2 tablespoons lukewarm water)
Sea salt and ground black pepper, to taste
1/2 teaspoon ground cumin
2 tablespoons olive oil
1 medium onion, chopped
2 garlic cloves, minced
For Hoagie:
2 hoagie rolls, halved
4 tablespoons ketchup
4 teaspoons mustard
Directions
Thoroughly combine all the ingredients for the burgers. Form the mixture into sausages and arrange them in a lightly greased Air Fryer basket.
Cook the sausages at 380 degrees F for about 15 minutes or until cooked through. Tun them over halfway through the cooking time.

Assemble your sandwiches with black bean sausages, hoagie rolls, ketchup, and mustard.
Bon appétit!

Cauliflower and Mushroom Balls

(Ready in about 20 minutes | Servings 4)

Per serving: 133 Calories; 3.9g Fat; 19.2g Carbs; 8.7g Protein; 6.4g Sugars; 3.7g Fiber

Ingredients

1 pound cauliflower, grated
1 small onion, chopped
1 teaspoon garlic cloves, minced
2 teaspoons butter, room temperature
1 pound brown mushrooms, chopped
2 ounces cheddar cheese, grated
Sea salt and ground black pepper, to taste
1 cup Japanese breadcrumbs

Directions

Mix all the ingredients in a bowl. Shape the mixture into bite-sized balls and place them in a lightly oiled Air Fryer cooking basket.
Air fry the balls at 400 degrees F for about 14 minutes, shaking the basket halfway through the cooking time.
Bon appétit!

Rustic Mini Cornbread Muffins

(Ready in about 20 minutes | Servings 4)

Per serving: 223 Calories; 9.7g Fat; 26.5g Carbs; 7.4g Protein; 3.2g Sugars; 1.6g Fiber

Ingredients

1/2 cup corn flour
1/2 cup plain flour
1 teaspoon baking soda
1/2 teaspoon salt
A pinch of grated nutmeg
2 eggs, whisked
2 tablespoons lard, melted
1 cup buttermilk

Directions

Start by preheating your Air Fryer to 350 degrees F. Then, spritz mini muffin cups with a nonstick cooking oil.
In a mixing bowl, thoroughly combine all the ingredients.
Pour the mixture into the prepared mini muffin cups and lower them into the Air Fryer basket.
Cook your tartlets in the preheated Air Fryer for approximately 15 minutes, or until a toothpick comes out dry and clean.
Bon appétit!

APPENDIX : RECIPES INDEX

D

CPSIA information can be obtained
at www.ICGtesting.com
Printed in the USA
LVHW011614280521
688752LV00002B/22